Praise for *The Memory of Music*

'Andrew Ford's wide-ranging musical autobiography is a pleasure to read. Accessible, informative and packed with anecdotes, it's an excellent guide to the life of a composer: what it entails, what matters, and how and why it happened in the first place.'—*Steven Isserlis*

'I love discovering how people become who they are. Andrew Ford's book took me into a new world: composition. His insight into how we talk about music and what it brings up for people is fascinating.'—*Julia Zemiro*

'Andrew Ford is one of the greatest music broadcasters around – and not just in Australia – yet *The Memory of Music* shows that he is much more than that. What is most striking is the extraordinary honesty in the way that he opens up how a composer really works and thinks, and the detail of a composer's everyday concerns – the ways that real life impinges on the artistic process. Having spent a lifetime in music myself, this book rings more true than anything else I have read. It's beautifully written, the prose flows effortlessly, and it's from the heart.'
—*Gavin Bryars*

The Memory of Music
Andrew Ford

Black Inc.

Published by Black Inc.,
an imprint of Schwartz Publishing Pty Ltd
Level 1, 221 Drummond Street
Carlton VIC 3053, Australia
enquiries@blackincbooks.com
www.blackincbooks.com

The National Library of Australia Cataloguing-in-Publication entry:

Ford, Andrew, 1957– author.
The memory of music / Andrew Ford.
9781863959490 (paperback)
9781925435696 (ebook)
Ford, Andrew, 1957– . Composers—Australia.
Music—Social aspects. Music—Philosophy and aesthetics.
Music—20th century—History and criticism.

Cover design by Peter Long
Cover photographs: music box by Fuse/Getty Images;
portrait courtesy of the author
Typeset by Tristan Main

Printed in Great Britain by Clays Ltd, St Ives plc

FSC
www.fsc.org
MIX
Paper from
responsible sources
FSC® C018072

For my family

CONTENTS

'In the end you understand music through your memory.
You go back to the same thing again and again and experience
it differently.'

—HARRISON BIRTWISTLE

Introduction

Top of the World

When I first met Ted Smith I knew nothing of his past except that he had once had a small reputation as an Al Jolson impersonator in the East End of London. It turned out his larger reputation rested on his association with the Kray twins, London's captains of organised, violent crime in the 1960s. They called him 'Mad Teddy' – he seems to have spent some years in Broadmoor Hospital for the criminally insane – and rumour had it he was Ronnie Kray's lover. Mind you, he was also supposed to be dead, Reggie Kray having confessed to his murder.

Yet there he was in Australia in 2004, rugged up and dying of lung cancer, his little apartment full of 'strange-but-true' books with an emphasis on conspiracy theories. And he was struggling to do Al Jolson for me, apologising each time his wheezy lungs let him down. Finally, he completed a rendition of the song 'If I Only Had a Match', an ironic choice under the circumstances. I suppose that was his last performance. When he got to the end, he gave a small, satisfied smile.

Then there was the retired postmaster who told me of his love of New Orleans jazz and wept with something like gratitude as he tried to put into words George Lewis's clarinet solo on 'Climax Rag'. And there was a six-year-old girl, so excited by Rossini's overture to *William Tell* that she could barely contain herself ('Ooh, *yeah!*') as she described the music to me. And a wide-eyed young woman with scars on her arms who spoke of the serenity and hope she found in 'Gabriel's Oboe', part of Ennio Morricone's music for *The Mission*.

I met these people because I'd been commissioned by the Casula Powerhouse, the arts centre in Western Sydney, to create an exhibition called *Local Portraits* with the photographer Jim Rolon. Jim took photos of our seventy subjects, thirty-five from Robertson, the rural town in the Southern Highlands of New South Wales where we both lived, and thirty-five from the 2168 postcode region near the Powerhouse – suburbs such as Green Valley, Miller, Sadleir and Cartwright. The idea was to show the differences and similarities between people living in the two locales. We chose subjects of all ages and from the widest range of backgrounds, and to complement Jim's photographic portraits I created secondary portraits in sound, interviewing each person about their favourite music. My theory was that if I encouraged them to speak about the sound of the music itself, rather than its associations, we might uncover quite personal things.

I usually began the interview with a general question: what sorts of music do you like? It was deliberately vague, designed, as much as anything, to let the interviewee feel in charge. The answer, invariably, was: 'Oh, everything!' Then we started finding examples, gradually narrowing them down to a single choice.

I was after a short sound bite to go with each photograph, no more than a minute long, and sometimes this was quite easy to achieve – but sometimes it wasn't. The longest interview lasted well over two hours, an elderly man from Robertson insisting I hear all about his life before he would share any musical enthusiasms with me (it transpired that most of his stories were fabricated). There were some predictable differences between Robertson and the suburbs around Casula, the former yielding more Slim Dusty fans, the latter more lovers of gangsta rap. But the surprising thing was how much common ground emerged when it came to strength of feeling, because it turned out that music, for most of these men, women and children, was very important indeed, sustaining them, encouraging them and restoring them, if only for the duration of a song.

I don't suppose anyone knew the full extent of Ted Smith's demons, but I know, because I witnessed it, that when he put on his Al Jolson voice, all else fell by the wayside. Listening to the recording now, I hear him relishing the nasal tone and flattened Jolson vowels. He pauses to apply the Jolson vibrato and dramatically delays the song's final cadence. Minutes after his performance he was still wearing that smile of satisfaction, and I would guess the memory of his singing continued to buoy him hours after I'd packed up my recording equipment and left. I imagine it was the same with the young woman with the scars. While 'Gabriel's Oboe' played, she felt somehow safe, and when she remembered the sound – for instance, when she described it to me – she felt safe again. But there's only so much that music can do to sustain you. I met her in 2006; I remember telling her I was about to go to Rome to interview Morricone, and that I thought he'd be happy to know how much his music meant to her. But by the time the exhibition opened in 2008, the woman who had drawn hope from 'Gabriel's Oboe' was dead.

Though I spent only a short while with most of them, these people made a lasting impression on me. One who particularly stands out is Rhonda, an irrepressible woman from a public housing block in Miller. This part of Sydney can seem like a dumping ground. There is a lot of unemployment, a lot of poverty, a lot of mental illness, a lot of crime. Amenities are run-down, vandalism is common and an outsider doesn't always feel safe, even in broad daylight. Many people would be surprised such places exist in modern Australia, but they do, and people like Rhonda try to turn them into communities.

Rhonda had taken it upon herself to create a thriving public garden in a courtyard area between blocks of units, and she was the person to whom many of the residents of those blocks poured out their problems. A rumour had started that she kept a large sum of money in her flat. It wasn't true, but it led to a string of burglaries, some of which occurred when she was at home. The first time I went to see her, she was out and I noticed her front door had recently been dusted for fingerprints. I returned the following week to find her at home and learn that, only the night before, she had gone to her door in response to banging, looked out through the spy-hole and seen a young man with a knife at a child's throat.

'Open the door,' he had said, 'or I'll cut her.'

But now here we were, sitting on Rhonda's sofa and talking about music. And she was laughing and remembering old boyfriends and sharing her enthusiasm for Karen Carpenter's voice.

'"Top of the World",' she said, 'was a good song always when you were in love. It's a lighthearted song that makes you feel good, and when you're feeling good already, it sort of ... *elates* that again. Coming through the generation I came through, there was a lot of yelling and screaming in music, and I didn't like that. So Karen Carpenter was nice: you could understand what she was singing, it was easy to learn the words, it had a good rhythm to it and you weren't banging your head against a wall when you were listening. So I guess it's all to do with romance and love and stuff like that.'

There's a lot in what Rhonda told me. Often we choose the music we listen to partly because it isn't like music to which we have an aversion. That's also one of the reasons composers compose: to create antidotes, to write the music we would like to hear. And most of us – composers or not – are drawn, like Rhonda, to music we seem to understand, music that speaks to us, that explains itself to us at some level, even if we're unable to put it into words. That is the music that imprints itself on our memories.

o o o

Ultimately, it is impossible to put music into words. At a technical level, you can be quite precise; you can say, 'This chord is a diminished seventh' or 'That rhythm is a hemiola'. But it's like stripping down a car engine and labelling the parts. When you are done, you still haven't explained how a car works, let alone why you might prefer a Mercedes to a Honda. Besides, most of the world neither knows nor cares what a hemiola is (it's three notes in the time of two, or vice versa).

All that said, the attempt to talk about music isn't necessarily futile. Whoever first insisted that 'Writing about music is like dancing about architecture' missed the point. In fact, you *can* dance about architecture. You may not be able, precisely, to convey the Sydney Opera House or the Taj Mahal in your dance, but you can try, and your attempt might be interesting. Talking about music is like that.

Since 1995, on ABC Radio National, I have attempted each weekend to engage other musicians in conversation about what it is we do. Someone worked out that I have spoken to more than 6000 guests in my time presenting *The Music Show*, and so you might think I would have it down to a fine art. But, to some degree, we are bound to fail. We aim to fail as interestingly, entertainingly and elegantly as possible, and the best we can hope for is a degree of illumination on the topic at hand – something about the motivation behind making music, about the work involved and how this or that person has approached the task, and perhaps something about the uniqueness of music and why it will not surrender its nature or its meaning to mere words.

We are told, often by composers and other musicians, that music is a form of communication, and so it is. But 'communication' is a twenty-first-century buzzword and its application to music is unfortunate. For as soon as we are agreed that music is about communicating, the question will arise: what is it communicating? There is a perfectly good and true answer to this question, but it doesn't satisfy many people. The answer is that music is communicating music.

A play or a novel or a poem may express a point of view. 'What's it about?' we ask someone who's just been to see a new film. 'What is it?' we ask of a painting, and we don't expect to be told, 'It's a painting.' But these are not questions we apply to music, because a piece of music is the thing itself. Music is not a language. You can't give someone directions to the shops in it; you can't translate it. Mozart's string quintet in C minor is about Mozart's string quintet in C minor.

Debussy said that music is 'pure emotion'. I approve of that, especially the word 'pure'. It's like pure mathematics. Musical emotion is not (necessarily) connected to anything except itself; it's also not (necessarily) intended. Of course you can sit down to write sad or happy music, but that's both rather basic and, at one level, manipulative. Music is capable of infinite subtlety.

Recently, in a cafe, I saw one woman throw another a glance that seemed to embody familiarity, affection, amusement, a little bit of disappointment (not in the other woman but in someone else) and a degree of resignation. How did I know that? How was I able to read this stranger's face? She said nothing, and if she had,

I'd have been too far away to hear. The glance lasted only a second, yet it seemed precise. I don't know what lay behind the wordless communication and I couldn't begin to describe the muscular movements of the woman's face that produced it, yet while I don't imagine her friend read her face in quite the same way I did, I feel sure I caught the gist of the glance. Did the woman consider how she was setting her expression to convey that complex range of emotions? Did she decide in advance how much to twist her mouth (just a little), how much to raise her eyebrow (a little bit more)? I doubt it.

This is similar to the way in which music operates and is composed. As with a facial expression, intuition is involved, even when the structure of the music is carefully planned. The precision of movement in facial muscles is not unlike the way a composer might place the notes in a chord, choose the instruments that play those notes, indicate how loudly they play and so on. And like the woman's expression, the chord is gone in a moment.

As a composer, I seldom give much thought to the emotion my music conveys as I work with my pitches and rhythms and dynamics, trying to get them right, but I know it's there and I feel it myself. And like the woman's wordless glance, my music – I hope – reveals itself without need of explanation, which is just as well because it's hard to account for pure emotion.

Sometimes on the radio I have encouraged my guests to grasp the nettle and say what they believe music to be. Father Arthur Bridge, a Sydney parish priest, commissioner of new music and director of Ars Musica Australis, once told me he considered all music to be 'the voices of angels'. Even if one doesn't believe in angels, this is quite good because it suggests communication at a level higher than words. The composer Larry Sitsky described music as 'a telescope into the unknown', which I like even better. But you see where this is going, don't you? We're in the realm of metaphor, of poetry, and try as one might it is hard to escape it. If you want to say what music is, you will end up reaching for an image.

I haven't avoided images in this book – you will find rather a lot of them – but I've attempted to be as direct and down-to-earth about music as I can. I did not especially want to write a memoir. When friends asked me over the past couple of years what the next book would be about, I hedged and said it's a *sort of* memoir. As it turns out, that's fairly accurate.

In writing my previous books and in making various radio series about music, I'd become aware that I was failing to answer with much clarity three key questions: What is music? What's it for? And how does it work in our lives? There is no single answer for any of these questions; it must be slightly different for everyone. But the questions belong together. Music doesn't fully exist unless it is being heard – or looked at on the page by someone who can read musical notation – or unless, perhaps, it is being remembered. It requires a listener, and listeners have lives. As we listen to music, it enters our lives and very often sets up camp there. Any attempt, then, to talk about the significance of music – which is finally what this all comes down to – must be undertaken in relation to life itself, and since my life is the one I know best, here we are ... with a *sort of* memoir.

I hope you will agree that what follows is more about music than about me; however, I'm aware that, like the people in *Local Portraits*, I probably reveal myself most when music is my subject.

1

The Monkeys of Colwyn Bay

They were wearing waistcoats, red with yellow trim; one of them had a fez. One monkey played cymbals and another a drum, a third strummed a guitar, and there was an upright bass.

The music still rings in my ears: Gerry and the Pacemakers' 'How Do You Do It', Billy J. Kramer and the Dakotas' 'Bad to Me', the Searchers' version of 'Sweets for My Sweet', Johnny Kidd and Pirates' 'I'll Never Get Over You', Freddy and the Dreamers' 'I'm Telling You Now' and, above all, 'From Me to You' by the Beatles.

The jukebox absorbed every sixpenny bit I could purloin from my parents. I watched as the record was selected from a rack and lowered into place; the toy monkeys strummed and hit their instruments and the music poured out, its effect thrilling, galvanising and immediate. The bright piano arpeggios at the start of 'How Do You Do It?', the strummed guitar chord before Billy J. Kramer's vulnerable, needy 'If you ever leave me', and the bold, wordless hook of the Beatles' 'From Me to You': 'Dada dah, dada dum dum *dah*!'

The jukebox was in Eirias Park, Colwyn Bay, a popular seaside destination for summer holiday-makers from Liverpool, with its promenade, donkey rides, Punch and Judy man, and occasional brass band. It was hardly any distance from Liverpool to North Wales, but the latter seemed exotic, another country with another language. At the beginning we took the ferry across the Mersey to New Brighton, then a steam train to Wrexham. Later, after my father learnt to drive, we went in the Morris 1000, its registration number imprinted on my mind along with all those songs.

The retention of the Morris's registration – and that of its successor, a Ford Cortina, and of the family's telephone number – is a child's memory at work. I have had subsequent phone numbers that I no longer recall, and have owned cars whose registration numbers I've forgotten; I struggle to remember the registration of my present car. But a child's mind is like a new piece of fly paper: things stick. There were records in our home that bore scratches – clicks and jumps – that I still expect when I hear the same music today, and there is something disappointing about their absence.

Of course music is meant to be memorable, and pop songs instantly so. The three-minute song doesn't have long to make itself known, so it typically employs a chorus–verse–chorus structure, a lot of repetition and a striking sonority or interval or melodic hook right at the very beginning. 'A Hard Day's Night' is a perfect example of a song that nearly everyone can identify – or at least recognise – from its first chord. If you spent your childhood listening to pop music, you will be able to pull off that same trick with dozens of songs.

Classical music is different. There are pieces with memorable starts – in terms of instant recognition, I suppose the fifth symphony of Beethoven is the classical equivalent of 'A Hard Day's Night' – but because classical works are generally longer than three minutes, and can sometimes last an hour or more, our memory tends to recall an impression of the music's structure, as much as its detail. I'm not suggesting that the average listener – even the average musician – will identify and retain a grasp of the key relationships in a piece, but the pacing of the music and the unveiling of its events in time leaves an imprint of its form on our unconscious minds. Sometimes, especially if we're children, we follow a piece of music as though it were a narrative, hearing a story, even where none is intended. Parents or teachers will sometimes reinforce this by playing children classical music that really does have a story, so that when the child runs up against a purely abstract piece – Beethoven's fifth, for example – she will transfer the technique and make up a story of her own. It's not a terrible way to listen.

In terms of memory, though, there's another aspect. Beethoven's fifth, which lasts approximately thirty-five minutes, creates its own world, and as listeners, we enter and explore it. We probably discover slightly different things each time, because there's a lot to find and thirty-five minutes allows us plenty of time. 'A Hard Day's Night', which begins fading from our hearing after just two minutes and twenty seconds, offers a different experience. Whereas the Beethoven symphony invites us to enter its world, 'A Hard Day's Night' enters ours. If we really want to hear the Beethoven, we put our day on hold, but 'A Hard Day's Night' makes itself part of our day.

I think it's probably for this reason that old pop songs induce nostalgia in a way that classical music generally does not. A chance encounter with a piece of classical music on the radio might bring back memories of the piece itself – a Brahms inter-mezzo or a Mozart sonata one has not heard for a long time – but when an old pop song suddenly jumps into our life, it often con-jures up the time we first heard it: a face, a place, even a smell. Play me Russ Conway's 1959 record 'Side Saddle', for instance, and I am in my Auntie Edna's front parlour. I can see the porta-ble record player – red and cream – and the record with its blue-green Columbia label spinning on the turntable, I can feel the leather pouf sticking to the back of my short-trousered legs, and I can smell something sweet and slightly soapy. It's a warm, welcoming smell that might be knitting wool; a lot of knitting went on in that room.

It's the early 1960s, and I'm living with my mum and dad and little sister Kate in a semi-detached house in the Merseyside sub-urb of Thornton, just north of Crosby. We refer to Crosby as the 'village', which indeed it was from Viking times until the middle of the nineteenth century, when the trains arrived. But even though it is just a few miles from the centre of Liverpool, it retains a village atmosphere. Sharing the house with my mother, father, sister and me is my maternal grandmother. My grandfather, who

has died before I was born, was a blacksmith by trade, latterly bed-ridden with chronic asthma.

Each Wednesday, we visit my father's parents in Kirkdale in the tiny rented terrace in which he grew up. It is not an exaggeration to call it a slum – there's no bathroom and only an outside lavatory, and the whole neighbourhood will be torn down in the late 1970s – but it is a well-scrubbed slum. Living with my grandparents is Dad's younger brother Harry, who has Down's syndrome. Harry was a late addition to the family, a replacement for Dad's elder sister Jean, who died of diphtheria at the age of six. My granddad is a pensioner and has known a lot of unemployment in his life. He was a tram-driver at one point, but like many unskilled men of his class in Liverpool also worked at the dockyard, arriving each morning to stand in a pen with other hopeful men, while a foreman decided who would work (and therefore, in some cases, who would eat) that day. In spite of their circumstances, my grandparents always vote Conservative.

On Sundays either Auntie Edna (Mum's sister) comes to visit us with her husband, Wilf, and their two teenage daughters, or we visit them and I request 'Side Saddle'. Quite a bit of my musical education occurs in that lounge, courtesy of my cousins. Sometimes they play the piano, but more often it is records, and soon enough Russ Conway gives way to the Beatles and other pop, and also folk, music. This is the folk-song revival, and my cousins have records by the Johnstons and the Watersons, Alex Campbell and the Spinners. We listen to them all.

o
o   o
o

I wasn't a discriminating child when it came to music. Perhaps no child is. I had favourites, but I don't think it ever occurred to me *not* to like certain records. My parents owned a few – mostly popular classics and 1950s pop – and I found them all fascinating. I can see them in my mind's eye spread across the carpeted floor of our living room: Mendelssohn's *Hebrides* overture and his violin concerto, Dvořák's *New World* symphony, Smetana's *Vltava* and two or three *Brandenburg* concertos, Ronald Binge's *Elizabethan Serenade* and Hugo Alfvén's *Swedish Rhapsody*, and there was a seven-inch EP of some of the character dances from *The Nutcracker*. I think these were all my mother's. There were also Dad's Frank Sinatra 78s – 'South of the Border', 'I've Got the World on a String' – and Ella Fitzgerald singing songs by Gershwin. And there were one or two records of sentimental value to both my parents, such as the Barcarolle from *Tales of Hoffman*, the Powell and Pressburger film they had seen on their first date, and Gertrude Lawrence singing songs from *The King and I*, which they'd seen in the theatre in London on their honeymoon. I listened to everything without judgement, and played the Sinatra records over and over until one day, in my enthusiasm, I knelt on 'South of the Border' and broke it.

My favourite music, however, was Beethoven's *Pastoral* symphony. It remains a piece that I like very much and find endlessly interesting. I listened attentively to my parents' recording of Erich Kleiber conducting the Amsterdam Concertgebouw Orchestra, hiding behind the settee during the storm, emerging for the 'Song of Thanksgiving'. According to family lore, my mother heard me singing that theme from the final movement while pedalling my tricycle round the back garden. I was either two or three years old, but lest this be taken as a sign of prodigious early talent, I must stress that there is no other evidence to support that theory.

Music also came into the home via radio and television. In the early 1960s, most households owned one radio and one TV set, so everyone watched and listened to the same things. There was a lack of specialisation in radio, which meant that a host of musical styles could coexist on the one station. On the BBC Light Programme, for instance, you would be as likely to encounter Frank Sinatra singing 'High Hopes' or Harry Belafonte and Odetta's version of 'There's a Hole in My Bucket' as the 'Flight of the Bumblebee' or a new song by the Beatles. Television was the same. Just about every evening was some sort of variety show that might feature any of the above, and each Sunday lunchtime there was a program from BBC Wales featuring the harpist Osian Ellis. I was transfixed by his fingers, positioning myself side-on to a dining chair so that I could strum its back with both hands and play along.

When it comes to inculcating musical sense into a child and encouraging listening and singing, a parent's own singing is more important than records, radio or television. In my mother's case, the song list consisted largely of traditional nursery rhymes that doubtless she herself had been sung as a child, rhymes dating from at least the eighteenth century (in some cases the sixteenth) that any English-speaking child would have grown up listening to in the twentieth century, and many still do. I like these rhymes for their lack of sentimentality and their sense of the past. I don't mean to suggest that they satirise moments of history – that's fanciful thinking: 'Ring a Ring a Roses', which is popularly believed to list the symptoms of bubonic plague, does nothing of the sort. The past that nursery rhymes capture is that in which mothers and fathers sang the same songs to their children a century ago, and two centuries ago and in most cases three centuries ago. It's a continuum that resists ever-hastening change, and there's a lot to be said for it. Children, after all, are still children.

At bedtime, Dad often recited poems to me – Wordsworth's 'Daffodils', say, or Leigh Hunt's 'Abou Ben Adhem' – but he also had a repertory of songs that was both more modern and less suitable than my mother's. He sang 'Frankie and Johnny', 'Cool Water' and 'Goodnight, Irene', 1950s hits that were among his favourites. He also did a fine, spirited rendition of Red Ingle's 'Cigareetes, Whuskey and Wild, Wild Women', complete with the cod temperance meeting at the top. But perhaps you don't know these songs?

'Frankie and Johnny', we learn at the outset, 'were lovers'; moreover, 'Lordy, how they could love'. The trouble was that while Johnny was 'her man', he had 'done her wrong'. So, several verses later, Frankie shoots him. It's a murder ballad, and as a very small child I found it darkly exciting.

'Cool Water' was darker still. In this one, the singer and 'Old Dan' pretty much crawl across 'the barren waste without the taste of water', mirages to the left of them, mirages to the right, until

Dan, evidently delirious, has to be slapped out of a demoniac vision: 'Don't ya listen to him, Dan, / He's a devil not a man.'

But 'Goodnight, Irene' was the darkest of all, even though it was the greatly sanitised Weavers' version of the song that Dad sang me, not the original Lead Belly song. There's a verse that goes: 'Sometimes I live in the country, sometimes I live in the town / Sometimes I take a great notion to jump into the river and drown.' It wasn't that I suspected my father of having suicidal thoughts – I was only three or four years old – but I did find the idea of his jumping 'into the river' alarming and can still feel the alarm.

But I loved Dad's singing. When a parent sings to a child, there is a special bond. To some extent, the actual song doesn't matter, it's the sound of the voice and the fact that it is a command performance. It is perhaps the first and best argument for live music.

My teenage cousins' records were another layer of musical experience on top of my parents' records, on top of their singing, and on top of whatever came out of the radio and television. Gradually, I came to regard their choices as cooler than my parents'; their tastes informed mine and were only reinforced when I started school. Pop music in general replaced most of my other musical interests, and I was soon saving pocket money for records. The first single I bought was 'I Want to Hold Your Hand'. What was happening, I suppose, was a temporary narrowing of my musical tastes. It's maybe inevitable, particularly at school: your classmates all seem to like the same music, so you do too. At least it was the Beatles; a decade later and it would have been the Bay City Rollers. Narrowing of taste, though, is always to be fought against, because it narrows our lives.

The fifth member of Auntie Edna's household was her mother-in-law, Mrs Roberts. I don't recall a conversation with Mrs Roberts. On our visits, she always seemed to be sitting quietly in the corner of the parlour – Dickens's Mrs Gummidge in a pale green housecoat – and I wouldn't mention her, but for a story that is illuminating of the way most of us restrict our musical diets.

Mrs Roberts might not have said much when visitors were present, but with her immediate family she was happy to voice her opinions, which included a strong dislike of the band leader Joe Loss. Who knows where this came from? It wasn't the music to which she objected, but the man himself. The trouble was that on television in the early 1960s, Loss and his orchestra were ubiquitous. Still, first they had to get past Mrs Roberts, who would want the TV set switched off the moment they appeared. In the end, Uncle Wilf came up with a neat solution involving a fictitious band leader he called Joe Low.

'Is that Joe Loss?' an agitated Mrs Roberts would demand to know.

'No, Mum. That's Joe Low,' Uncle Wilf would reassure her.

'Oh, that's all right then,' Mrs Roberts would acquiesce, settling down to enjoy the music. 'As long as it isn't Joe Loss.'

Though mild enough, it was musical bigotry in a nutshell, and we're most of us guilty of it. We discount certain music without listening – usually certain sorts of music – and, unless we're tricked into hearing it with innocent ears, may never know what it is we've missed. I'd say the three forms of music most susceptible to this today are hip-hop, country music and the sort of stuff I write – modern music for the concert hall. All that's needed for the bigotry to take hold is a single bad experience.

Once, on a train in London, I ran into one of the modern language teachers from my school. He'd just been to a concert where he'd heard the first performance of a piece by Hans Werner Henze, and he was personally affronted.

'I'm never going to a first performance of anything again,' he sulked. It was as though this music, which he'd heard once and hadn't immediately liked, had ruined his life. For me, the conversation was evidence that teachers are just like other people, and some of them are fools. But it also shows the difference between music and some of the other arts. If we begin a book we don't like, we might tell a friend that we're finding it a bit heavy-going or difficult to get into; perhaps in the end we give up. And isn't it the same with a TV series? We'll watch an episode or two and then leave it. Music's different. It gets past our defences and sometimes, if we are not feeling receptive to it, it can seem like violation. But being ravished by music can also be one of life's most intensely pleasurable experiences.

o   o
o

The only ambition I have ever had was to be an actor. When I was a small child, the standard answer (for boys at least) to the question,

'What do you want to be when you grow up?' was 'A train driver', but I always wanted to be an actor. Perhaps it was simply that I was a show-off, or perhaps it was an early manifestation of the artist's need of an audience, which may be the same thing. At high school, when I was finally given the chance to act, it turned out I had no special aptitude for it, but I am still fascinated by what actors do and how they do it, by their make-believe, their 'let's-pretend'. I probably got this from my dad, who always seemed to know the names of the actors playing even the smallest roles in TV dramas and old movies. When I stumble across a Western from the 1940s or 1950s and recognise Andy Devine or Edgar Buchanan, Walter Brennan or John Carradine, that's my dad's doing.

I was not an avid reader in my early years, much as my parents encouraged it (my mother was a primary school teacher). Instead, I watched television. My favourite shows were what one might call costume dramas: *Ivanhoe* (with Roger Moore), *Sir Francis Drake*, *The Adventures of Robin Hood*, *The Adventures of William Tell* and, above all, *Richard the Lionheart,* a wholly fictitious account of the absentee Plantagenet king's reign, in which he spent his time riding around the English countryside with a few knights doing good deeds, Robin Hood in a crown. You can find episodes on YouTube. Richard is played by Dermot Walsh, an actor so wooden he could give you splinters, but the program's signature tune continues to stiffen my sinews. Like pop music, TV themes are intended to grab our attention and stick in the mind, all the more so when TV consisted almost entirely of weekly programs. You'd hear the music from another room and come running, especially, in my case, if the music meant that knights were involved.

Knights were an obsession of mine to the extent that one Christmas my mother knitted me chain mail. It was, no doubt, partly an early interest in history – those summer holidays in Wales included visits to the ruins of once imposing medieval castles in Caernarfon, Conwy and Harlech – but mostly I wanted to *be* a knight, or at any rate an actor playing a knight. I did understand the difference, as I sat watching *Richard the Lionheart* in my woollen armour.

Accessorising was an important part of my viewing. Another favourite TV program was the Western *Laramie*, which I always watched with my dad. At least, he watched it; I spent much of each episode getting myself properly attired. *Laramie* had two principal characters, Slim Sherman and Jess Harper. Slim wore a grey hat (at least it was grey on our black-and-white TV), Jess's was black. I had both grey and black cowboy hats among the dressing-up clothes out in the washhouse. As soon as *Laramie* came on, and it was apparent which of our heroes would be the main character that week, I was off to find the appropriate hat and get myself in character. If it was one of Slim's episodes, the transformation was relatively swift: I needed my grey hat, gun and holster. Becoming Jess took a little longer. He was a tough-talking, hard-riding kind of cowboy, and the front of his black hat was generally coated in dust. I discovered that my mother's flour shaker could simulate this with considerable accuracy, and so, having located the hat, would make a detour to the kitchen cupboard in order to complete the effect, before racing back to the television to catch what was left of the show. Fortunately, one didn't have to watch the first part of an episode of *Laramie* to understand the basic plot.

Understanding plots is not, in any case, the strong suit of most children watching television. They see but do not always listen, not to the words. While the theme music of my childhood TV favourites is still evocative, I couldn't describe the plot of a single episode and doubt that I could have done straight after the show. I watched my young daughter watching the television – she's another dresser-up – and it was exactly the same. If I had asked her to fill me in on the plot of an episode of *Charlie and Lola*, she would have given me a version of what she had seen on the screen, with her own rationale for the pictures.

What children *do* hear, in addition to music, and perhaps because of it, is atmosphere. Sometimes the atmosphere will even focus the child's attention long enough to take in a few words; a sudden change of tone can achieve it. The announcement of President Kennedy's assassination in November 1963 falls into this category for me. It was teatime and we were watching television as a family when a news flash cut dramatically into the regular program. I would not normally have paid attention to the news, but the change in mood was arresting. Something about the newsreader's countenance and sombre tone of voice seized my six-year-old attention. He was talking only to me. I remember urging my parents to listen, and being hushed because they were trying to hear the details of the shooting.

By the time Kennedy's death was announced about half an hour later, Mum had left for a Friday night 'coffee evening' at our next-door neighbour's house and I was dispatched to inform her of the news. It was the first time I had been entrusted with a task of any solemnity.

'Don't make a fuss,' Dad coached me. 'Just go up to her and say, very quietly, "He's gone."' And so off I went with my weighty responsibility, rehearsing my two words: out of our front gate, in through the side door of Mrs G's house, through her kitchen, down the hall, into the front room where I sometimes listened to records with her son, Kevin, through a forest of ladies holding coffee cups, and up to Mum with my whispered intelligence of a presidential assassination.

o
 o
  o

Back in those days of coffee evenings, Kevin G was what we called a spastic, his form of cerebral palsy having left him physically quite able, but happy to play knights and cowboys with a boy several years his junior. Indeed, he was sometimes reluctant for the games to end, my grandmother once finding him on our doorstep holding me in a neck lock to prevent me going indoors for my lunch. I saw the panic on her face and decided she was overreacting.

Kevin provided much of my early musical education. In that front room, we listened to the Applejacks' 'Tell Me When', Peter and Gordon's 'Nobody I Know' and a succession of Beatles records. Kevin always seemed to have their latest single, and we played them over and over – the B sides as well as the A sides.

Since it was only ever the A sides we heard on radio, I associate 'You Can't Do That', 'Things We Said Today' and 'She's a Woman' with Kevin and his impersonation of Ringo Starr. There was nothing wrong with this boy's powers of observation. He mimed the basic drum pattern to 'I Feel Fine' pretty well, but it was the detail he brought to Ringo's demeanour and facial expressions that was uncanny: the faraway look, the exaggerated overbite, the nodding head and the occasional flash of a conspiratorial smile. Holding Kevin's sister's tennis racket, I was John.

That the Beatles should have been such a big part of our play was hardly surprising. You didn't have to live in Liverpool to be taken by the mania, but Liverpool felt an appreciable degree of civic pride about the group's success. There hadn't been much to be proud of in those postwar years; Liverpool's glories were behind it and its grand buildings (paid for by trade in cotton and slaves) looked out of place in a landscape characterised by destruction. After London, Liverpool had been the most heavily bombed English city of World War II, and even in the early 1960s the rubble was still being cleared; from the top of a double-decker bus as I travelled into town with my mum, I could see the bombsites – 'bommies' to the locals. There were houses with roofs and first floors missing, while the remaining interior walls were distinguished by wallpaper that changed from parlour stripes to bedroom flock where the ceiling would once have been. I was struck by the sight, not I think because of any real sense of the bombings my parents had lived through as children, but by the thought that we were looking inside the remains of people's homes. I'd seen my dad hang wallpaper, and I imagined the people who had once lived in these ruins hanging theirs: choosing the patterns from a big book, laying the paper on a plank and lathering it with paste, climbing a ladder with the heavy, pasted sheet. The people had long gone – many of them must have died in the blasts that damaged their homes – but the patterned wallpaper remained.

The fact that, more than fifteen years after the end of the war, the city still had bommies gives some indication of the economic state of postwar Britain and Liverpool in particular. The Beatles, then, were a reason to celebrate, and their popularity was not limited to the young. When they appeared on *Sunday Night at the London Palladium*, I was allowed to stay up to watch with my parents and grandmother; on Saturday mornings, Dad and I would listen to *Saturday Club* on the BBC Light Programme, and on Sunday mornings *Easy Beat*, and often the Beatles would perform. In the early 1960s, listening to the radio in the UK meant listening to the BBC (unless one tuned into pirate radio or searched the static-ridden short wave for European stations), and listening to the BBC meant one of three possibilities – the Home Service, the Light Programme or the enigmatically named Third Programme (later, Radio 3), purveyor of classical music, drama, poetry and discussions about philosophy. In our house, we oscillated between the first two: the Home Service for news and current affairs; the Light Programme for entertainment, which included comedy and sport in addition to that wide range of music from vaudeville and musical theatre via light classics, jazz and country music to rock and roll. It isn't a coincidence that the Beatles, who had grown up with the BBC and now found themselves on it, had a routine that included nearly all the above, including the comedy. Indeed, one of the defining features of British pop in the 1960s, from the Kinks to the Small Faces, was its vaudevillian roots. Even the Rolling Stones had it. Their music might have come from the blues bands of Chicago, but Mick Jagger's camp posturing and pouting lips were pure pantomime dame, Howlin' Wolf meets Frankie Howerd.

The excitement that greeted each new release from the Beatles was keenly felt, even by a child. I have strong memories of hearing individual songs for the first time and of where I was when I heard them. I was taken to see the films *A Hard Day's Night* and *Help!* at a local cinema, but quite separately recall hearing the songs on radio and the thrill they created ('thrill' is the word). I also recall the first time 'Yellow Submarine' came on. In some ways, this was an equally important moment in my childhood, for as I listened, it dawned on me the Beatles might have feet of clay. Patently, the song was not up to their usual standard of harmonic invention, though of course I couldn't have told you that in so many words, and having 'Eleanor Rigby' for a B side didn't quite redeem it. If I had gone through the first nine years of my life uncritically liking everything, I suddenly realised that with music – even with the Beatles – some things were better than others. I saved up my pocket money and bought the single of 'Yellow Submarine' anyway, but even today when I hear the song, I can't shrug off that sense of disappointment.

It was around this time that an upright piano was delivered to our front room. Front rooms had pianos in those days. There was the instrument at Auntie Edna's – the cut-down modern upright, played by my cousins – and, more mysteriously, the piano at my paternal grandparents' home. The mystery surrounded their parlour more than the piano, for in my grandparents' tiny terraced house the front room was never used. I can only guess that they were saving on heating bills, because the door to the parlour was kept shut, the darkened room always cold in a tactile sort of way. I only went in there on my own and to play the piano. The instrument was an imposing old thing, its casing a mottled, tortoiseshell brown, its ivories a slightly lighter brown. It was resonant in that special way that out-of-tune pianos generally are, and I don't know why it was there at all, because as far as I knew nobody in the house had ever played the piano. But as a small child I was fascinated by its capacity to come roaring to life, and it was on this instrument I composed my first piece, an assortment of repeated tone clusters – it can't have been anything more – entitled 'The Animals in the Jungle', which I announced and then performed to my parents and grandparents listening from the back room. I guess I was about five.

I must have banged on this piano many times, so why I remember this performance I don't know. Perhaps it's because I gave it a title, and perhaps that, in turn, means that I thought I had found something – some structure, some musical scenario – that was worth naming. It could be that the moment is memorable because of something someone said, some response I have now forgotten but which cheered my five-year-old ego, or maybe wounded it. It's all gone. I just recall 'the boom of the tingling strings' (to quote D.H. Lawrence), the dark, cold, damp of the room, and the title. And now, aged eight or nine, I was to put away childish things and learn how to play the piano properly – at least that was the plan. For hard on the heels of our new piano came Miss Halliday, a gentle soul in a felt hat for whom the term 'spinsterish' might have been coined. She had a look of Margaret Rutherford – pale blue, twinkling eyes and pink cheeks a tangle of cross-hatched capillaries – and she arrived at our front door each week to give piano lessons to me and my sister.

I've often wondered what went wrong. I am, after all, a professional musician. For many years I taught music at a university; I've written operas and concertos and string quartets, and my music's been sung and played by famous people. In 2008, the Sydney International Piano Competition commissioned me to write a test piece for their quarter-finalists. Yet I still can't play. My wife, who once overheard me tell someone 'I can't really play the piano', pointed out that in that sentence the word 'really' is redundant.

It is true that I was and still am to some extent uncoordinated, but while hamfistedness might have explained why I disappointed my sports-mad father when it came to throwing and catching a ball, and certainly accounts for why I am not a *brilliant* pianist, I am, as my wife will testify, far less than that. When our daughter was about three she rushed to our piano after my wife had been playing and placed her own fingers on the keys. Her face fell.

'It doesn't work,' she said. I knew how she felt.

I don't think any of this was Miss Halliday's fault. At nine, I liked the idea of playing the piano, and had a teacher who was full of encouragement. But wanting to be a pianist was like wanting to be a knight, or at least an actor playing a knight, the piano itself the equivalent of knitted chain mail. I was a fantasist – not in itself, perhaps, a bad thing in a child (or a composer) – but I was also lazy and found it hard to apply myself to practising the pieces Miss Halliday brought. My only mitigating plea is that the music in question was *Scenes at a Farm* by Walter Carroll, an album of pieces with titles such as 'On the Lake' and 'Going to the Hayfield'. Each consisted of a few bars of blandness prefaced by an impossibly twee poetic quatrain. I was interested in most music, but could work up no enthusiasm for this, even though the pieces were easy enough to play. Without consciously rebelling, I began to alter and 'improve' Dr Carroll's works, syncopating their rhythms and adding notes to their dull chords. Miss Halliday was more bemused than anything.

But our lessons were short-lived. This was not because I gave up – that came later – but because our family was about to move to the other end of England.

Dad had worked at the Liverpool factory of British American Tobacco since he'd completed his national service (he'd been just too young to be called up in the war). I never knew exactly what he did there – he certainly wasn't making cigarettes; whenever I asked him what I should put on a form that required 'Father's Occupation', he'd say: 'Just put "clerk".' So clerking was taking us south, where Dad would work at BAT's head office in London.

2.

'Libera Me'

In the 1960s, as now, there was a cultural chasm between the north and south of England, indeed between the south-east of England and everywhere else in the British Isles. Moving to Kent from Liverpool, then, was not a straightforward matter. Suddenly, turnips were swedes and swedes were turnips, and it wasn't just that there were different names for things. There were also different customs.

For example, in Liverpool people ate 'salt fish' for breakfast on Good Friday and sometimes on Sundays. This was cod that had been salted and dried, in the process hardening into an unattractive yellowish-grey that resembled an ancient piece of chamois leather. The fish could be reconstituted by soaking it in water for a day or two, then simmered in milk on the morning of its consumption and made palatable with the addition of a knob of butter, white pepper and possibly a poached egg. The flavour was salty, of course, and very slightly rotten. It was sailors' food, originally from Scandinavia, cheap and basic, almost a symbol of frugality, which I imagine is why it was eaten on Good Friday. The first time my mother attempted to buy it in Kent, she was looked at askance and informed she might possibly find something of this nature in a specialist delicatessen in London. Harrods' food hall was mentioned.

Even for a nine-year-old, things were different in lots of small ways. In Liverpool, our house had been on a suburban street; now we lived in a long, winding lane with hedgerows and old cottages. At the top of the lane was a T-junction where, according to legend, a gibbet had once stood. Our house was modern, but it was next to a sixteenth-century farm, which in itself seemed exotic after suburbia. Where once we had looked out at a back garden with a back fence and, beyond it, another back garden and another house, now we saw fields and horses. Because my father took the train to London each day, we all ate our evening meal later. And it had a new name: dinner instead of tea, a subtle form of embourgeoisement that made me feel we'd gone up in the world. But perhaps the most consistent difference in our new surroundings was the way people talked.

The Liverpool accent comes in many forms, partly because it is itself a hybrid. There is a lot of Lancashire in it, but also a lot of Irish, and depending upon the speaker, one or other of these influences will often be quite prominent. Also, it seems to me that the sing-song lilt evident in some versions of the accent probably comes from across the border in North Wales. Beyond that, though, there is a wide range of what might best be called intensity. It's the same with the Australian accent, and while the level of intensity is certainly related to class, it is also something one may choose to modify.

So the Liverpool accent stretches all the way from the relatively posh tones of the conductor Simon Rattle to the impenetrable Scouse of any number of Liverpool or Everton footballers. Neither of my parents had a particularly thick accent, but after fewer than five years at a Liverpool primary school, I did, and I was determined to hang on to it in my new surroundings, in spite of the fact that people in Kent (especially people's mothers) found it cute. This was partly a Beatles thing, of course.

As far as I was concerned, southerners were soft and I was not going to sound like one of them. I stubbornly continued to pronounce words such as 'bath', 'path' and 'grass' with a short, flat a – as opposed to 'bahth', 'pahth' and 'grahss' – until I went to university. This was back up north, but nearly all my friends were from southern England and gradually my accent was acculturated into something rather nondescript. Even so, if today I find myself speaking to someone from Liverpool, the accent can come back quite quickly and strongly, tiny vestiges of Scouse remaining in my everyday speech.

Most noticeable to others is the hard g in the sound 'ng'; in the phrase 'singing a song', I tend to pronounce all the gs, where someone from the south of England or Australia would swallow them. But the element of Scouse I am most aware of is the fluctuating 'er' sound, particularly when several similar words come in a row. 'Her hair is fair' would be an example. As far as I can tell, everywhere in the English-speaking world, the word 'hair' is pronounced with a more open palette than the word 'her'. Everywhere except Liverpool, where for reasons that elude me, it is the other way round. A Liverpudlian is more likely to say 'Hair her is fur' and 'I went to the fun fur' and 'She's whirring a fair coat'. Small children tell their mothers: 'But it's not *fur!*' I am still occasionally tripped up by 'er' sounds, especially if I am obliged to read a sequence of them off the page.

° °
 °

I mentioned football. In the mid 1960s, both Merseyside teams were riding high in the English Football League, and it followed that to hail from Liverpool was almost as glamorous in terms of sport as pop music. I am no good at games. With a cricket bat, I have – or had – a reasonably convincing forward defence, but I was never able to score runs, and that was the full extent of any sporting prowess. Even that skill was never put seriously to the test. When it came to football, I was as much a fan as the next boy – a Liverpudlian, in contrast to my father, who was an Evertonian – and I can still name the players in the Liverpool team that won the League Championship in 1966. As for kicking a ball, I was useless.

In my primary school playground in Liverpool, I had hung around with the other boys in improvised football games, rolled up pullovers serving as goalposts, but I was never in danger of gaining possession of the ball. However, Liverpudlians are a sentimental lot – I think, like Australians, they get it from the Irish – and on my last day at the school my mates conspired to let me score. Time and again, the ball was passed to me a metre or two in front of the goal, the keeper falling over or bending down to tie a shoelace, thus affording me an unimpeded shot. Time and again I would miss. I can hear the other boys' exhortations: 'Give it to Fordy!' To no avail. I returned to the classroom for my final afternoon of a Liverpool education, touched by the attention but shamefaced at my inability to repay the other boys' confidence in me.

Just a few weeks later, at my new primary school in Kent, everything was different. Football hadn't happened in a formal sense at my school in Liverpool, but here we had games lessons, and the boys were divided into teams, identifiable by different coloured vests. The new school was not especially well appointed, but there was a playing field, with real goal posts and even some markings on the grass. Mr Jones, a kindly Welshman, refereed with a whistle, just like in a real game, and it all appealed to my sense of showmanship. For the first few minutes I was able to pretend I was a footballer, but suddenly everything went wrong.

I was minding my own business at the edge of the penalty area when the ball landed at my feet, so I booted it in the direction of the goal. Somehow or other I really connected with it. The timing, though solely a matter of luck, was perfect, and the ball flew with considerable speed and accuracy past the helpless keeper. Had there been a net, it would have bulged gratifyingly out of shape. As it was, I can still hear the thwack the ball made against the wire fence several metres behind the goal. Boys whose names I had not yet learnt ran across the field to pat me on the back.

But my elation ended when I saw the faint smile on Mr Jones's face and the faraway look in his eyes. He was staring at me without quite focusing, and I knew what was going through his mind. Here was this new boy in his first games lesson – a new boy from *Liverpool* – and he had just scored a brilliant goal. It was as though the great Liverpool and England striker Roger Hunt had suddenly enrolled at Green Street Green primary school.

I saw all this and more. I saw the future, in which I was destined to prove a major disappointment to Mr Jones. Should I have said something? Ought I to have walked up to him and confessed that what had just happened was a fluke? Of course I didn't. I was nine. But I recognised what was coming and knew there was nothing I could do to stop it. The following week, a notice was posted announcing the teams for the forthcoming game between the school's third-year and fourth-year classes. Taking the field at centre forward for the third-year team would be 'Ford, A.'

For a fleeting moment I felt proud. Part of me wanted to believe that a hitherto unsuspected talent for football had been discovered in me by the nice Welshman, but I knew the truth, and it was confirmed by the look that passed between my parents when I told them the news of my selection. A dreadful error had occurred; the only possible outcome was my mortification, and the rest of the story is sadly predictable. The following week, the fourth years beat the third years 10–nil; and the third years' centre forward, in his first and last representative game in any sporting code, had the ball at his feet precisely eleven times during the match – kicking off at the start and kicking off after each of the ten goals his side conceded.

Strangely enough, my meagre skills with a football were about to be shared with thousands of British cinemagoers. One of the first people I met at my new school was a friendly boy called Victor, who could play Eric Coates's *Dam Busters March* on the piano. This was something I found beguiling, my own piano lessons having stalled, but I was just as taken with the fact that Victor's father was an actor. My ambitions in that area, though undimmed, were no nearer being realised, but knowing Victor brought me tantalisingly close to the mysterious art. The fact that his dad landed roles in which he hardly ever spoke did not for a moment diminish the magic of this association. His biggest claim to fame, as ubiquitous as it was anonymous, was as the chef on the Paxo packet, Paxo being a brand of instant stuffing (add boiling water and stir). Dressed in chef's whites, with a toque on his head, he smiled winningly from a shelf in our kitchen cupboard. He also had a role in a new TV series called *Dad's Army*. As usual, it didn't require him to say anything, but you could see him standing in the second row of the Walmington-on-Sea Home Guard platoon. He was, in other words, an extra, but I looked out for him each week and felt a buzz of excitement when he appeared.

One day, Victor's mum rang mine. A casting agent wanted three boys to take part in a film shoot for an advertising campaign in cinemas. Victor would be one of these boys, and he had suggested my name. It would be shot in London, and there was a fee of ten guineas. There wouldn't be much to do, we were told. We'd just have to kick a ball around in a park.

The advertisement was either for a camera or a brand of film – if I was ever told, I have forgotten – and the plot, such as it was, involved a man with a camera creeping out of the bushes to snap a young woman in a yellow bikini sunning herself on the grass. Meanwhile three boys (that's me on the left) are playing football, when one of them (Victor, the star) kicks the ball in the direction of the man, who is concentrating on the woman, knocking the camera from his hands.

So it wasn't Chekhov, but I learnt quite a lot that day. There were many things I liked about the process of filming, from eavesdropping on the director ('Maybe you could lick your lips,' he told the actor in the bushes), to the novelty of my proximity to a woman in a bikini, to riding around in the back of the camera van. But above all, it was what happened at lunch that impressed me.

We'd begun shooting in Holland Park, only to be ejected by a council official, so we drove out to Isleworth, where the film crew knew of a bushy park near the famous film studios. Lunch was in a restaurant round the corner. It must have been fairly up-market, because I remember a red velvet interior and curtains drawn against the bright sunshine. The crew and cast (if I may call us that) sat at a long table with candles, and I found myself opposite the make-up lady, a rather grand, theatrical woman, the like of whom I had never met. One of the things that struck me about her manner was her confidence. She had a deep, fruity voice like the actor Hermione Gingold, and was given to proclaiming her thoughts on the smallest matters.

'Well! *I'm* going to have the mushroom omelette,' she announced to the table with abrupt finality, as though we'd all been waiting on tenterhooks for her decision. When my family went out for lunch nobody made such important-sounding declarations; I'm not sure food was even discussed. Yet somehow she managed to make a mushroom omelette sound like the most sophisticated thing you could eat.

Next, the restaurant door opened and a shaft of sunlight brightened the interior as two men stepped inside. As the door closed behind them and the candlelit gloom settled once more, the place fell suddenly, respectfully quiet. The men, nodding to some of the other diners as they moved through the restaurant, disappeared into a private room at the back.

'The Master!' whispered the make-up lady dramatically.

I couldn't see him very clearly, and probably wouldn't have recognised Noël Coward in any case, but I certainly knew his lunch companion, because John Le Mesurier was Sergeant Wilson in *Dad's Army*. Today a bit of research suggests they must have come to the restaurant from a morning's shooting on *The Italian Job*, which was filming at the Isleworth Studios. So it was a brush with fame that might have been a bigger brush with even greater fame, yet what I remember most about it is the make-up lady. As for my advertisement, for years I went to the cinema expecting to see it, but I never did.

o   o
o   o

There was more music at my new school than there had been in Liverpool, and certainly plenty of singing. The headmaster – who had a shockingly bad voice – liked to take these classes himself, and we worked our way through a wide repertoire of songs from around the world. They included 'Donkey Riding', 'Green Grow the Rushes-O' and 'Kookaburra Sits in the Old Gum Tree', the last of which we sang with gusto and, as its composer intended, in canon. Fifteen years later, having learnt that I would be moving to Australia, part of my preparation involved immersing myself in as much Antipodean culture as possible. Australian classical music was thin on the ground in the UK, but Australian pop was enjoying something of an international golden age, and I was pleased to discover 'Kookaburra Sits in the Old Gum Tree' making a cameo appearance in Men at Work's big hit 'Down Under', along with what I later discovered were numerous other bits of Aussie popular culture (at the time, for instance, I had not the slightest idea what a Vegemite sandwich might be). Twenty-six years after that, I found myself an expert witness in the Federal Court of Australia, giving evidence that 'Kookaburra Sits' really was in the Men at Work song, as though the song itself were not evidence enough. It still amazes me that the case ever went to court.

It wasn't long after my family's relocation to Kent that a new piano teacher was found for my sister and me, as different to Miss Halliday as it was possible to be. Harold Dresser was a loud, brusque, almost boorish man with a club foot, who boomed though our front door every Wednesday afternoon after we returned from school and frankly intimidated me and my sister, who had lessons with him one after the other. Part of the intimi-dation was physical, I now see, and I suspect his closeness to me on the piano stool might these days have been deemed unaccept-able. There was also a lot of leg squeezing, though nothing more. But what Mr Dresser brought to our house, at last, was real music: Bach and Haydn and Beethoven, and no more Walter Carroll.

The trouble was, I couldn't actually play Bach and Haydn and Beethoven. I liked the music, indeed I was fascinated by it, but as a pianist I was a poseur. I practised the beginnings of cer-tain pieces until I could play them with a degree of flair. I recall I was quite convincing, at least in my own mind, with the start of Beethoven's *Pathétique* sonata, but I couldn't get beyond the introduction. It was the same with the three piano preludes of Gershwin. I could play the slow middle one until the right-hand octaves arrived, and I could manage the start of the first. I wanted people to believe I could play, and I would happily perform for anyone who was prepared to listen to a recital con-sisting mostly of the starts of pieces. But over the years I simply failed to get any better. I lacked concentration, and as soon as a difficult passage came along, I gave up. In later life, working in universities, I often had an office near to practice rooms and I could always hear the students who were like me, and whose practice regimens, such as they were, involved giving little recit-als for themselves, the same mistakes always occurring in the same places.

By the time Mr Dresser retired, when I was about sixteen years old, I had not truly progressed at the piano from a technical point of view, though my knowledge of music theory was quite advanced and I had begun composing with a degree of earnestness.

Six years later, I tried again. By now, I had won the music prize at my grammar school, completed a first degree in music and been appointed Fellow in Music at the University of Bradford. As a composer, I'd just received my first commission. I suppose it could fairly be said that not playing the piano – or any other instrument – wasn't holding me back. But I felt that my work would be enhanced by the ability to play reasonably advanced music tolerably well. That was all I ever aimed to do; I was never going to perform in public.

I asked a friend, Joan Dixon, a wonderful pianist with an excellent reputation as a teacher, if she would give me lessons. It would be easier this time, I reasoned. Music was now my life: I didn't have all the distractions of childhood and adolescence; I could devote a fair proportion of my time to the piano. We began with the easier pieces from Bartók's *Mikrokosmos* and Stravinsky's *Les cinq doigts*; and we ended with them too. It took a few weeks of mounting embarrassment on both our parts before I faced the fact that I was coming up with excuses for not having practised, or worse, claiming that I *had* practised, when it would have been evident to any teacher I had not. It's one thing to do this as a child, but at the age of twenty-two?

If my keyboard skills would never advance beyond those of a lazy child, my listening, always avid, deepened significantly in the years after we moved to Kent, and this was at first thanks to the Beatles, who remained the centre of my musical imagination. In this I was no different to most of the rest of the world, but something was happening with the Beatles and their music that coincided with our family's move away from Liverpool. Within weeks of our arrival in Kent, the Beatles released a single bearing two of their best songs, 'Penny Lane' and 'Strawberry Fields Forever'. Everything about it seemed strange. Instead of a generic, bottle-green Parlophone sleeve, this record came with a picture of the Beatles on the cover, and they didn't look like the Beatles I knew. They all had droopy moustaches, they weren't smiling and they were sitting in the dark.

Musically, too, something was afoot. 'Penny Lane' included a high trumpet that, to my knowledge, none of them played. 'Strawberry Fields' had a melodic line that was far removed from anything I'd heard in pop music. And there was one more thing with which I particularly identified as I clung to my Northern identity: these were the Beatles' most Liverpudlian songs. Both were named after places in Liverpool – a bus terminal and an orphanage – and they contained flashes of Scouse ('it's a clEEn m'-shEEn' and 'the barber shaves a-NUH-ther CUHS-tomer') and Liverpool slang ('nothing to get hung about' and 'finger pie' – not that I had the remotest idea what the latter was).

At the same time the Beatles were moving from the poppy energy of 'I Want to Hold Your Hand' to the dreamy, druggy multilayers of 'Strawberry Fields Forever', I went from being six to nearly ten, a lifetime for a child. Looking back, it seems astonishing that the Beatles' musical development should have taken them so quickly from simple chords and rhymes to tape loops and Bach trumpets. Their entire output, from first single to last, spans little more than seven years. Had they been songwriters alone, the Beatles' production of more than 200 songs for themselves and others would have been impressive, but we should also remember their range, for there is really no such thing as a typical Beatles song. While writing and recording, they pursued an onerous touring schedule for the first four years. They influenced every other popular musician on the planet, and became 'more popular than Jesus' while garnering critical attention such as pop had never before received, their later albums reviewed in the *Times* by its classical music critic, William Mann (who called them the 'Beatle Quartet' and compared them to Mahler). At the time of their break-up, all four were still in their twenties. You do sometimes encounter people who are dismissive of the Beatles' achievement, but that's always seemed to me a posture.

o   o
o

In 1968, Britain still had what was known as the 11-plus, an exam undertaken by all students at the end of primary school to decide, in effect, how academically bright they were. Those who passed went to grammar schools; those who 'failed' – the word was used – were sent to 'secondary modern' schools. My general feeling about exams is that they waste valuable resources and time that might be better spent educating children. Sometimes they measure a child's understanding of a subject – though they seldom tell teachers what they don't already know – but the only thing they consistently reveal is a child's ability to pass exams. Anyone who has ever taught in a school or university knows that students develop at different rates, and that eleven is both an early and arbitrary age to condemn a child to woodwork instead of Latin, which was more or less the choice. I got Latin, doing well enough in the exam to go to grammar school, but I was no academic star. The first and only time I did really well in exams was in my university finals, ten years after the 11-plus. It's hard not to wonder about the millions of children who never had the chance to develop that far, whose prospects were shut down after being told they were eleven-year-old failures.

The 11-plus exam was only introduced in 1944, so my father never sat it, but having left school at fourteen he was conscious his whole life of a want of formal education and often spoke of it. This was a quick-witted man, interested in everything, who solved the *Guardian*'s cryptic crossword puzzle most days (even now I can't manage a single clue), and yet who carried with him a profound sense of academic failure. The night before my 11-plus, he came into my bedroom to wish me good luck. He hoped I would do well, because then people would say I took after my college-educated mother; he didn't want anyone to say that I took after him. I found this sad and still do.

Years later, on one of my visits home from university, Dad made a pun on the French expression *faux pas*. I didn't get it; I didn't know the expression.

'Don't be so sodding superior,' he said, when I looked at him blankly. I realised later he must have thought he had mispronounced it and that I was pretending not to understand, whereas I was genuinely mystified – so much for a French O-level! That made me sad, too. Dad wouldn't have snapped at me without cause, and while on this occasion he was wrong, there must have been earlier occasions when he'd thought I was lording it over him.

St Olave's and St Saviour's Grammar School for boys probably hadn't helped in this regard. It was a 'voluntary aided' institution, state-funded but with its building program privately subsidised by a foundation that dated back to 1560-something, its original charter bearing the seal of Elizabeth I. So it was a privileged set-up – there were language laboratories, a swimming pool and Eton Fives courts (I never found out what Eton Fives was) – and the staff, whom we addressed as 'Sir' and in a few cases 'Ma'am', wore academic gowns. They included some inspiring figures, among them Giovanni Baldelli, the author of *Social Anarchism*, who taught modern languages, and an Australian teacher of English, Reg Renshaw, who ran the debating society and encouraged in his students the ability both to frame an argument and to listen critically to what others had to say. As so often goes with educational privilege, the staff also had its admixture of sadists and paedophiles: a games teacher who made us stand barefoot in the snow for twenty minutes; a history master who groped his favourite boys until two police officers took him away, mid-lesson. But there were no fees, the only price exacted being two religious assemblies a day. At these an organ played and the choir often sang an anthem or an *a cappella* four-part setting of the Lord's Prayer. It was what you would call a musical school.

In my first week at St Olave's I was auditioned for this choir, not because I was keen to join it, but because the music master auditioned all the new boys. Along with anyone else who could hold a tune, I was told to be at the Small Hall the following Wednesday lunchtime. On arrival, we were handed copies of Fauré's Requiem, and by the end of the half-hour rehearsal I had had my first taste of singing from a vocal score, singing in harmony and singing in Latin.

Desmond Swinburn, the music master, was a sour man with a sharp tongue. Perhaps he was bitter to be wasting his talents on schoolboys, because he was undoubtedly talented; in particular, he was an excellent organist. But he was the worst teacher of any subject I ever had. His classes were devoid of inspiration and enthusiasm, and I imagine in the course of his career he must have ruined music for hundreds of his pupils: Richard Gill he was not. Lessons consisted of copying bits of music theory from the blackboard, but without reference to the sound of actual music. We were expected to learn about crotchets and quavers for their own sake. Occasionally we sang Benjamin Britten's setting of Eleanor Farjeon's 'The Jazz Man', or Stanford's stirring song to Henry Newbolt's words, 'The Old Superb'.

'Westward ho! for Trinidad, and Eastward ho! for Spain, / And "Ship ahoy!" a hundred times a day,' went Newbolt's poem. That got us all sniggering. 'A hundred times a day,' you see, was related to sex in our schoolboy minds; everything was related to sex, though none of us knew the first thing about it.

'Colony,' whispered Martin Holland one day at the bus stop.

'What?' I said.

'Colony,' he repeated, rolling his eyes. 'It's *rude.*'

'I don't think so,' I said.

'It *is*,' he insisted. He looked around to make sure we were weren't being overheard. '*Nudist* colony.'

I suppose being cooped up in a classroom with these sorts of adolescent minds might alone have accounted for our music master's caustic demeanour, yet in spite of his myriad shortcomings, I liked Desmond Swinburn. Partly, I think, I felt sorry for him, but I was also fortunate to be in that choir, where one saw a different side of the man. He was still sharp-tongued, but when he raised his baton, his musicianship communicated itself instantly. A former conducting student of the great Adrian Boult, he had a calm clarity to his beat and every movement indicated something important; nothing was wasted.

Fauré's Requiem is not an obvious choice to inculcate a lifelong love of the choral repertoire in children. Its harmonic subtleties, you might think, would be lost on the average child. I was a very average child – I'd never heard of Fauré and had no idea what a requiem was – yet this music swept me away. I remember relishing, as you'd expect, the boisterous central section of the 'Libera me', with its depiction of 'that day of wrath' (it was as though Fauré had set the phrase 'calamitatis et miseriae' with eleven-year-old boys in mind). But the delicate soprano solo 'Pie Jesu', which all we trebles sang in unison, was no less affecting, while the graceful viola melody at the start of the 'Agnus Dei' still makes me catch my breath.

By the time of the concert at the end of that first term, I was hooked. It wasn't that I was a natural chorister, or really any kind of chorister. After the concert, my mother commented that I hadn't appeared to be singing at all, my lips having barely moved. I suppose what I was doing, standing in the middle of that glorious noise, was soaking it up, and after six years at the school – by which time I was singing and reading music fluently – I had absorbed Handel's *Israel in Egypt*, *Samson* and *Messiah*, Bach's *St John Passion*, *Christmas Oratorio*, *Magnificat* and the cantata *Sleepers Wake!*, Vivaldi's *Gloria*, Schütz's *Christmas Story*, Britten's *St Nicolas*, and smaller works by Parry, Stanford, Elgar, Vaughan Williams, Holst and Delius.

Being in Swinburn's choir was perhaps the most important part of my music education – more important than university, more important than composition lessons – because it formed the foundation. I wish all children had the chance to sing at that level: you learn to concentrate for long stretches; you learn to cooperate as a group, as a community; you learn above all to listen. And you carry the music with you ever after.

One of the immediate effects on me of the choir was that I began to explore classical music with greater curiosity. I still listened to pop music, but as the 1960s became the 1970s and I became a teenager, my horizons broadened. I finally began to read voraciously, I listened to the radio – not only pop radio, but classical music, drama and book programs – and, I suppose, I began to think for myself.

Paradoxically, thinking for yourself requires assistance, even guidance. There isn't time to explore everything off your own bat;

anyway, how would you know where start? So you follow the recommendations of those you admire, particularly those who have previously recommended books or films or music you have enjoyed or been impressed by. You need teachers and you need your peers – I was fortunate, particularly in the latter, because there were other boys whose curiosity was awakening at the same time as my own. You also need role models, and they can come from anywhere. Some are public advocates.

On the radio, the pop broadcaster John Peel was as import-ant to me as to many thousands of others, his witty laconicism never quite masking a genuine enthusiasm for the music he pre-sented. I sat by the radio with my family's cassette recorder, pointing the microphone at the loudspeaker and recording hours of music that I would later pore over. Peel presented not only new recordings but also live sessions, such as Joni Mitchell singing the new songs from her album *Blue*, and James Taylor performing songs that would shortly appear on *Mud Slide Slim*; there was also harder-edged and more experimental stuff: the searing Scottish soul of Maggie Bell and her band Stone the Crows ('Mad Dogs and Englishmen'), the jazz rock of Soft Machine and, a little later, the avant-garde collages of the German band Faust. There was a serendipitous quality to my discovery, as there always is with good radio, and my cassette tapes thinned as they were played back, then recorded over, then played back, then recorded over again.

Sometimes the most important role models can be right there in your home. On my mother's advice, I read Richard Hoggart's magisterial study of working-class culture *The Uses of Literacy*, at least as relevant today as when it was first published in the year of my birth. Mum was relieved that I was finally reading and would often push things my way. When I was fourteen, she gave me D.H. Lawrence's *The Rainbow* for Christmas, which we discussed at the time as a slightly risqué choice. And it was Mum who encouraged my classical listening. Somehow I had discovered Stravinsky's *The Firebird*; Mum told me I should try *The Rite of Spring*. She was also good at correcting my sometimes wayward taste. Overhearing me listening to Waldo de los Ríos's *Symphonies for the 70's*, Mum suggested I might want to try Mozart's Symphony No 40 in G minor without the rhythm section. When I borrowed a friend's copy of Emerson, Lake and Palmer's *Pictures at an Exhibition*, she recommended listening to Musorgsky's original piano suite. And when Miguel Ríos came on the radio singing his (let's face it, execrable) 'Song of Joy', which I quite liked, it was Mum who pointed out that the tune was Beethoven's and I'd be better employed listening to his ninth symphony.

3.

'Freude, Schöner Götterfunken'

I lost my religious faith the day I discovered my father was a fifth columnist.

I say lost, though it is perfectly possible I never truly had it. But there I was, sixteen years old in my school uniform, wearing a paper badge that read 'Jesus Saves!' or perhaps 'Smile, Jesus Loves You!' – something of the sort. It was about five centimetres in diameter and stuck to the lapel of my blazer. The words, whatever they actually proclaimed, were in orange lettering on a purple background. It was the early 1970s.

'Why do you wear that?'

As soon as Dad framed his question, I knew I'd been rumbled. I'm sure I blushed. Yet it was the obvious question, and what was this badge if not an invitation to ask it? Now that I'd been called to account, I floundered. Not only could I think of nothing to say to my father, I couldn't even explain the badge to myself. At length, I mumbled something about God, to which Dad replied that he didn't believe in Him.

Now, this was a surprise. My father was a man who could – and did – recite chunks of the Book of Common Prayer. Of course, it's a quotable book, and Dad's recitation of passages from the Creed or the General Confession were not of a particularly pious nature.

'We have erred, and strayed from thy ways like lost sheep,' he once observed in the car, having taken several wrong turns; 'Have you done those things you ought to have done?' he was fond of asking in relation to my homework. And it wasn't just the prayer book: there were quotes from oratorio too. He needed little prompting – a closed garage door would do it – to burst into 'Fling wide the gates' from Stainer's slice of Victorian piety, *The Crucifixion.*

So there was all that, but there was also family legend. I imagine all families must have this, parents asked to regale their children with stories about the times before they were born. In our house, many of these tales revolved around my parents' attendance at St Lawrence's Anglican Church in Liverpool. All their oldest friends had been in the congregation and my sister and I called them uncle or aunty. I had the sense that St Lawrence's formed a kind of bedrock to our existence.

'Well, what about St Lawrence's, then?'

'I was recruiting for the Labour Party,' Dad replied matter-of-factly.

Whether this was the whole truth, I never found out, but coupled with my shock at suddenly learning Dad was not a believer, and a second shock – slightly smaller and tinged with relief – that perhaps neither was I, came welling pride. My father was a man of mystery. An infiltrator, a spy. Almost a double agent.

Learning secrets about one's parents can be discomfiting. When, as children, we demand to hear their old stories yet again, we want them to be the same as last time – legends become legends in the retelling, the listener waiting for familiar, reassuring words and phrases; we do not want to encounter elements in the stories that weren't there before. But although Dad's undercover work was all new to me, I was impressed.

So the badge was removed, and God went with it. But just as my father remained a quoter of the prayer book, so the accoutrements of Christianity never left me. Lines from hymns and verses from the Bible (and, yes, the prayer book) pop unbidden into my head as they did into Dad's. Since I don't believe in God and don't wish to, I must be an atheist, but I am not a militant atheist, and when people such as Richard Dawkins insist that religion in history has only been a force for evil, I disagree. Setting aside everything else, there is the art that would not exist without religion, art that was inspired by faith and often paid for by the Church. That includes the poetry of Cranmer's prayer book and the King James Bible.

In 2015 I was commissioned by four Australian cathedrals, two Catholic and two Anglican, to compose a mass – to be precise, a *missa brevis*, or short mass – for liturgical use. When I told my friends, their most common response, after a beat of incredulity, was the tentative enquiry: 'But aren't you an atheist?'

Let me say this was not a question asked by the cathedrals themselves, and there was no reason it should have been. They were commissioning a piece of music from me, so my relevant credentials were musical. The temptation to set to music Latin words previously set by Byrd and Bach, Haydn, Mozart and Beethoven, Bruckner, Dvořák and Stravinsky was irresistible. And while many composers have been devout – in sixteenth-century England, Byrd risked his life for Catholicism; Bruckner's whole musical output was an act of devotion – there's also nothing to stop an atheist writing a mass. Moreover, if you remove from the list of liturgical music all those pieces composed by nonbelievers, you will leave a significant hole. Brahms is gone, for a start, and probably Schubert. Not that they wrote a lot of church music, but Strauss and Tchaikovsky can join the list, along with Sibelius, who composed some of Finland's best-known hymn tunes. And the Anglican liturgy will be especially affected, for there will be no music by Parry (the composer of 'Jerusalem') or Holst ('I Vow to Thee, My Country') or Britten (*A Hymn to the Virgin*, *A Ceremony of Carols* and the *Missa brevis* he wrote for Westminster Cathedral).

Ralph Vaughan Williams, editor of *The English Hymnal*, was described by his second wife as 'an atheist who occasionally lapsed into agnosticism', yet he took to his editorship with gusto, even writing some new tunes for the publication ('Come Down O Love Divine', 'For All the Saints'). John Ireland, who composed one of the English-speaking world's most beautiful hymns, 'My Song Is Love Unknown', once declared: 'I am a Pagan. A Pagan I was born & a Pagan I shall ever remain.'

Strictly speaking, I suppose we are all born pagans, but growing up in England, where the separation of powers has been compromised since Henry VIII, it is hard to avoid religion. As a small child in Liverpool, I was sent to Sunday school, which I disliked, and at my primary school sang hymns and Christmas carols, which I liked very much. In those twice-daily assemblies at St Olave's, there were hymns, anthems, Bible readings and prayers. And there was the school choir: if a choir sings classical music, it will tend to be religious. But none of this accounted for that badge. My moment of teenage fervour can only be explained by two things, music and sex. Only the music was real.

As a teenager, I listened to everything I could lay my ears on: rock music, particularly the more progressive sort (for which I now have little patience), folk music, classical music and some jazz. In addition to my avid radio listening, I brought home, each fortnight, an armful of classical LPs from the local public library. This music became so important to me that I began, consciously, to explore the repertory. If, for example, I heard a Schumann symphony on the radio, I would borrow his others from the library. It seemed important to be familiar with the whole body of work. And some of it moved me to tears.

But there was one particular moment, an epiphany I suppose you'd call it. Nothing like this had happened to me before, and as epiphanies go I've had very little since that has matched it. I wish I could claim it had been something more recherché, but the music that floored me so unexpectedly was Beethoven's ninth symphony, and the choral finale at that. It wasn't the first time

I had heard this music. On the contrary, the recording was the one I had bought a couple of years earlier at my mother's bidding and since listened to numerous times (Franz Konwitschny conducting the Leipzig Gewandhaus Orchestra, since you ask).

The moment that got me comes midway through the finale, following the variation on the famous 'Ode to Joy' theme that Beethoven turns into a Turkish march, the tenor soloist joining in with a tune that always seems to have escaped from a bier-keller. This is followed by a serious fugal workout for orchestra alone. But then comes a mysterious, ruminative passage in which the French horns have repeating F sharps in a rhythm reminiscent of a heartbeat. Over this, oboes and bassoons play a tentative ascending figure in D major, which leads nowhere; they try it in D minor, still nowhere; finally they settle for the dominant key of A and, without warning, we are whisked abruptly back to the chorus, loudly and triumphantly punching out Schiller's ode in D.

That was the moment – and it shook me, literally. I was physically affected. There were tears, but there was also something harder to explain, something like possession. I felt the music had taken me over, taken me in. The music was inside me – in my head – but I was also in the music. This must be God, I thought.

Actually, I wanted it to be God, because I secretly hoped He'd help me locate a girlfriend. At a school for boys, it wasn't immediately obvious how I might meet members of the opposite sex, but a couple of my friends attended the local Methodist youth club, and I knew there were girls there. Now that I had

God, I could go too. Maybe there would be sex. In fact, there was table tennis, but at least there were girls in the room.

I don't mean to mock my teenage self here, because something significant had indeed occurred in my life. C.S. Lewis wrote a late memoir of his conversion to Christianity called *Surprised by Joy*, taking his title from Wordsworth. For Lewis, the 'joy' in question might have been termed 'longing', since he also uses the German word *Sehnsucht*, and he describes it as coming in the form of 'stabs' of feeling for something far above him. I had been surprised by the 'Ode to Joy', and for a short time – no more than a year – was serious enough about religion to attend church, where I listened attentively to the sermons of the minister Hugh Temple-Bone. He was a gifted public speaker, perhaps the first intellectual to whom I paid regular attention. His sermons generally pushed past the half-hour mark, and I looked forward to them more than any other aspect of the services. I also enrolled in his confirmation classes and finally got confirmed. If my father had a problem with any of this, he never mentioned it; it was only when I took to badge wearing that he raised the matter.

Hand in glove with my brief commitment to religion went an ever-deepening engagement with music and art in a broader sense, a curiosity that eventually took over from God. I began to explore books and music willy-nilly, in the process often lighting on works of art that remain important to me today. I bought a copy of T.S. Eliot's *Selected Poems*. I must have heard about Eliot on the radio. In bed that night I read *The Waste*

Land, and while I don't suppose I understood more than about twenty per cent of it – there's much about the poem I still don't understand – it made a big impact, largely because of the way it sounded in my head. It wasn't quite Beethoven's ninth, but the music of *The Waste Land* captivated and affected me and I began to burrow into its meaning as best I could. George Orwell became another favourite writer, particularly his essays, and here there was no problem at all with meaning. Other books were bought or borrowed: *The Mersey Sound* – a bestselling anthology of poetry by three Liverpool poets, Adrian Henri, Roger McGough and Brian Patten; Leonard Cohen's *Poems 1956–68*; Huxley's *Brave New World*, Zamyatin's *We*, Sartre's *Nausea*. Some of these were recommendations from school, where like-minded friends were also reading avidly, meeting in each other's homes to read plays by Friedrich Dürrenmatt, Max Frisch and N.F. Simpson. With a blend of irony, surrealism and high preten-tiousness, we called ourselves the Metalwork Club. Sometimes music was involved. Somebody brought the LP of *Stockhoven–Beethausen* to one session, a version of Karlheinz Stockhausen's *Kurzwellen* – his work for short-wave radio receivers – in which fragments of Beethoven's music were heard through the white noise. We thought it was weird, and therefore good. There were also girls at the Metalwork Club.

It would be easy to dismiss us as a bunch of teenage pseudo-intellectuals. On my first genuine date with a girl, I got the time of the film wrong and ended up boring poor, hapless Eileen Buckley for more than an hour with my thoughts on the

Communist Manifesto. I had read only the first four pages and the last – and never did get around to the rest – but somehow believed she'd be interested in hearing all about it. She must have been mightily relieved when we finally went in to see *The Poseidon Adventure*, a disaster movie, the theme of which nicely summed up the evening.

But a word in defence of pretentiousness. Just as small children learn by pretending, so do older children. We try on ideas as once we tried on cowboy hats; we want to be like our peers and so pretend to like the same things, the same books and films and music. Sometimes, we discover that we actually do like them. Our pretensions have guided us; we have learnt from them and they are pretensions no longer.

It's not impossible that my interest in religion had been pretentiousness of a sort, though one that failed to develop. When I stopped going to church I began attending concerts – new music and early music, symphony concerts, chamber concerts and operas – and music became something to proselytise about. I might have been half-hearted when it came to religious evangelism, removing my Jesus badge the first time I was called upon to justify it, but my advocacy for music was tireless. I seldom attended concerts alone, and often dragged along half a dozen friends.

I find it interesting that Richard Dawkins has almost as little time for art as he does for God. I think he detects a similar irrationality of response by adherents of both, and it bothers him. It doesn't bother me – quite the contrary – and it didn't bother the musicologist Wilfrid Mellers. The last time I spoke to him, he was in his late eighties and had just written a book about religious music in the European classical tradition. It was called *Celestial Music?* (note the question mark). I asked him what he thought about religion, to which he replied that he thought it was 'non-sense really'. Then he added: 'But perhaps we need more non-*sense* in our lives.'

I suppose my response to Beethoven's ninth was irrational. I still find that moment exhilarating, but it has never again bowled me over in quite the way it did this particular day. What, at the time, I thought was God, now I think was Beethoven. Either would condemn me in Dawkins's eyes. My feelings at that sudden choral entry, blazing away in D major, were, it occurs to me, something like Stendhal's syndrome. The Frenchman had his dizzy spell while viewing Giotto's frescoes in Santa Croce, but if a wall painting can provoke such a reaction, how much more likely is music to do it, an art form that takes over the body? And isn't this all fairly close to the way that some Pentecostals respond to the divine presence? Isn't this what they call being 'slain in the spirit'?

I can't recall a single religious inclination from the past four decades, but I do think that perhaps what I and others get from music is what a lot of people get from their faith. And of course it's not all bursting into tears or feeling faint – in fact hardly ever. Proper listening involves engagement with a musical work. We have to concentrate, to contemplate, but mostly we must listen. I often think that an important aspect of music is that it forces us to stop talking, an attitude similar to prayer. If listening takes place in the concert hall, then sometimes the experience will be amplified by the presence of others. By sharing the experience, even wordlessly, we seem to make it more intense: the audience as congregation, music as communion. This is not, however, to suggest that everyone in the concert hall is having the same experience. If there are a hundred listeners, there are arguably a hundred slightly different pieces of music, because we hear and process music, and certainly understand it, in our own unique ways. We make it – or at least remake it – in our heads. Perhaps it's the same with God.

I am not, of course, suggesting that with music and religion it's either/or. Most of the world's religions use music as an aid to worship, and you can see why. But there are some religions or branches of religion that don't permit music at all, or don't permit certain types of music. Or perhaps they redefine the term to suit their needs.

I was once in a Melbourne taxi with a driver who was listening to the most magnificent singing. I was captivated and asked him what the music was.

'It's not music,' he replied. 'It's the Koran.'

'Oh, right … But it's being sung,' I said.

'No, it's not,' he said.

'He's singing,' I insisted. 'It's beautiful.'

'He's not singing.'

I finally got the driver to agree that the man was 'chanting', and that this 'chanting' was a way of helping to focus the listener on the text. Not that I mentioned it, for fear of starting another argument, but the chanting of the Koran was reminiscent of an ornamented plainsong.

In the music of Christianity, medieval plainsong (sometimes generically, and wrongly, referred to as Gregorian chant) led to Renaissance polyphony – to many voices in communion (the symbolism was intended), and to more complex, multilayered forms of composition. At which point – the mid sixteenth century – the Council of Trent questioned the place of music in the liturgy. Was music now too beautiful? Was there too much detail in the masses and motets of Palestrina, too much to take in? In a nutshell, was music getting in the way of doctrine? I understand this concern. Music can seduce us. Music seduced me into thinking I was having a religious experience, when I was having a musical one.

My best attempt to make sense of religion is to regard it as a branch of poetry. Art, it seems to me, is humanity's attempt to explain itself to itself, and so, I believe, is religion. Some people would find that notion blasphemous. Hey ho.

As a composer, I want people to pay attention to my music. I want their ears, their concentration and their critical faculties. And I have to confess, I am delighted when I'm told by an audience member that my music has moved them. It means that something inexplicable has occurred, some wordless exchange between me and the listener, some non-*sense*.

My *Missa brevis* was commissioned by St John's Anglican Cathedral in Brisbane (their director of music, Graeme Morton, was the ringleader), St Stephen's Catholic Cathedral in Brisbane, St Patrick's in Melbourne and St George's in Perth, in consortium with Ars Musica Australis. I had been impressed by the stance taken by many cathedrals and other churches in support of the rights of refugees. Australians have never much cared for 'reffos', and since the start of the twenty-first century the nation's politicians have tended to exploit this streak of xenophobia, some while ostentatiously proclaiming their deeply held Christian beliefs. It was, in a way, brave of the churches to stand up against popular sentiment and hypocrisy, but then there's nothing in the teachings of Christ that says we should reject desperate people who ask for help. In recognition of this, then, my *Missa brevis* is dedicated to 'all who seek asylum', and each of its sections makes use – sometimes quite subtle use – of the tune of the spiritual 'Sometimes I Feel Like a Motherless Child'.

Late in 2015, I found myself at St John's early one Sunday for a final rehearsal before the choir sang the mass at that morning's Eucharist. After the rehearsal, Graeme Morton asked me when was the last time I'd been to church, not counting weddings and funerals (they can tell, you see). I did a quick sum and replied that it must have been forty-two years. At the end of the service, as the choir walked up the aisle and Graeme, bringing up the rear, passed my pew, he muttered under his breath, 'And when was the last time you were in a procession?', grabbing my arm and pulling me into line behind his choristers as they left the church.

The whole business was fascinating to me: composing the mass, writing for an organ for the first time in my life, discussing the work with the commissioners, hearing it sung in a liturgical context dotted through a ninety-minute service. Still, the single most interesting part was when it was all over and the tea and biscuits came out. This was when I was approached by a number of parishioners who told me that their worship had been enhanced by my music. Now, I have had compliments over the years, but never of this nature, and while, of course, I said thank you, I admit the words gave me pause for thought. Only for a moment. Then I realised I was never so pleased in my life.

o   o
o

The first concert I attended off my own bat was a Prom at the Royal Albert Hall played by the BBC Symphony Orchestra. I chose it for Gustav Holst's suite *The Planets*, but it was significant in other ways. For one thing, it contained a piece by a living composer, Elisabeth Lutyens. *De amore* is a cantata for soprano, tenor, chorus and orchestra to words by Chaucer, lasting more than half an hour. I found it hard to comprehend and fairly tedious. Although this was its first performance, the music had been written in 1957, the year of my birth. The fact that a large-scale piece by a significant composer might wait sixteen years to be heard should perhaps have served as a warning to a boy who was already thinking a lot about composing. But if it registered at all, it was eclipsed by the thrill of the composer herself walking on to the platform to acknowledge the applause. Lutyens, the daughter of Edwin Lutyens, the architect of New Delhi, was one of the first British composers to take Schoenberg's twelve-tone system seriously – this was before the war, when British music was typically a mixture of arch pastoralism and pastiche jazz with added-note chords and syncopated rhythms. Lutyens's music, in contrast, was spikily modern, and as likely to turn up on the soundtrack of a Hammer horror film as in the concert hall. In the 1950s and 1960s, she influenced many of the next generation of modernist composers, including Richard Rodney Bennett and Malcolm Williamson. Now here she was on stage, glamorous, bohemian and very serious. In years to come I would often see her in the audience at concerts, but I was too shy to speak to her.

The rest of the concert consisted of *The Planets* and Elgar's *Introduction and Allegro* for string orchestra, the latter unfamiliar to me but making an instant impression that evening and still a favourite today. Both these pieces were conducted by the 84-year-old Sir Adrian Boult, Desmond Swinburn's old teacher. Not that I registered it, but I was in the presence of history. In 1930 Boult had been the founding conductor of the BBC Symphony Orchestra; he had numbered both Holst and Elgar among his friends and conducted the first performance of *The Planets* as long ago as 1918. I couldn't see a lot from my cheap balcony seat, but I was taken with Boult's evident authority and already interested enough in the art of conducting to pay attention to how he beat the five-in-a-bar of 'Mars – the bringer of war' with a pattern involving a second, smaller downbeat.

Boult disapproved of conductors who made themselves the centre of an audience's attention, and once insisted that you do not go to see a concert, but to hear it. And fair enough: it's a distinction I've subsequently been careful to make, and when I hear others say they've 'seen' music, it jars. But over the next few years, I attended a lot of Boult's concerts, and I watched as much as I listened, more often than not from a seat behind the orchestra. I heard and saw Boult conduct three of the four Brahms symphonies, as well as music by Wagner, Beethoven, Mozart, Elgar and Vaughan Williams.

Like his own teacher, Arthur Nikisch, Boult used a long stick by modern standards – it must have measured at least half a metre – but otherwise moved very little. He conducted from the wrist and his beat was clear and patient. His face was as impassive as his stance, yet you could never say that his conducting lacked expression. Where other conductors show through their gestures how they feel about the music, and by extension how you should feel, Boult showed the music itself. It wasn't the stick alone that did this, though his manipulation of the baton was certainly expressive; it was also the sparing, unfailingly poetic use of his left hand, and the focus of his eyes. He never wore glasses and the pale blue intensity of his gaze was impossible to avoid, even from the choir stalls.

In interviews, Boult talked about music as architecture, and his hope that he could, above all, convey a sense of a whole piece from start to finish. My experience of his conducting was just that, and in several cases, as with Elgar's *Introduction and Allegro*, Boult's concerts provided my first exposure to the piece. I had never, for instance, encountered a Mozart piano concerto until I heard André Previn play the C minor concerto with Boult; in the same concert

I had my first experience of Elgar's *Cockaigne* overture. Boult's conducting of the *Siegfried Idyll* was the start, for me, of a long journey into Wagner's music. With all these pieces, I took away, as Boult had hoped, an impression of the whole work, but there were also details from those performances that remain vividly in my memory. Previn's first entry in the Mozart was breathtaking – this was largely Mozart's doing, of course, but there was a simple fragility to the moment, set up by Boult's dramatic phrasing of the long orchestral introduction; in absolute contrast, I was pinned back in my seat by the timpani thwacks at that moment when a marching band arrives in *Cockaigne* – the player that night must have had particularly hard sticks, because ever since I've found this moment anticlimactic; in the *Siegfried Idyll* there was a sudden pianissimo that I've never heard more elegantly achieved than in that first concert with Boult conducting.

The other conductor I watched a good deal was Pierre Boulez, who from 1971 to 1975 had Boult's old job as chief conductor of the BBC Symphony Orchestra. Because the orchestra was publicly funded, it could take programming risks the other London orchestras could not. A radio orchestra's concerts are broadcast and heard by many thousands, so if the concert hall itself isn't completely full, it doesn't necessarily matter. But there was something about Boulez that pulled audiences anyway, even when the music in his programs was well off the beaten track. It's hard to say what created the magnetism, for, like Boult, Boulez was hardly a showman. Businesslike is perhaps the best description of his technique. Where Boult had a very long stick, Boulez had none at all, but otherwise they were rather similar. There was no extraneous movement from Boulez; each gesture was related to a musical imperative. Watching him, one was taken directly into the score, rather than into a personal fantasy of the conductor's. And then of course there was the music, much of which, again, I was hearing for the first time. The second Viennese school, Varèse, Berio, Stockhausen, Boulez himself: in the 1970s there were still those who regarded even Stravinsky and Bartók as difficult, but Boulez conducted it all with such precision and style that many of the difficulties fell away. Schoenberg had once remarked that his music wasn't difficult, just badly played, and here was Boulez proving the point. Schoenberg's orchestral textures can seem clotted, but Boulez rendered them transparent; you could hear everything. Applying the same technique to familiar music – Berlioz, Schumann, Mahler, Debussy, Ravel – Boulez's results were equally revelatory.

As well as summer visits to the Proms, I was now regularly making the 25-minute train journey up to London to attend concerts in the Royal Festival Hall and Queen Elizabeth Hall at what is now called the Southbank Centre. Today this part of London is a thriving riverside hub of bars and cafes, street performers and carousels, but in the 1970s it was an empty, concrete space, like something from Jean-Luc Godard's *Alphaville*, the poorly lit off-white facades of the concert halls emphasising their 1950s brutalist style. I thought it was fabulous.

The excitement I felt at attending these concerts was partly a matter of anticipation. Sitting in an audience, waiting for this or that musician to emerge and perform, the frisson of expectation is always the same, even if, when the concert begins, there may be disappointment. Perhaps the performance isn't very good; perhaps the music doesn't appeal. Sometimes we discover we're simply not in the mood, as I wasn't for Lutyens's *De amore*. But when one is receptive and expectations are met, time flies by. And one of the most magical things that can occur in a concert – or with any other experience of art, a novel, a play – is when we are taken by surprise. A piece of music we hadn't expected to enjoy suddenly sucks us in, or it might be something we have heard a hundred times that now speaks to us with renewed intensity. What I'm describing doesn't always happen, or even happen often, but when it does the experience is so powerful it keeps us returning with renewed anticipation. Sometimes it also has the effect of making us wonder about the music and want to try to get to the bottom of it. We go off exploring: we search the internet, we buy a book or a recording, we scour the radio.

My favourite concerts were by the Early Music Consort of London and the Fires of London, both directed by young, intense, charismatic men, the music historian, broadcaster and multi-instrumentalist David Munrow and the composer Peter Maxwell Davies. Munrow's concerts were informal yet carefully devised explorations of music from the Middle Ages and early Renaissance; I don't suppose I had previously heard even a single piece that he presented. It was scarcely any different at concerts by the Fires of London, except that here the music was mostly brand new. Both groups contained some remarkable musicians – the keyboard player Christopher Hogwood was in the Early Music Consort, along with the counter-tenor James Bowman, while the Fires had that fearless clarinettist Alan Hacker.

Maxwell Davies would bound on stage, wired and wiry, his hair a profusion of black curls, his eyes a mix of penetrating focus and pixie-like glint, his conducting all elbows, his sharp, military bows always from the waist. At a Prom concert in 1974, the two ensembles shared a program, the Early Music Consort marking 500 years since the death of Guillaume Dufay with a performance of his mass, *Se la face ay pale*, the Fires playing Maxwell Davies's no less monumental *Hymn to St Magnus*, the two groups joining forces for music from Ken Russell's film *The Devils*.

In those days Munrow was ubiquitous. Besides the Early Music Consort, with which he made countless recordings, personally playing forty-three instruments, there were his film and TV scores (including *The Six Wives of Henry VIII* and *Elizabeth R*), and his *Pied Piper* radio program for children on weekday afternoons. I would not have been the only child who rushed home from school to hear these carefully scripted, twenty-minute explorations of this or that instrument or of the music of Mexico or Egypt or Berlioz or Villa-Lobos (there was an ear-opening week's worth of episodes given over to the Brazilian composer), or of dance music down the centuries or ceremonial music or some aspect of jazz. By 1976, when he hanged himself in a state of severe depression at the age of thirty-three, Munrow had written and presented 665 of these finely crafted programs in just five years. That alone should have been a full-time job.

Radio was a vital resource for any young person seeking to explore music, and it remains so, even if there are those, especially on the commercial networks, who would narrow its stylistic range. A knowledgeable presenter makes all the difference, and my own rapacious teenage listening was hugely enhanced by broadcasters such as Munrow and John Peel choosing and ordering the music (these days, I suppose, people would call it 'curating', though I wish they wouldn't) and pointing out the connections. I like to think some of their skill rubbed off on me in my radio work. Their enthusiasm certainly did.

Munrow's programs went out on BBC Radio 3, the rebranded Third Programme, and this was where most of my own listening was now directed. My cassette recorder was employed to record music by Tippett and Birtwistle more often than Soft Machine or Faust, though I still paid attention to Peel. My school friends also ensured that rock music wasn't neglected, the sixth-form common room ringing to the sounds of Emerson, Lake and Palmer and King Crimson, Uriah Heep, Bowie and the Mahavishnu Orchestra. Bowie, I hardly need say, was extraordinary, but closer to my taste was the Mahavishnu Orchestra. At the time we thought of it as heavy rock – we didn't know much about jazz besides Dave Brubeck – but now it seems less like rock and more like jazz all the time. It also stands up remarkably well forty years on. An international, jazz rock fusion 'super group' – which is what Mahavishnu amounted to – should really sound its age, but the first two albums, *Inner Mounting Flame* and *Birds of Fire*, remain fresh and exciting, John McLaughlin's guitar demonstrating, like Charlie Parker's alto sax, that you can play thrillingly fast, the music pouring from your instrument with seeming spontaneity, and yet every note is justified and necessary.

The other band of which I was a huge fan, and which seems as fresh today as it did then, was Pentangle, with the guitarists Bert Jansch and John Renbourn and the redoubtable Danny Thompson on double bass. Because the bulk of their material was traditional folk music, Pentangle are lumped together with Steeleye Span and Fairport Convention as folk-rockers, but in fact rock music was one of the musical idioms they never embraced. Blues, yes, jazz, yes, even a sort of 'world music' *avant la lettre*, with banjo, sitar and piano jangling together on certain tracks. Pentangle's official singer was the slightly pallid Jacqui McShee, but it is Jansch's soulful, doleful, never-quite-in-tune voice that I hear when I think of the band. Actually, 'band' really won't do. Pentangle neither sounded nor looked like a 'band'. They sang and played a form of chamber music; they even sat down on the job – 'bands' don't use chairs. To my ears, the folk-rock of Steeleye Span and the Fairports now sounds very much of its time, while Pentangle sound as though their time is yet to come.

One of the first composers I explored in depth was Vaughan Williams. His music seemed to speak to me directly and I grew slightly obsessed by it. Vaughan Williams's centenary, in 1972, was marked by many concert broadcasts, but the most important concert to me was the one I sang in with the combined choirs of Bromley schools – an event attended by the composer's widow,

Ursula, who made a speech. She was rather posh and struck me as young, given that her dead husband was 100 years old. The music in this concert was mostly minor stuff, including *A Song of Thanksgiving* and *The Sons of Light* (for which Ursula had provided the astrological text), but Vaughan Williams is one of those composers with a strong idiolect, his music recognisable from a few bars, so even his lesser achievements are distinctive. Thanks to Radio 3 and the Orpington library, I quickly became something of a Vaughan Williams expert.

Michael Tippett's third symphony and third piano sonata date from these same years, and I heard the premieres of both works in radio broadcasts. The torrent of notes from Paul Crossley's hands at the beginning of the sonata produced in me something like the excitement of John McLaughlin's guitar playing. Again, I supplemented my radio listening with library trips, and one LP in particular stands out, an abstract blue and white wave framed in black on its cover. It featured the Academy of St Martin in the Fields playing Tippett's music for string orchestra under Neville Marriner, and it was the sort of recording that changes the way a composer is regarded. When Tippett's *Fantasia Concertante on a Theme of Corelli* was new, the conductor Malcolm Sargent had found it so intimidatingly complex he'd refused to conduct its premiere at the 1953 Edinburgh Festival, but just nineteen years later Marriner revealed the lyrical strength of its counterpoint. Far from the arid 'intellectualism' of which Sargent complained to Tippett's publisher, the *Fantasia Concertante* emerges here as a bit of a tearjerker. The final minutes of the piece were used again and again by Peter Hall in his 1974 film *Akenfield* to evoke a sort of pastoral bliss.

The piece that leaps at the listener off Marriner's Tippett LP, however, is the Concerto for Double String Orchestra. I can think of very few pieces that come so quickly, vividly and *happily* to life as this – Beethoven's eighth symphony, perhaps? Mendelssohn's *Italian* symphony? Schumann's *Rhenish*? The first movement of Tippett's concerto is an exuberant display of modal melody and sprung rhythms, crisscrossing each other and the bar lines, and it starts in bar one, bounding into our consciousness like a delighted dog. In his television film *Poets in a Barren Age*, first shown in 1972, the same year Marriner's LP was released, Tippett spoke of the necessity of inventing music whether 'society' wants it or not, and of how the composer's role includes the provision 'in an age of mediocrity and shattered dreams' of 'images of abounding, generous, exuberant beauty'. He might have been describing the start of this piece composed in 1938 and 1939, a time of violently 'shattered dreams'.

The ability of a piece to reveal itself in its first seconds is also exemplified by Boulez's *Le marteau sans maître*, another oft-borrowed library LP of my teenage years. The music bursts straight into life, but unlike the purposeful start of Tippett's double concerto, *Le marteau* shoots off in several directions at once, a dazzle of sound that is simultaneously disorientating and beguiling in its use of alto flute, guitar, viola and tuned percussion. The sonority is a big part of the appeal of this music – the instrumental colours glittering at least as much as the darting shards of melody – but it's also the energy that Boulez generates that captivates us: this music is very fast and yet harmonically stable. For all the teeming activity at the start of *Le marteau*, we're not really going anywhere. This piece is the aural equivalent of a kaleidoscope.

My next discovery came when I brought home Leonard Bernstein's recording of recent pieces by two American composers, Aaron Copland and Elliott Carter. I did this entirely on the strength of the Copland, who was an early favourite (and another recommendation of my mum's), but this wasn't the cowboy Copland I knew. *Connotations* and *Inscape* were thorny, twelve-tone creations that had their moments but didn't quite come off. I couldn't have said why, but it seemed to me the composer himself wasn't convinced by the music. The pieces seemed like dutiful fakes, and they still do, but they are interesting nonetheless, because Copland was a great composer and sometimes a great composer's forgeries are more interesting than a third-rate composer's greatest hit.

I hadn't heard of Elliott Carter, but as soon as I began listening to his Concerto for Orchestra, I knew there was something authentic going on. I'd never encountered such multilayered complexity, but just as impressive was the energy that erupted from the orchestra early in the piece. Unlike those works by Tippett and Boulez, it wasn't at the very beginning – there's a minute of undulating calm preceding this explosion, and when it comes, it takes us by surprise. It evidently took the sound engineer by surprise, too, because you can hear the fader being hastily pulled back as Carter detonates his orchestra. This moment of this recording remains for me a sort of touchstone for musical excitement, and I would go on to follow Carter's music for the rest of his very long life. He was sixty when he wrote the Concerto for Orchestra, and he was still composing at 103. I interviewed him at his home in New York on a number of occasions, and he was always generous with his time. He called me Mr Ford, and naturally I called him Mr Carter, so I treasure the copy of his *Collected Essays and Lectures* he gave me when I visited him in 1999, inscribed from 'Elliott' to 'Andrew'.

The energy that Carter's Concerto generates takes different forms, depending partly on how you listen. This is music of interlocking layers or strands – each with its own instrumentation and set of harmonic and rhythmic parameters – and one method of listening is to follow a particular strand; Carter said the piece consisted of four movements playing simultaneously. But there's also a cumulative energy to the music. You feel, as the listener, that you are borne aloft by this music, moving at great speed. When, after twenty-something minutes, the forward momentum abruptly ends over wispy string harmonics and gently chiming bells, you keep going like one of those cartoon characters who has run over the edge of a cliff and is now running in midair before plummeting to the bottom of some chasm. Carter's ending provides a parachute. I often return to this work, but associate it especially with the student house I lived in at university, where more than once we put all the lights out and listened to the Bernstein recording very loud, lying on our backs. It was never less than a shattering experience.

There's another piece by an American composer that is almost the negative of Carter's Concerto for Orchestra. Lucia Dlugoszewski's *Fire Fragile Flight*, for just seventeen instruments, doesn't have Carter's complex multilayers. but shares its energy and sense of momentum. The difference is that listening to Dlugoszewski's piece you don't seem to be moving at all. On the contrary, the music hurtles past your ears while you stay rooted to the spot. The effect is like being inside a vortex, and occasionally you want to duck as some musical debris flies by.

In January 1974, I sat holding the cassette recorder's microphone to my transistor to capture a broadcast of Harrison Birtwistle's orchestral piece, *The Triumph of Time*. Like most of my other listening, it was a whim. I'd never heard of the Lancastrian composer before this broadcast and I tuned in largely, I think, because there was something vaguely provocative about his name. I've been enthusing here about fast music by Boulez, Carter and Dlugoszewski, but *The Triumph of Time* is very slow, a funereal procession through a blighted landscape. The composer, I believe, came to think less of the piece the more it was performed, but it has never grown stale to me and I have listened to it a lot, especially that first cassette tape. The meandering cor anglais tune, always outwardly the same, always different in detail, one of the most plangent sounds in the music of the past fifty years; the amplified soprano saxophone, its three note motto magically ringing out from the centre of the orchestra; the culminating peroration for unison winds as the percussion department goes wild: even though I now know to expect these things, they never pall.

Part of the power of Birtwistle's piece is its dramatic timing, and this was also a feature of the instrumental concertos of the Scottish composer Thea Musgrave. Her Viola Concerto was played at the Proms in 1973, the first year I began paying attention to those concerts and the first year I attended. But it was her Horn Concerto for Barry Tuckwell that really seized my imagination. From time to time in Musgrave's orchestras, players stand to declaim solos, and sometimes they move. There's one moment in the Horn Concerto where the four orchestral horn players leave the orchestra, walking to the four corners of the auditorium from where they play answering signals to the soloist on stage. At this point in the piece, there's a sharing of control between the conductor (Musgrave herself on the recording I discovered in Orpington Library) and the horns whose calls are independent of the conductor's beat. It was that rather fluid aspect of the piece that most appealed to me.

Besides the Dlugoszewski (which I heard later), all the works I've mentioned impressed me as a teenager; they all affected my early musical thinking, and I still bear their influence. They are very different pieces – Tippett's double concerto and *Le marteau* have little in common – but they were the pieces I latched on to, while others left no mark. These pieces seemed authentic, to repeat the word I used in relation to Carter's music, and I sought to own them. In the first place, this was a literal matter: I gradually acquired my own copies of the LPs so I could listen whenever I wanted to. But they were subtly different to earlier purchases – the Beatles, Beethoven's ninth, Pentangle, Mahavishnu Orchestra or whatever – because even as I bought this music by Birtwistle and Musgrave, Carter and Boulez, I could feel they were part of something new in me, something *creative*.

I was coming to the end of my schooling, and there was the question of what to do next. It would be university, but which one? St Olave's had a tradition of sending boys to Cambridge and a group of us was taken to look around the place and stay over-night in Selwyn College. I think most of the other boys in the party ended up going to Cambridge, but I was put off by the atmosphere of the place and came home adamant that I didn't want to go there. It's hard to explain. I certainly detected an air of privilege to which I took a strong and instant dislike; I was also put off by a weight of tradition that is hard to miss even on an overnight visit.

What did attract me was the concrete and glass modernism of the new universities built in the 1960s, and my choices reflected this. I applied to five of them. York was at the top of my list; Lancaster at the bottom. I forget the others. The first four insti-tutions neglected to make me an offer; Lancaster gave me an interview. And this was just as well. For all my obsession with it, music was still a hobby. At university I intended to study English, and would have ended up with an English degree had I not been lucky enough to be rejected by my first four choices. The University of Lancaster was about to be my salvation.

4.

Permission to Compose

The first of my friends to claim to be a composer (as opposed to a composition student) was in fact not a composer at all for very long. He quickly turned into a baritone and, after that, an actor. These days he is a well-known face on television; the last time we had a drink together, following his stint on *Game of Thrones*, we were interrupted by teenage girls wanting selfies. But at some point in 1976, over a cup of coffee in Lancaster University's Cartmel College refectory, Roger Ashton-Griffiths was bold enough to begin a sentence with the words, 'Speaking as a composer ...' I have no idea what he said next, because I was so taken aback by those first four words.

My surprise at hearing them was multifaceted. For one thing, the phrase sounded absurdly grand. We were eighteen or nineteen years old and could scarcely have claimed to be anything at all, least of all something so exalted as a composer. Bach, Beethoven and Stravinsky were composers, Benjamin Britten was a composer, our teacher Edward Cowie was a composer: by comparison – could one even make a straight-faced comparison? – we were just fumbling around in the dark. (I now know that blind fumbling is part of the job.) But what Roger said also provoked a frisson of possibility. Because while I couldn't have spoken those words myself at the time – and would still find them hard to utter – there was nothing I wanted more than to be a composer.

But how do you become a composer? The French novelist and philosopher André Malraux said that you don't turn into a painter by looking at landscapes, but by looking at paintings. By the same token, you become a composer by listening to music and not by contemplating the heavens or the human condition. And yet there must be more to it, because most people listen to music but do not become composers. Unless you count those childish thumpings on my grandparents' piano and my improvements to the works of Walter Carroll, the first inkling I had that I might want to compose music came late in the evening of Saturday, 10 March 1973, a week before my sixteenth birthday. Actually, it was more than an inkling.

Now it's hard to credit that BBC television had a live Saturday-night program devoted to contemporary arts, involving not only interviews and discussions, but also performances of drama, poetry and music. It was called *Full House*, and this particular night the guests included the composer Karlheinz Stockhausen and the London Sinfonietta, a chamber orchestra specialising in twentieth-century music. They rehearsed and performed a new work, *Ylem*, that had had its first performance at the Queen

Elizabeth Hall only the night before. The actor and comedian John Bird – a devotee of new music – interviewed the composer and they took phone calls from viewers. Someone – a schoolboy – rang in to ask if he might dedicate his latest composition to Stockhausen, and Stockhausen told him to dedicate it to God.

Even if I didn't understand it, I was already fascinated by the music of Stockhausen that I'd encountered on recordings since my first, puzzled exposure to *Kurzwellen*. In particular *Hymnen*, operating on a broad canvas, its lonely national anthems battling their way through radio static, seemed almost romantic in scale and intent, yet at the same time daring and of the future. But hearing and seeing *Ylem* rehearsed, performed and discussed was perhaps the most formative musical moment in my life.

This was a new piece of music by a so-called difficult, modern composer, and I was able to grasp it completely at one hearing. The shape and structure of the music were clear, the premise was beguiling, the fabric of tones and timbres was vivid and provocative, and the commitment of the players was completely convincing. I couldn't turn away. More importantly, I realised that this was not only something I wanted to be part of – the creation of such bold new sounds – it was something I *could* be part of. Though I was able to read music and follow a score – those piano lessons had to have been good for something – I wouldn't have known how to begin notating a conventional work for an orchestra like the London Sinfonietta. But I could very quickly see how I might devise a piece along the lines of *Ylem*.

Stockhausen was always interested in the stars (he once dreamt he was born on Sirius, and occasionally stated this as fact). *Ylem* was inspired by the theory that every 80 billion years the universe explodes and reforms. Reflecting this, his music had a strong spatial element, most of the performers playing portable instruments so that they could move from one place to another.

At the outset of *Ylem* the players gather, heads bowed, around a piano with its lid off. A sharp tam-tam stroke is the signal for them to jerk suddenly to life, repeating, fast and loud, either an E flat or an A in the middle of their ranges. These will be the only stipulated pitches in the whole piece. The mobile players now begin to drift away from the piano, leaving the stage and spreading out to encircle the audience. Bit by bit their range of pitches and style of playing broadens until by the central moment of the piece we are hearing the very shortest sounds and the very longest, the loudest and the quietest, the highest and the lowest, and also silences. Then the music goes into reverse as the players gradually converge once more on the piano, their tonal ranges shrinking in the process until the piece has returned to the loud, fast repetitions of the initial E flat–A tritone. When this interval reaches maximum intensity, there is a second tam-tam stroke, the music abruptly jerks up a whole tone and off the players go again, this time leaving the concert hall or, in this case, television studio. Even those players who didn't move before – the pianist and percussionist and others whose instruments couldn't be carried – now pick up toy instruments and follow the others out, the music eventually fading from earshot.

Ylem was a revelation in all sort of ways, but the aspect of it that most grabbed my imagination was that this was one of its composer's 'intuitive' pieces. That previous paragraph was more than my attempt to describe the music; it was a precis of the score. For there is no notation in *Ylem*, no crotchets and quavers for the players to read, only a few pages of verbal instructions, which I've summarised. The instructions are quite specific – the piece is anything but a free-for-all – but a good performance depends upon the players listening to each other (when not walking, they play with eyes closed) and establishing sonic connections with each other across the room.

Only a few weeks earlier, the same TV program had broadcast the first UK performance of David Bedford's audience-participation piece *With 100 Kazoos*, also involving members of the London Sinfonietta and with the composer himself conducting. Bedford's piece had been commissioned by the BBC for Boulez to conduct, but he had thought it trivial, and didn't believe the audience involvement would work. The eleven instrumentalists played and, from time to time, the audience would blow the kazoos of the title in imitation of what they'd heard. Much of the instrumental music was conventionally notated, but as the piece went on the camera moved in on the players' music stands to reveal that they were also playing from drawings and diagrams. There was a star chart and illustrations from children's stories, including a picture of a rabbit. Boulez was right, the piece was trivial, but the sight of that star chart on the violinist's desk got me thinking, especially after I'd seen and heard *Ylem*. I started to compose my own music.

Anything I might have attempted to notate with standard notation would have sounded dull and simplistic because I lacked the technique. I wanted to create the sorts of sonorities I'd heard in *Ylem* – spiky points of sound, and long, sustained smudges of tone – and by using diagrams and a few verbal instructions, I was able to construct a score that represented this. One diagram consisted of shard-like shapes, reminiscent of vorticist art; another had layers of horizontal lines of different lengths. The players would interpret the diagrams vertically (pitch) and horizontally (time), and I would be a composer. Except that I didn't have any players.

In an act of extreme chutzpah, I decided to approach my friends at school, who, between them, played a range of instruments. I put together a mixed ensemble of six or seven players from which quite a variety of colours could be extracted and I wrote my piece for them. Though they must have been surprised to learn I was suddenly a composer, they entered fully into the spirit of the occasion. The piece, in three movements, was called *Short Suite* – I don't know why the neutral title – and was full of all the unusual sounds I could come up with. Thinking the idea was mine alone, at one point I had the pianist pluck the strings inside the piano. I was disappointed, later, to learn that composers had been asking for this effect for fifty years. Some of the music used simple standard notation, some diagrams. Most of the conventional scoring was in the middle movement, where the music – a sort of warmed-up English pastoralism – was as conventional as the notation. But the diagrams produced fresher sounds. There were also parts of the piece in which both sorts of notation coexisted. To the extent that the music required a conductor at all, the job was really just that of a coordinator, indicating the beginnings and endings of sections. But I was not about to pass up the opportunity to make my debut as a maestro. I couldn't lay my hands on a baton, but had a paintbrush with a long handle. Armed with this, I stood in front of my little orchestra and waved my arms enthusiastically. If my friends thought me absurd, they were kind enough not to mention it.

So that was opus one, and having been taken seriously I was in no mood to stop. Opus two was a cello sonata, built around a folksong – Stockhausen never ousted Vaughan Williams from my affections. But it was a listless thing, largely because, again, I was attempting to notate the piece conventionally and lacked the skill. A more ambitious notion was an oratorio called *Moses* with a libretto by one of my school friends, Richard Brown. I'm not sure he ever finished writing it; certainly the score never advanced beyond about page four.

But I was composing, and the experience was teaching me some valuable lessons, most importantly that this was hard work. While it might have seemed like a good idea to write an oratorio, evidently it was going to take an enormous amount of my time to do it properly. The other issue, not unrelated, was that I had better find myself some notational skills. This reliance on graphic notation was a stopgap. A spiky diagram was unlikely to produce more than a spiky musical texture, and increasingly I was imagining specific musical ideas – melodic lines, harmonic fields, precise combinations of instruments. I had to acquire the ability to write it all down accurately, because diagrams weren't going to be much use. I had no composition teacher. My piano teacher, Mr Dresser, had retired, but wouldn't have been any help. When I showed him my first scores he was kind enough, but he had nothing to say.

I believe that all composers and probably all creative artists are largely self-taught. Teachers can set examples (good and bad) and can certainly save you time, but you have to find your own way, own metier, own voice. For a composer, as Malraux's comment implies, that starts with listening to a lot of music and looking at it too. So I set about the task.

Cassette recorder at the ready, I was already an avid radio listener when I encountered Bernard Rands's *Wildtrack I* played by Boulez and the BBC Symphony Orchestra in a concert broadcast from Stuttgart. What was so captivating about *Wildtrack I* – and, later, other pieces by Rands, whose music I began to seek out – was his placing of fully notated passages alongside music that was less determined, perhaps with lines the players repeated at will and in their own tempos. In some cases the two sorts of music alternated, but at others they occurred simultaneously, like the horns playing independently of the orchestra in Musgrave's Horn Concerto. And there was a dramatic quality to *Wildtrack I* – also reminiscent of Musgrave's music – in that the orchestra begins the piece before the conductor comes on stage, making visually apparent those musical lines that are synchronised by the arrival of the conductor and those that are free-floating. I tried this out on a small scale and discovered it gave me textural richness (from the players' rhythmic independence), yet harmonic control (because I was still stipulating the pitches). I felt I'd made a real discovery. Still, what I'm describing requires some context, and the context is this: I was a schoolboy preparing to take A levels in English, history and economics with a Special Paper in history, prior to a degree in English and a life in primary-school teaching like my mum. The idea that I might one day call myself a composer like Rands and Musgrave hadn't entered my head.

o   o
o

Because Lancaster University was at the bottom of my list of choices, I hadn't read the prospectus very carefully. During my interview with the English department, I was asked which other two subjects I hoped to study in my first year. At the time, taking three subjects of equal weight was a Lancaster requirement for first-years, but I knew nothing of this and had to improvise. Instead of mentioning history or economics, I heard myself asking about Lancaster's music department and, before I knew what was happening, I was sent to meet Richard Langham Smith. His office was just off the balcony of the Great Hall and next to it was another door marked 'Edward Cowie'. At last, I thought, I am going to meet a composer.

In fact I wasn't, not that day. Langham Smith, a nice man who gave the impression of only just being able to contain his amusement at life, was a specialist in Debussy and music of the French baroque. He began with an apology.

'Of course Ed should be seeing you,' he said, 'but he's in Liverpool.' At that very moment, he told me, Alan Hacker was rehearsing Cowie's clarinet concerto for its premiere by the Royal Liverpool Philharmonic Orchestra under Sir Charles Groves. I could almost reach out and touch this exciting world. Instead, I was told to take a seat while Langham Smith proceeded to ask me questions about my compositions and my interests, my favourite composers and so on; moving to the piano, he gave me a series of aural tests, which I seemed to answer to his satisfaction. Finally he played a sequence of chords.

'Who uses suspensions like this?' he asked. The sequence was dimly familiar, but I couldn't place it.

'It's Britten,' he said. 'The Agnus Dei from the *War Requiem*.' Far from feeling crushed, I was elated. If these were the sorts of conversations that went on here – Britten's harmonic writing pulled apart and examined – I wanted to join in. Langham Smith was encouraging and I promised to send my scores to the department when I got home. As I was about to leave, his phone rang.

'Is Ed all right?' I heard him ask. It transpired that the orchestral parts from Cowie's publisher were full of mistakes and the rehearsal had been a disaster. The premiere of the clarinet concerto was cancelled – permanently, as it turned out – and Alan Hacker would play Mozart instead. I suppose you could say this was my first composition lesson from Edward Cowie: make sure your parts are accurate or you will waste the players' time and sabotage your performance.

So after school, I went to Lancaster and had lessons with Edward, who was charismatic and inspiring in many ways, chiefly for his energy and voracious inquisitiveness. He read a lot of science – D'Arcy Thompson's *On Growth and Form* was a sort of bible for him – and painted curious little watercolours involving plants and birds, with little bits of musical notation in ink, which he exhibited publicly. I couldn't get along with D'Arcy Thompson, but I took up drawing and painting with enthusiasm. In three years with Edward I can't say I learnt much specific musical knowledge – when he was on sabbatical I got more of that from his replacement, John Buller, in a single term – but I picked up a healthy attitude to work. You couldn't show up to a lesson with some puny excuse about having had no time to write, because you knew that Edward had been working since dawn, completing a watercolour and sixty bars of a string quartet before coming to the campus. As a professional composer, I've always delivered my work on time and often early, and I put that down to Edward.

Tutorials consisted of his looking at my work, asking me questions that forced me to justify my choice of pitches and making suggestions for improvements, always trying to get to the bottom of what I was doing. Later, when I taught composition, this was also the way I taught. You ask questions in order to have students clarify their intentions, but you allow them the space to make discoveries for themselves (because that's how we learn best); occasionally, like a doctor, you prescribe something that will help – you say, 'I think you'd better take a look at the bassoon writing in Stravinsky's Octet.' This approach works with good students, though not so well with those who need constant motivation.

By the end of my first year, it was clear that I was well enough motivated. I was devoted to composing music in a way that I was not devoted to writing essays about *The Dream of the Rood* or *Paradise Lost*, though I enjoyed that too. But could I switch my major from English to music? Edward called me in.

'I think you're a composer,' he told me. 'I don't say that to everyone.'

I felt as though I had been given permission to compose. This is what every artist needs at some point: a more experienced artist giving their imprimatur. Otherwise, how do you know that your obsession — and it must, first of all, be an obsession — isn't just a fantasy? For me, music and composing were obsessions, but I'd come to university to get an English degree. I wanted to be a primary school teacher and in my mind had already settled on St Martin's College in Lancaster for my postgraduate year of teacher training. This was not just what *I* thought I was going to do, it's what my parents thought I was going to do. But Edward thought I was a composer. Not that the two were mutually exclusive — most composers, I was aware, supported themselves by doing other things — but since music, to this point, had been a sort of hobby, it was still going to be hard telling my parents I intended to pursue it professionally.

As it happened, I never had to tell them. I had had the same girlfriend since my last year of school and while now we were at different universities, we visited each other every couple of weeks. She had come up to Lancaster just before the end the year and we'd discussed my dilemma. I fancy she may even have talked to Edward. Then she went home, her term having ended a week before mine. By the time I got home, she'd visited my parents to explain the situation and they were reconciled to the notion of my pursuing composition. I don't know what became of Becky S. – a few months later, the relationship fizzled, as these things will – but I remain grateful for her diplomacy.

My parents were always supportive of my decisions, even when they would have preferred me to make different ones. Indeed, they were so supportive that I mostly didn't realise what their preferences were. For example, it was years after I moved to Australia that it dawned on me that they would much rather I hadn't. At the time, they'd offered only encouragement. On one occasion, when I was working at Bradford University – my first job – and called to inform my parents that I'd decided to accept the offer of a one-year extension to my initial three-year contract, Mum asked if I didn't think that might be playing things a bit safe.

'You're supposed to advocate safe choices,' I said. 'You're not meant to be encouraging me to take risks.'

The University of Lancaster was good for me. The city itself, on the River Lune, inland from Morecambe Bay, is full of history – a medieval castle, a fifteenth-century priory – and the Lake District is only a short drive. The university campus is a mile or two out of the city, a small town in itself. The music department was pretty intimate, with just four full-time staff, but while I've sometimes felt a more rigorous musical training might have been helpful, nearly all my pieces were performed, and I was able to hear for myself what worked and what didn't. Because there weren't many contact hours in the week, there was also time for me and the other students to put on our own concerts. Rather than being taught an off-the-peg technique, then, I was given the chance to work one out for myself. It meant making lots of mistakes in public – both as composer and conductor – but if your performers are your friends and fellow students, and the public consists largely of other people on campus, it's not a bad way to learn. Soon enough – and this is if you're lucky – your music will be played by professionals who don't know you, may not like your work and may tell you so; they will certainly point out any errors, probably loudly enough for the other players to hear. The public, meanwhile, will be mostly total strangers who have paid to hear your work, or more likely paid to hear the other pieces in the concert and resent the presence of yours. A day or two after the concert, more people you don't know will publish their judgement of your music. Young composers should make as many mistakes as possible while they're still students.

I always tell student composers to write songs or at least set words to music. I did a lot of this as an undergraduate, and learnt a great deal from the experience. Working with a text takes some of the decisions out of your hands and helps you become more fluent. You're not having to devise structures – or not necessarily – because the poetry has its own structures, some of which you can borrow. Phrases also have structures, and so do individual words, and to some extent tell you what notes to write. This helps a young composer be less self-conscious, and that's always a good thing. I made settings of Japanese haiku in translations by Kenneth Rexroth, as well as words by cummings, Yevtushenko, Eliot and Pound. I even set some of my own poetry to music, though it turned out that late-adolescent pretentiousness will seem only more pretentious when sung. After the first performance, I rewrote the vocal line for clarinet and changed the title from whatever it had been in the first place to *Songs without Words*. Both scores are lost. In fact, none of my student scores survives, just a few recordings.

There's an orchestral piece called *Rounds and Hollows*, the best thing about which is its title, taken from the opening of *The Return of the Native*. It's a short, brooding landscape of a piece that owes a debt to *The Triumph of Time*, though it includes canonic structures (inspired by the 'rounds' of the title) that Birtwistle would never have used. Another recording is of those first-year haiku settings. I called the piece *A Salt Girl* and scored it for tenor voice – Andrew Murgatroyd, who it was obvious, even at the time, would become a professional singer – flute, harpsichord, piano, tuned percussion and string trio. Listening now to the recording, the word setting is poor, the harmony is worse and the piece depends almost entirely on pretty gestures. But there's something there – atmosphere, I suppose, partly the result of that glittery instrumentation, partly the timing of the gestures. Timing is one of the hardest things to get right in a piece of music, and listening back to the songs, forty years after the fact, I think perhaps I hear the flicker of talent that Cowie heard, though it's very much a flicker. I remained fond enough of this piece to recycle both the title and the words in 1994 in a new setting for tenor and piano. Before I did so, though, I sought permission from the publisher of Rexroth's translations, something I failed to do with any of my student settings. Not until it was too late.

In my second year at Lancaster, I set to music two rather sensual (not to say sexual) poems from Ezra Pound's *Lustra*. I understand why the poems 'Coitus' and 'Doria' might have appealed to a nineteen-year-old, but I can't say I like them much anymore, and I certainly can't imagine setting to music the line, 'The gilded phalloi of the crocuses are thrusting at the spring air'. The resulting piece, *Flowers of Orcus* for soprano and small ensemble, didn't seem to me as effective as *A Salt Girl*, and unusually we didn't give it a performance at Lancaster. At Edward's suggestion, however, I submitted it to the Society for the Promotion of New Music (SPNM) in London, and forgot about it until I received a letter informing me that the piece had been selected for inclusion in their 1978–79 season. The concert would be at London's Southbank, the conductor would be the highly respected John Carewe (Simon Rattle's teacher), and this would be my first ever professional performance. Unfortunately, I didn't have permission to use Pound's words.

I wrote immediately to Pound's publisher. I could hardly tell them I'd already used the poems, let alone that the piece had been scheduled for a London performance, so I played the helpless student card. This was an error. It was a while before I heard back, but when I did it was in the form of a letter asking me to provide references addressing my ability to make 'a satisfactory musical work' from Pound's poetry. I was running out of time. The performance was only a few months away. One of the women I shared a house with, Jayne Gill, wrote poems and so together we set about the task of ripping Pound's words out of my score and putting in Jayne's. This was a less straightforward task than my giving the vocal part to an instrument, because in order to fit the notes the new words had to have the same stresses as the old and, where possible, the same or similar vowels and consonants. They had to sound like Pound's words, without actually being Pound. They also had to make sense, and ideally share the same mood as the original poems so that the music seemed apt.

The day came for the performance of Ford and Gill's *Flowers of Orcus*. It was a rehearse-and-record session in which the public could hear a new piece rehearsed from scratch, then performed (and recorded) a couple of times. Lynda Richardson sang it admirably, John Carewe was affable and assiduous, and a boy came up to me at the end to say how much he had disliked the piece. A year later, I received a letter from Fabers granting me permission to use the two poems by Pound.

The biggest event of my second year at Lancaster was the week Michael Tippett spent in the music department. We were told in advance that he would not be looking at our scores or listening to recordings of our music because he was in the middle of writing his fourth symphony. I understand this much better now than I did at the time, when we all felt a little short-changed.

There are two sorts of influence on a composer. The first consists of the aggregation of early musical experiences that go to shape a composer's voice, the sort of thing I've been writing about here. But the second is a less welcome sort of influence that can come from bumping into a piece of music almost by accident. It doesn't have to be a good piece: encounter it at the wrong moment and it will throw you.

In 2016 I was composing *Comeclose and Sleepnow* for Gian Slater and the Monash Art Ensemble. The piece is a song cycle, subtitled 'six Liverpool love songs', that puts to music poems by Henri, Patten and McGough, the poets of *The Mersey Sound*, whose work I'd first fallen for more than forty years earlier. Before I had finished these songs, their commissioner Paul Grabowsky sent me the Ensemble's new CD, which included *Aerea* by my friend Mary Finsterer. I badly wanted to hear this piece, not least because it was for the very ensemble for which I was composing, but I delayed listening until I had completed my own work and was glad I that I did. Had I listened to *Aerea* before I'd finished, I'd have been in trouble. Mary's very powerful music was utterly different to mine, and the moment I heard it I began to have doubts about my songs. Should I have had some of Mary's sound world in my piece? Should my songs have been more rough-hewn and harmonically repetitious? Should the whole cycle have been more dissonant? The novelist Peter Carey once spoke about the danger of reading other writers' books while engaged in writing your own. You come across a beautiful description of rain and are suddenly, sickeningly struck by the complete absence of weather in your novel.

In asking not to hear our music at Lancaster, then, Tippett was being careful, because you can be derailed by any music, and even a student piece will do it. But he gave talks and attended concerts of his own music, including *A Child of Our Time*, which we sang in the University Choral Society (by the end of the performance he was in tears); he conducted a memorably touching performance of the *Fantasia Concertante on a Theme of Corelli* with the visiting Royal Philharmonic Orchestra; and, most importantly, he talked to us informally over lunches. I told him about a string quartet movement I had planned down to the last detail. It had taken me a whole term to compose and I could have explained the significance of every single note and shown you how it was derived from a set of charts. I was proud of my achievement until the Delmé Quartet played the piece and I heard how boring it was. I told Tippett of my disappointment and he listened, a little amused, never having been one for systems himself.

'Just use your ears, love,' he said.

It's not perfect advice – you need more than your ears – but it was what I needed to hear. I went off and composed *Flowers of Orcus* and have seldom used a musical system since.

Of course, being a composer isn't just about organising your musical ideas. You must also learn a professional attitude to the job, and much of that comes down to practical experience. As a non-instrumentalist, I was in danger of ending up an impractical, academic, even theoretical, sort of composer. But in addition to singing in the university choirs, I could conduct a bit. I had started at school with my own first pieces, graduating to a few items of standard repertory. There was a performance of William Walton's *Façade* that I organised as well as conducted. I had no training, but I'd watched Boult and Boulez very closely, studied Walton's score well and sought advice from Desmond Swinburn about how to beat a bar of 5/8.

At Lancaster I carried this on, first conducting my own music and my fellow students', then adding in other twentieth-century pieces. I began to plan little seasons for which we needed posters and therefore a name. Lancaster University New Music Group seemed cumbersome. The equivalent group at York University, I noted, was called Anemone. One of my housemates was our violinist Michael Rafferty, who after finishing his studies in physics would go on to become the respected conductor of Music Theatre Wales. Mike picked up the copy of *The Tao of Love and Sex* we had lying around our student home to impress girls (which I'm sure it didn't) and more or less randomly lit upon the expression 'moon flower', a term for female ejaculate. So Moonflower we became, with a nice logo involving a many-petalled flower growing from the letter 'f', though when anyone asked what the name meant we tended to temporise.

Not all the players in Moonflower were brilliant – it was a university department, not a conservatoire – and I was far from being a good conductor, but there's something about youth: you don't always see the problems. Early on, we performed Ravel's delicate, sinewy *Three Poems of Stéphane Mallarmé*, the soprano part sung by the future Emmy-winning documentary maker Cesca Eaton. The day before our concert, I was in the university library reading that these songs were seldom performed because of their difficulty. I was surprised. The writer didn't say exactly what was difficult about them and, apart from a tricky piano break in the middle song, there was nothing I could think of. But in the years that followed I conducted the songs again with other singers, and each time they seemed harder to pull off, as though the more experience I had, the more difficulties I saw. Years later, I came across a cassette recording of our Moonflower performance, and it wasn't bad at all: simple, unfussy (the best way, in my view, to approach Ravel) and rather poised.

Our repertoire was broad. We did lots of Stravinsky and Maxwell Davies, works by Schoenberg, Webern, Martinů, Walton (*Façade* again), the wonderful Italian composer Luciano Berio, the American experimentalist Christian Wolff, Stockhausen and student composers from the department, including Andy Vores and John Woolrich. At the end of my last year, we staged a festival of three concerts. The first was made up entirely of student works, the second was an all-Stockhausen program that included *Ylem*, and the third featured Maxwell Davies's *Eight Songs for a Mad King*, another important piece for me and in some ways a cause celèbre of the new music repertoire.

The king of the title is either George III or someone who believes himself to be George III. He's played by a singing actor who, across five octaves, screams, barks and howls words by Randolph Stow, some of them borrowed from the historical George, while four of the six instrumentalists sit in giant bird cages representing the monarch's bullfinches. *Eight Songs* had been composed in 1969 for the South African actor Roy Hart and his impressive range of extended vocal techniques. There must have been some falling out between Hart and the composer, because the actor did it only a few times. Maxwell Davies and the Fires of London continued to perform it with other soloists, usually classical baritones. The multiphonics that Hart could produce eluded most subsequent performers, including me when I did my one and only performance as the king at Wollongong University in the late 1980s.

Because of the work's extremes, which can be confronting, audiences often laugh. It's a defence mechanism, but the laughter is encouraged by the composer's disorientating collage of styles, ranging from Handelian pastiche – and even a quote from *Messiah* – to a 'smoochy' foxtrot to the most ear-splitting avant-gardisms you could wish for. For all that, it is a serious work. At one London performance I witnessed a burst of nervous laughter quelled by Maxwell Davies himself, whipping round to glare at the offending audience member while continuing to conduct one-handed. These days, performances of *Eight Songs* are common enough all over the world, but in 1978 the piece was less than a decade old and seldom tackled by anyone but the Fires of London conducted by the composer. Our Moonflower performance, then, was another of those instances of youthful confidence trumping all practical consideration.

We rehearsed for weeks – someone constructed rather beautiful cages for the players with vertical bars made of rope – and the performance was a triumph, largely due to the fearlessness of our king, Roger Ashton-Griffiths in a nightshirt, who screeched and howled as though to the manner born. Even after we all left

Lancaster, we continued to perform our *Eight Songs* in other venues, for one tour borrowing the Fires of London's own cages.

The most memorable Moonflower performance was on a Sunday night in January 1979 at Wildsen Village Hall, on the edge of the Yorkshire moors. Soon after we arrived at the venue it began snowing quite heavily, and ten minutes before the concert a blizzard was raging, the hall still empty. Then people started to arrive – not many of them, ten or twelve perhaps, and with one exception elderly women, but we had a quorum. From backstage we scanned their faces through a crack in the door and decided they were not going to enjoy our first half (Berio, Stockhausen, Ford), so the players rummaged through their bags, our flautist Edward Blakeman coming up with Debussy's *Syrinx* and a Mozart flute sonata. I think Geoffrey Brown, our keyboard player, had some Bach. The audience hated it all.

Having exhausted our alternative repertoire, and with the cages for *Eight Songs* already nailed to the stage, there was nothing for it but to go ahead with the second half as planned. Backstage we had the sort of meeting I imagine sporting teams have in their locker rooms before facing a tough opponent. We decided to go out and give the performance of our lives.

I have always had doubts about the musical merits of *Eight Songs*. The piece seems to have been composed in a great rush and the score amounts, in the composer's own words, to 'a collection of musical objects … functioning as "stage props", around which the [actor's] part weaves'. Compared to Maxwell Davies's other collaboration with Stow – the complex, detailed *Miss*

Donnithorne's Maggot – Eight Songs is musically thin, as the composer once acknowledged. But dramatically it is a tour de force, and in my experience never more so than in the performance Roger unleashed that night on those unsuspecting Yorkshire women. In fact, it wasn't only the performance he unleashed.

The conductor gets in the way in *Eight Songs*. The audience wants to concentrate on the king and his interaction with the players; it doesn't want to watch the conductor's back. Where possible, then, I always did what I saw Maxwell Davies himself do, and stood in the audience with my score on the edge of the stage. The players could see me very clearly – they didn't even have to look up – and I wasn't in the audience's line of vision. My own line of vision was more or less at stage level, and this was how I came to see Roger Ashon-Griffiths's penis lolloping towards me that night in Wilsden. For in his enthusiasm for the performance, he had got down on all fours and started crawling to the front of the stage, the neckline of his nightshirt hanging low to reveal his pink body beneath.

Conducting with my right hand, I beckoned furiously to Roger with my left, imploring him to stand up. He thought I wanted him to sing louder.

At the end, the ladies cheered. We took our bows and went backstage. When we returned to the hall to dismantle the cages some time later, the audience was still there. A couple of the women were poring over my score. They wanted a discussion and they got one. Roger, the ensemble and I talked to them for a long time. They had never encountered anything like this piece before, but had understood it completely. Some said how moved they'd been. I was never sure if they'd seen Roger's willy. I like to think they hadn't.

But the whole night was a lesson in not underestimating your audience. If you give them your best shot – and we certainly did – there's no reason they shouldn't respond. Whenever I see orchestras heading off on country tours with a repertoire of popular old warhorses, I remember those Yorkshire women and their response to *Eight Songs*. I also remember their response to under-prepared Debussy, Mozart and Bach.

I learnt another lesson from my involvement with Moonflower, though it wasn't one I immediately understood. The art – or maybe it's a skill – of making something happen at a practical, organisational level, of getting everyone together and going out and doing something ambitious, isn't as common as you would think. There were other people who could conduct a bit, some of whom could do it better than me, but when I graduated from Lancaster and tried to pass on the organisation of Moonflower, nobody wanted to run it.

My talent for making things happen – having ideas and getting others to help me see them through – was doubtless what lay behind a last-minute change in my postgraduate plans. Just as I was settled on studying for a teaching diploma, three of my four music lecturers independently handed me the same newspaper clipping. It was a job advertisement, for the post of Fellow in Music at the University of Bradford. I applied for the job and got it, my career as a primary school teacher over before it had begun.

5.

Work

'Not the 21-year-old,' the memo read, or words to that effect.

For obvious reasons I never saw it, but later I heard this was the gist of the Vice-Chancellor's message to the chair of the appointment committee. Six applicants had been shortlisted for the job of Fellow in Music. I was the 21-year-old.

The University of Bradford in West Yorkshire was established, like Lancaster University, in the 1960s, but was a very different place to its counterpart on the other side of the Pennines. Bradford University wasn't on a campus out in the middle of nowhere, but in the city itself. Next door was the Bradford School of Art, which David Hockney had attended, but the university was technological – modern languages being as close as the university came to the humanities – and the arts were the domain of the fellows in theatre and music. There was nothing academic about these roles. It was the fellows' job, simply, to makes theatre and music part of the daily life of the campus.

The chair of the appointment committee, the professor of pharmacy, was a cultured Scot named David Mathieson, and he elected not to share the VC's advice with his colleagues. I forget how I finally found out about it. Following a first round of interviews, six candidates were whittled down to two – me and Charles Rae, now Charles Bodman Rae, the distinguished Sir Thomas Elder Professor of Music at Adelaide University. And after another round I was offered the job. It might easily not have happened.

As Professor Mathieson was wrapping up the interview, Kenneth Whitton, professor of German, spoke up.

'Just out of curiosity, this new music group of yours ... What exactly *is* a moonflower?' I scanned the faces of the panel, attempting to size up the members' combined botanical knowledge, then explained about a pale yellow flower, native to the Morecambe Bay area of Lancashire. It was a bit like a primrose, I said. I couldn't remember the Latin name, but the locals called it the moonflower because its petals reflected moonlight.

As Fellow in Music at Bradford, I had several responsibilities and I wasn't truly qualified for any of them, though at the time this never occurred to me. The first part of the job was to run the University Music Centre. This was easy enough, consisting largely of accepting bookings from students who wanted to use one of the centre's practice rooms. But there were two choirs to conduct – a large choir for all-comers and a small, invitation-only chamber choir. And there was a concert series to run, with a budget to pay for it. The 1978–79 season was already planned and announced by my predecessor, Philip Jones, and included a recital by the great mezzo-soprano Janet Baker at St George's Hall in the city.

To my surprise, when I walked into the Music Centre on my first day, I discovered that I had a secretary. Brenda H. was a kind, jovial, middle-aged woman with a rare talent for malapropisms ('Anthony Wood can't come to the rehearsal, because he's having an autopsy'). Brenda was as surprised by my arrival as I was by her presence, mistaking me at first for a new student. It was partly my age, partly my clothes. I later learnt that Philip Jones had worn a suit to work, but I turned up that first day in dungarees and a tartan bomber jacket. Brenda was an old-fashioned secretary who expected to type my letters and generally be told what to do. Since I barely knew what I was doing myself, this was tricky; it might have been better for the first few weeks had she told me what to do. But we soon worked each other out and in time became good colleagues.

My counterpart at Bradford, the Fellow in Theatre, was the writer and director Graham Devlin, and to start with he was as wary of his 21-year-old colleague as the Vice-Chancellor had been. But we discovered a shared sense of humour and, because of our parallel jobs, often found ourselves fighting similar battles. Graham was nine years older than me and ran his own touring theatre company, Major Road, which had once come to my school to perform, so I tended to look up to him. Among other things, Graham helped broaden my musical tastes, which had narrowed at university as I concentrated on contemporary art music and my own composing. It's probably good for a young composer to be single-minded, but I'd gone so far as to sell my rock LPs, eschewing pop music in general, with the exception of some rather mainstream jazz. I hadn't been oblivious to rock – punk was impossible to ignore, and I developed a lasting admiration of Elvis Costello when his second album came out in my final year at Lancaster; I was also immediately drawn to Kate Bush's *The Kick Inside* and the magnificent weirdness of 'Wuthering Heights' – but on the whole, I think I had developed a slightly snobby attitude to music. Today I would argue no one sort of music is better than any other sort, only different, but back then I had come to consider pop music to be shallow (of course some of it is) and too easy to be worth an investment of my time.

Graham had a devotion to American rock, and through him I found myself listening properly to Dylan and discovering Springsteen. *Darkness on the Edge of Town* had just appeared; it is still my favourite Springsteen album, its emotional energy almost overwhelming. This wasn't shallow at all and it wasn't that easy. Some of the best rock music took effort and persistence. It was, for instance, years before I understood the appeal of Van Morrison, and that was despite having a girlfriend at Bradford, Diana W., who was a Morrison fan (it wasn't till we eventually moved in together that I appreciated the richness in Morrison's voice). Ry Cooder was another discovery I made through both Graham and Diana, and listening to those early albums – *Boomer's Story*, *Paradise and Lunch* and *Chicken Skin Music* – whole swathes of America's musical past opened up. I had never taken country music seriously, but Graham had just returned from the United States, having directed the lighting on a tour by Waylon Jennings and Willie Nelson. He had *Red Headed Stranger* – one of the great albums of the 1970s. Among his other mementos was Willie's recipe for mixing a margarita: one part lime and lemon juice (you need both); one part triple sec; four parts tequila. You mustn't drink too many of these, but by the same token, once you've tasted Willie's recipe, all other margaritas seem like soft drinks.

o o
o

My first challenge at Bradford was the two choirs. In the concert schedule left for me by Philip Jones there was a December date on which the large University Choir was to perform in Bradford Cathedral. I had never conducted a choir in my life and my chamber ensemble repertoire consisted almost exclusively of twentieth-century music, the single exception an ill-advised Moonflower performance of Wagner's *Siegfried Idyll*. For my first concert with the choir, I programmed two pieces I had sung at school and knew thoroughly: Bach's cantata *Sleepers, Wake!* and Vivaldi's *Gloria*. To my relief, rehearsals went well. I discovered that I enjoyed conducting this music and had a rapport with the choir. But you also need an orchestra to perform these works and there wasn't one.

Philip Jones had scrapped the University Orchestra – I soon discovered why – preferring to engage a professional chamber orchestra for these concerts. But I felt that a university ought to have an orchestra, and so should a city of nearly 400,000 people, so I put out a call for players in the Bradford *Telegraph & Argus*. The initial response was not encouraging. Of the four or five violinists who turned up on the first night, only one, an elderly man named Stanley, showed flair, and with Stanley there wasn't much except flair. Still, in the absence of anyone else, I asked him to sit in the concert master's chair and we began our weekly rehearsals. In addition to the Bach and Vivaldi, I also programmed Tippett's Little Music for String Orchestra. It's not such a difficult piece to play, but it was too much for these players. While the choir improved all the time, singing the Bach and Vivaldi with real feeling, the orchestra made little headway. I couldn't even count on the same players coming each week. Some weeks, even Stanley didn't come.

The difficulty was that Bradford had no music department. In most universities, the music students form the core of the orchestra, talented players from other departments making up the numbers. We had no numbers to make up. Our players were chemical engineers and mathematicians, physicists and pharmacologists. There were some good ones, too, but they never seemed to be violinists. As the concert drew nearer, I realised I would have to bring in other players, so I asked old Lancaster friends to come and give the orchestra some body – and indeed some accuracy. I didn't handle it well. At the final rehearsal, Stanley arrived to find someone else in his seat. Much of my job at Bradford required interpersonal skills. By the time I left there, four years later, I think I had acquired some, but along the way I offended people.

The concert wasn't exactly a disaster. The singing was good. But my resurrection of the University Orchestra looked like a poor decision. Spotting the Vice-Chancellor in the audience – the man who had advised against my appointment – a member of the choir said with Yorkshire bluntness that he expected one of two things to happen as a result of the concert: there would either be more money for music or there would be less.

Next came my first concert with the small chamber choir. No one had mentioned the university's annual carol service until someone asked which carols we'd be singing this year. I discovered that usually the chamber choir sang a handful of items *a cappella*, the audience joined in for the big numbers, and the singing was interspersed with readings. So it was a version of the Festival of Nine Lessons and Carols at King's College, Cambridge. Apparently it was the Fellow in Music's job to devise it and it was four weeks away.

As a child, like most children, I had loved Christmas, and ever since I married a Finn – and particularly since we had a child – I've come to love it again: the traditions, the food and especially the music. But in between I was at best ambivalent, and as a young man, I'm sorry to say, I regarded the whole thing with disdain. With the Bradford carol service looming, it was too late to wriggle out of my responsibilities, but I was determined that if this was to be *my* show, we'd do something a little less predictable than a pale imitation of Christmas at King's. I told Graham Devlin my difficulty and asked if he had any ideas.

'What about the Towneley *Second Shepherds' Play*?' he said.

Mystery (or miracle) plays were common in medieval England, retelling Bible stories from the back of a cart, often in a rambunctious manner. Benjamin Britten's children's opera *Noye's Fludde* is based on a mystery play from Chester, Mrs Noah portrayed as an incorrigible drunk, her refusal to cooperate nearly scuppering her husband's plan to save the world.

The Chester plays form one of four complete or nearly complete cycles of mystery plays, another being the so-called Towneley cycle from Wakefield in Yorkshire. And since Wakefield was just down the road from Bradford, it made sense to perform one of their Christmas plays. But the *Second Shepherds' Play* is pretty unconventional. The shepherds visit the Christ Child in time-honoured fashion and the infant is identified as the redeemer of humankind, but only after a knockabout first act in which the same shepherds find a stolen sheep lying in a manger. It's not the *same* manger, but we don't know that yet, and a modern audience, such as the one attending my carol service, might easily be confused. Theatre had never been part of the service before, and seeing the play announced in the printed program, there were those who expected a traditional Nativity play. An hour after the service finished my phone rang. It was Professor Mathieson.

'I'm hearing from various sources that this year's carol service was blasphemous,' he said. He was deadpan, yet thankfully I could tell he was amused. But from all this I learnt a lesson. The Christmas concert had not been *my* concert, it had been the university's. And while I never set out to offend anyone, only liven things up, not everything needs livening up. For the next three Christmases, we did the thing properly.

There was still the problem of the orchestra. Having brought it back from the dead, I felt I now had to keep it going. Playing it safe was hardly an option, so I decided to aim bigger. For our next concert I programmed Carl Orff's *Carmina Burana*, having once been impressed by an amateur performance of the piece. I reasoned that it might give the orchestra some confidence since it's not hard to play and you are obliged to make a lot of noise. My instinct was correct. After ten weeks rehearsing *Carmina Burana* I had come to loathe the piece for its simple-minded plundering of Stravinsky – so much of Orff is a cheap pastiche of *Les Noces* – but the performance was a success. And we made a very big noise indeed. The trick was to find the right repertoire. I came to realise there is some music orchestras shouldn't touch unless they can really play. Mozart is top of the list. An average amateur orchestra can destroy Mozart and we did just that to his clarinet concerto. On the other hand, Schubert, which you might think would be a similar case, seems to stand up much better to a rough-and-ready approach. We played his first, third and eighth symphonies, with the third, which involves a degree of bluster, coming off best. Bluster, indeed, is what you're looking for if you conduct an amateur orchestra. For instance, while there's not much Wagner you can play successfully, you can pull off the prelude to *The Mastersingers*.

We also tackled more recent music – Elizabeth Maconchy's early Suite for string orchestra and David Bedford's *The Tentacles of the Dark Nebula* (with my old friend from Lancaster, Andrew Murgatroyd), then, more ambitiously, Lutosławski's *Venetian Games* and (with the choir) Birtwistle's cantata, *The Fields of Sorrow*. And I staged Stockhausen's *Ylem* again, the players at first sceptical, because there was no music to read, but gradually coming round until, after many rehearsals, they gave one of the best performances of the piece I've ever heard. This was an orchestra that mostly had difficulty playing in tune, but *Ylem*, which depended on intuition and listening and playing single notes, turned out to be something they could perform with insight. We even took our performance on a little tour, playing it at universities in London and Southampton. Two years earlier there had been no orchestra at all at Bradford University, then there'd been a ramshackle orchestra that had made a hash of Bach and Vivaldi. We were still ramshackle, but for a moment we'd found our mojo and toured it, playing Stockhausen at universities that had actual music departments.

Touring was something the chamber choir had always done and sometimes we gave concerts outside England. We sang Monteverdi and Purcell in churches around Yorkshire and Lancashire, Dufay and Dowland in Dundee and St Andrews, Gesualdo and Victoria in Kilkenny and Dublin, and Byrd, Allegri, Bruckner and Stockhausen (*Atmen gibt das Leben*) in Amsterdam, Gouda and The Hague.

The Ireland tour took place in the summer of 1981, at the height of the Troubles in Northern Ireland. This was the year of the hunger strikes in the Maze Prison, a number of republican prisoners starving themselves to death. The first to die was Bobby Sands, two months before our tour. Since we were going to the Irish Republic, not Ulster, it hadn't crossed my mind that the choir might be in any danger until I was contacted by the Irish Special Branch. They also didn't believe we were in danger, but said they would be keeping an eye on us all the same. The night we arrived in Dublin, a member of the Special Branch called at the house where we were staying and told us there would be officers at all our concerts and rehearsals. But not to worry.

On the day of our first concert the fifth hunger striker died. We arrived at a big barn of a church in the Dublin suburb of Finglas West, to find the letters IRA carved into the front doors. A couple of Special Branch men came to say hello and stayed for the rehearsal. The first half was secular music, Italian and Elizabethan madrigals along with the first performance of my own *Wedding Songs*, sung by the baritone Austin Allen. The second half included more music of the Renaissance, this time liturgical in nature and enthusiastically received by the audience, culminating in an extraordinary piece for twenty-four solo voices by a friend, Vic Hoyland. It was called *Em*, its text a deconstruction of the Anglo-Saxon poem 'The Ruin' – a ruin of 'The Ruin'.

Em is an exceptionally intense piece, performed – you would hardly say 'sung' – by opposing 'phalanxes' (the composer's word) of male and female voices, twelve and twelve. The two lines stand facing each other but as far apart as possible and utter loud, high-pitched shrieks across the divide in a complex, violent polyphony. Vic himself had attended an early rehearsal, encouraging the singers to push their voices until they hurt. By the end of the ten-minute piece, the singers are reduced to quiet guttural noises, slowly fading to nothing. Then there's a long silence. We always did it last on a program, because no one could really sing after it, and once it was under our belts we seldom rehearsed the piece. Never on the day of a performance.

So at the concert that evening our Special Branch protectors, chatting in an anteroom with the parish ladies busy preparing sandwiches, were ignorant of *Em* until the moment it started. In that cavernous building it sounded very much like a massacre. The police went for their guns, one hitting the floor while another flattened himself against the wall, edging his way into the main part of the church (or so the ladies told us later). Once in the church, it took the officer a few moments to realise that the reason he couldn't see the choir wasn't that its members were lying dead on the ground, but that they were hidden from his view behind pillars. Fortunately, he could see me conducting, it slowly dawning on him that this appalling, blood-curdling din was a piece of music.

o o o

The Fellow in Theatre's office was in the still-new Theatre in the Mill, a converted wool mill that now housed a small performance space. The seating was flexible and the theatre could be set up with the audience at one end or on any two sides. It seemed ideal as a space to present little workshop concerts. We did these on Sunday evenings, performing one or two pieces of twentieth-century chamber music, with an illustrated introduction, followed by a discussion. One of these evenings was devoted to Schoenberg's *Pierrot lunaire*, with the Australian soprano Margaret Field. I was surprised when she asked me which language I'd like her to sing the piece in, because I'd only ever heard it in German. But Margaret had also performed it in English, and so we took advantage of this to present all the introductory examples in English, with the subsequent performance in German.

The Sunday-night events were an example of my growing interest in the way music is presented. Ever since I'd dragged schoolmates along to concerts there'd been an element of missionary zeal in my attitude to music. At Bradford, I invited guests not only to perform but also to talk about music. A favourite was Wilfrid Mellers, Professor of Music at York University. He came a few times, on one occasion speaking about Hebridean mouth music, on another the music of the Spanish composer Federico Mompou and on a third about tradition in the songs of Dolly Parton and Joni Mitchell. Largely through his books, Wilfrid was an important role model for me, but in his lectures the occasionally purple prose of his writing style translated into an irrepressible fountain of enthusiasm for whatever was the music at hand, and he always emphasised that you could talk about any music at all. I was soon emulating him, giving a series of my own talks that ranged from Kate Bush to Edgard Varèse, speaking before concerts in Leeds Town Hall and writing occasional articles about music for the Yorkshire Post.

Another aspect of musical presentation is program building, which at Bradford became a favourite game. It's to do with mixing and matching pieces of music so that they illuminate each other. The trick is not to be obvious. You can put chamber music in an orchestral concert; if you play an overture, it doesn't have to go first – it can end the evening. We're used to mixing old and new, and to the familiar pieces providing context for the unfamiliar, but occasionally the more recent music might be better known than the older works, even when the older works are by famous composers. The Bradford concert of which I was most proud began with Bach's Cantata No 50 (for the Feast of St Michael), followed by *The Fields of Sorrow* by Birtwistle, then Bartók's Piano Concerto No 3 (with Geoffrey Brown). After the interval, we performed Birtwistle's *Nenia on the Death of Orpheus* for soprano (Poppy Holden), three bass clarinets, percussion and piano, and finished with full choir and orchestra in Beethoven's late cantata, *Calm Sea and Prosperous Voyage*, a piece that feels like the ninth symphony condensed into ten minutes. You can easily imagine a concert in which the Bartók concerto would be the novelty item, but on this evening it was the most familiar work, and there were more audience members who knew one of the Birtwistle pieces than had heard either the Bach or the Beethoven.

In addition to those concerts I was conducting, I was able to indulge in building programs for visiting artists, and we had some great names in those four years. Besides Janet Baker, Ravi Shankar came, the great recorder player Frans Brüggen gave a solo recital and Christopher Hogwood visited twice; we welcomed the Carla Bley Band, the medievalists Syntagma Musicum of Amsterdam, the Dutch contemporary music group Hoketus with composers Louis Andriessen and Frederic Rzewski (narrating his impassioned piece about the Attica Prison Riots, *Coming Together*); the Arditti Quartet played Debussy, Bartók and Ligeti, the Lindsay Quartet played Tippett and Schubert, the University of London Orchestra visited with Nicola LeFanu's *Farne*, and Julian Lloyd Webber played cello sonatas by Ireland, Bridge and

Delius. There were regulars, such as the Fitzwilliam Quartet who came from York three times a year, and old heroes of mine: the harpist Osian Ellis, who had once inspired me to strum the back of a dining chair, the counter-tenor James Bowman, the clarinettist Alan Hacker and the pianist Peter Donohoe.

Because everywhere in the United Kingdom is close to somewhere else, there are touring musicians constantly crisscrossing the country, You can perform in Bradford and then, if you've planned your tour well, drive the forty miles to Manchester or fifteen miles to Huddersfield or eight miles to Leeds for the following night's concert. It's very different to touring in Australia. So, as a concert booker, I spent much of my time discussing not only dates but also geography with these artists or their agents. I also discussed repertoire, and was surprised to learn that this was unusual. When I was booking Peter Donohoe, for instance, I asked if he would include Boulez's first sonata on his program, since I knew he played it and thought it might fit well with the Berg sonata he'd said he wanted to play. To my delight, he agreed. Later he told me that since none of the other promoters on the tour had expressed any preferences about music – they just wanted Peter Donohoe to come and play their pianos – he played the Boulez for them too. I hope they were grateful.

Being a concert promoter involves financial risk, of course, and even though it wasn't my money on the line, it was my reputation as far as the university's finance officer was concerned. In my first year we lost a packet on Janet Baker. I don't know why the tickets didn't sell – I even put advertisements on buses – but the hall was half-empty and Janet Baker didn't come cheap. In those days, she charged £2000 a concert, which was nearly half our annual budget.

A good way of making money, I found, was organising children's concerts. This wasn't simply a fundraising exercise. An important aspect of the fellows' job was what universities in the 1970s were pleased to call 'outreach'. By putting on concerts and plays, we were bringing audiences from the town to the university, and filling the place with children seemed an especially worthwhile form of outreach. I put on at least one children's concert a year, and they generally sold out; if I booked the University's Great Hall, I could finance a number of other projects with the money taken. The flute player Atarah Ben-Tovim came one year, and on another occasion the percussionist James Blades, who in addition to being able to hold an audience of small children in utter thrall at the age of eighty was the source of wonderful stories over supper. He told me about playing *The Soldier's Tale* for Stravinsky, and working with Britten, who had written many of his percussion parts with Blades in mind and often on the strength of his advice. Blades had provided J. Arthur Rank with the sound of his gong, and the BBC with its wartime call sign 'V for Victory', tapped out in Morse code on a drum.

One year, I booked a double bass player for the children's concert, but when I tried to secure the Great Hall I was told this would be a problem, because two days later it would be required for graduation and preparations would already have begun. I went to see the building manager, Mr Jack, who was not happy about having hundreds of small children in his hall just forty-eight hours before the Chancellor, Harold Wilson, was due to lead an academic procession into the same place. I gave him my word that the morning after the concert he wouldn't find so much as a sweet wrapper on the floor.

On the evening of the children's concert, I was due to be in London for a concert in which a piece of mine was being performed. But I had enlisted a small army of student volunteers, to whom I gave the same talk Mr Jack had given me, and I had no doubts they would cope. As it turned out, they never had to cope, because the children's concert never took place.

Late in the afternoon, the bass player and her pianist arrived to set up as planned. Apparently the Great Hall looked splendid. Special blue velvet curtains bearing the university's insignia in gold had already been hung either side of the stage in readiness for graduation. With only the house lights up, it was a little gloomy on stage and the pianist couldn't see her music, so she went off in search of a light switch. Backstage, she discovered a lever and pulled it. But it wasn't a light switch.

At first the water came as a trickle, but before long the emergency sprinkler system was in full flow, and by the time it was switched off several thousand gallons of water had fallen on the stage. Forty-five thousand is the figure I remember. It wasn't just water, either, but quite dirty water that had been sitting for years in a large tank on the roof of the Great Hall. Obviously, in the event of a fire, the first thing to go up is the curtains, so that's where most of the water was directed. Alarms went off. Fire engines arrived. There was a photo of three of them on the front page of the next day's *Telegraph & Argus* under a headline about 'Water Music'. The cleaners were called back; a security guard slipped on the wet stage, fell into the auditorium and broke his leg; the stage lights were put on full to dry the floor, but the heat warped the boards and the following morning a team of carpenters had to lay a whole new stage. I know these things because Mr Jack told me.

Sometimes it's hard to remember what life was like before mobile phones and instant messaging. Whenever I want to remind myself, I recall the sound of Brenda's voice when I rang from London to ask how the children's concert had gone. But the face-to-face meeting with Mr Jack was more memorable still. You must imagine the following delivered in a Yorkshire accent by a fundamentally kind man pushed well beyond his limits. I was told he had once been a sergeant major, but to begin with he spoke surprisingly quietly:

'You may remember,' he said, 'that when you came to see me six months ago and told me you wanted to have a concert in the Great Hall two days before Graduation, I was reluctant. But I agreed on condition that there wouldn't be a single sweet wrapper dropped. Do you remember that?'

I nodded. I was tempted to point out that in fact no sweet wrapper had been dropped, but I was biting down so hard on the side of my mouth I couldn't speak. Perhaps Mr Jack could see what was going through my mind, because now he became more emotional.

'Well, then. On Thursday night I went home as usual. While Mrs Jack and I were having our tea, the phone rang and a security man told me that some ... *clown* ... had turned my hall into a ... *swimming pool* ...'

o o
 o

When I arrived at Bradford, I wasn't, technically, a professional composer, because I had never been paid to write music. My first commission came courtesy of a lovely man, the composer Philip Wilby, director of the Aulos Ensemble. This was a contemporary music group based in Leeds and it regularly gave concerts at Bradford University. The clarinettist was Ian Mitchell, already an important figure in new music; the pianist was Martin Roscoe, his fame still ahead of him; and Phil himself played violin and viola. Phil was a real mentor: he was wise, experienced, encouraging of me and my music and, where necessary, also questioning and gently critical. The encouragement was the important thing.

Artists thrive on encouragement. Naturally, there's an element of ego about this. Everyone likes praise, but from time to time artists actually require it. It goes without saying that you wouldn't want to listen to music composed by someone with a low opinion of themselves and their work, so for this reason alone it's a good idea, now and then, to bolster an artist's ego. But the opposite of confidence is doubt, and with that comes vulnerability, which is every bit as important. We may work best when we're feeling confident, but the motivation to work comes when we're vulnerable, because that's when we know we can do better; that's when we say to ourselves, 'The next piece will be my best.' Vulnerability is also important to art itself. Art that is only a series of bold statements, brooking no opposition, might dazzle us for a moment, but will eventually push its audience away. The best art asks questions and opens its audience to doubt.

Encouragement is also important, because it demonstrates to the artist that contact has been made. As a composer, I spend my time putting dots and squiggles on paper – I still use pencils and paper. Some pieces take months to write, occasionally one might take years. You know what it sounds like, of course, or you wouldn't be writing it down in the first place, but no one else can hear it, and it might easily be that the first performance occurs a year after the piece is finished. So to learn that the music has meant something to a listener is reassuring. In fact, it's more than reassuring, it's a justification for doing what you do. Your work isn't pointless and you're not deluded, because someone else found it worthwhile.

It doesn't take much. A well-timed email or card, even an approach from someone in the street saying they have enjoyed a piece of my music can set me up for days (I do see how that might sound a little pathetic), but the best form of encouragement is a commission for a new piece. That is the sort of compliment about which there can be no doubt, and it also helps you pay some bills. An artist's first commission is a milestone in their career, and perhaps the biggest encouragement they'll ever receive. I responded to Philip Wilby's commission for the Aulos Ensemble with my best piece so far, a chamber concerto (these days called Chamber Concerto No 1) that they performed in the Theatre in the Mill in June 1980. I conducted. It earnt me my first review, Ernest Bradbury writing in the *Yorkshire Post* that the piece 'had air in it and light'.

Other commissions followed, but I was able to use some of my time at Bradford to compose works that hadn't been commissioned. At this point in my career, no one was likely to pay me to write a Concerto for Orchestra, so I did it off my own bat. It was quite a dramatic piece and not for a conventional orchestra so much as an imagined one: double woodwinds; four horns; just one each of trumpet, trombone and tuba; three percussionists; a piano; eight double basses. I dedicated it to Edward Cowie and sent the score to the SPNM. Surprisingly quickly a letter came back informing me that the composer Oliver Knussen would conduct it with the London Sinfonietta in a concert at St John's Smith Square. It was April 1982, and this time there were lots of reviews. In those days they appeared the next morning in the national press and you could wait up for them, which I did, reading about the premiere in the *Financial Times* and the *Daily Telegraph*. The following Sunday, more reviews appeared in the *Observer* and *Sunday Times*, and finally the monthlies came out with an especially nice review in the *Musical Times*. The reviews were mostly positive, while the *Sunday Times* ran one of the most honest pieces of criticism I've ever read, Desmond Shawe-Taylor writing that as he hadn't been able to make head or tail of the piece, he would resist writing anything about it at all.

By the end of my three-year appointment at Bradford I felt like a professional composer, and when Graham Devlin and I were offered a fourth year, we decided to accept it if we could farm out some of our regular duties (including conducting, for me) and write an opera together. The subject was Edgar Allan

Poe, his life more than his stories and poems. It was a steepish learning curve, and not only because the piece was approximately six times longer than anything I had previously composed.

One of the most interesting things about Poe's life was his death, which remains mysterious. En route from Richmond, Virginia, to New York in September 1849, the writer disappeared. He turned up a week later in Baltimore, drunk and delirious outside a bar, and died in hospital two days later. There are different theories regarding the disappearance, the most common – and the one we opted for – that Poe had been a victim of 'cooping'. The day of his discovery in Baltimore was also that of an election, and it may be that in the days leading up to it Poe was rounded up by a political press gang, plied with alcohol and held ('cooped') with others until the polling booths opened, whereupon he would have been forced to vote a certain way and probably more than once. The practice was common in nineteenth-century America; the press gangs looked for loners and Poe would certainly have qualified. He was also a dipsomaniac who would have found the offer of a drink hard to refuse. More recent theories have called into question the circumstances of his disappearance and death (was he even an alcoholic?), but still no one is sure, and the capture of Poe and forced inebriation gave us a framing device for the opera, which we called at first *Poe: The Terror of the Soul*, then just *The Terror of the Soul*, and finally simply *Poe*.

As part of my research, I made my first trip to the United States, visiting Poe's houses in Richmond and Baltimore, and giving a talk about the opera at the Peabody Conservatory. Even before it was written, the piece created interest. Clive Wilson, who ran the prestigious Harrogate Festival, agreed to mount the premiere, and with the festival's imprimatur Graham and I took the idea to a television company in Manchester run by a producer called Tony Sutcliffe, who was keen in spite of Graham's tendency to call him 'Peter' (Peter Sutcliffe was the recently captured Yorkshire Ripper). Rather than making a film about the opera, however, he wanted to turn the opera into a film. He proposed three directors, Ken Russell, John Schlesinger and Jonathan Miller, all from the realms of fantasy casting, and one afternoon I had a pleasant phone conversation with Schlesinger, talking through the possibilities.

None of it happened. The Harrogate Festival suddenly pulled out with no explanation, though not before they had sent provisional program details to the press. The TV film simply withered as most TV projects will. I was neither surprised nor especially disappointed by the latter, having never for a moment believed we'd see a film of our opera directed by Ken Russell, but Graham and I were both angry about Harrogate, not least because we continued to read in newspapers, including the *Sunday Times*, that the opera would be happening there. One of my new American friends even sent me a clipping from the *New York Times* mentioning *The Terror of the Soul* at the Harrogate Festival in a round-up of British cultural events for 1982, at which point I decided to become a nuisance. Ringing the festival box office with my best American accent, I explained that I was a tour manager from New York. The Edgar Allan Poe Society of America was arranging a party of seventy to attend the premiere of the opera, and I wanted to enquire about a group discount on tickets. An embarrassed voice explained to me that the opera had been cancelled, and when I asked why – a question that genuinely interested me – he was unable to provide an answer.

But an important lesson had been learnt amounting to not counting chickens before they're hatched. We had no contract with Harrogate and we'd received no money – in fact money had barely been discussed (Graham and I regarded the commission as part of our university work). We had made the mistake of taking an artistic director's enthusiasm as a guarantee and now found ourselves with a half-written opera and no home for it. The try-out scheduled for the Theatre in the Mill also had to be cancelled, since, without Harrogate's involvement, we couldn't afford the twelve singers and fifteen players. But you only make that sort of mistake once. I no longer believe anything will go ahead until I've signed a contract or at least received written confirmation, and I don't begin work without a down payment.

While we pondered what to do with our opera, one pressing matter was how to replace it in the university schedule. Four years earlier, I had seen a music-theatre piece called *Bow Down* by Harrison Birtwistle and Tony Harrison, at the National Theatre in London, and been taken with its simplicity of design, musically and dramatically. Nine performers sat on stage in a semicircle telling and retelling a story common to traditional ballads from Scandinavia, Scotland, England and the Appalachian Mountains in North America. The basic elements are always the same. Two sisters, one dark and one fair, love the same man. The suitor chooses the fair sister, and the dark sister kills her out of jealousy. In several versions, this is done by drowning, the fair sister's remains found by a blind harper who constructs the frame of a harp from her bones, stringing it with her hair. He plays at the wedding feast of the dark sister to the suitor, the harp mysteriously telling of the murder. There's a related German version of the story, collected by Jakob and Wilhelm Grimm, in which the sisters are brothers and the harp a flute. Mahler used this version in *Das klagende Lied*, and I turned it into *Once Upon a Time There Were Two Brothers . . .*, a piece for a speaking flute player, first performed by Sally Walker at the 2013 Melbourne Festival.

In Birtwistle's *Bow Down* many different versions of the story overlap, the nine performers all speaking, singing and playing instruments in the cyclical retelling, while taking it in turns to get up, adopt characters and act out scenes. So that summer we put on the second-ever season of *Bow Down*, Graham directing the student cast, while I was music director. A late dropout forced me to perform in the piece too. I don't know whether he'd been booked in advance to review *Poe*, but to everyone's surprise Felix Aprahamian, the august music critic of the *Sunday Times*, turned up to the show.

Soon after the short season ended, two of the students who had taken part in *Bow Down* asked to meet Graham and me. Nick Chapman and Nikki Axford announced that they would like to continue to perform *Bow Down* and make the group into a professional company. Since Nick was an environmental science student and Nikki a linguist, Graham and I felt a degree of responsibility. We'd done our jobs a little too well and now were about to ruin the lives of two young people. As ideas went, starting up a contemporary music-theatre company had to be one of the more doomed, but Nick and Nikki were not to be dissuaded. Very much against our better judgement, Graham and I agreed to help.

To begin with, a name had to be found. Nick and Nikki favoured Breath. Graham pointed out that the company's first negative review would be headlined 'Bad Breath', and so he and I decided to come up with something better. We were talking about this one afternoon as we watched cricket on the TV in Graham's parents' flat. The enormous West Indian fast bowler Joel 'Big Bird' Garner was in action.

'How about "Big Bird"?' Graham said.

Neither Graham nor I had spent much time watching *Sesame Street*, and so we didn't know that this was where Garner's nickname had originated. But Big Bird Music Theatre, though essentially meaningless, had a certain ring to it, and it stuck. Graham and I agreed to revive the production of *Bow Down*, and some dates were lined up. By the start of the tour, two performers had dropped out and so this time both of us ended up on stage.

Nick and Nikki successfully applied for small grants and new pieces were commissioned, but full Arts Council funding proved elusive and Big Bird remained a part-time company. My involvement as a performer ended with my move to Australia in 1983, though as a composer I was involved till 1985, when Big Bird performed in New South Wales and Canberra. The production for which I wrote music was *From Hand to Mouth*, an evening-long work devised from an oral history project in the Yorkshire Dales. Beyond my schoolboy cello sonata, this was the first time I had worked with folk music, but ever since this piece folk songs and dances have proved an endlessly rich mine of material for me. Even when a folk tune all but disappears into the fabric of one of my pieces, it can leave behind a vibrancy that couldn't have come from anywhere else. I have a love of drones that comes from folk music, and often techniques drawn from folk fiddling can be found in my scores.

I was proud of *From Hand to Mouth*, but because it was more devised than composed there never was a score, making the ninety-minute piece hard to repeat. And because the four performers all had to be able to act (above all) as well as sing and play musical instruments – and do Yorkshire accents – those Big Bird performances were the first and last.

In 1986, after several unsuccessful attempts, Nick and Nikki finally learnt that Big Bird Music Theatre had secured continuing funding from the Arts Council of Great Britain. Flushed with success, they wound up the company.

These days, Nick is an environmental scientist in Sydney and Nikki an arts administrator in Glasgow, so apparently Graham and I didn't ruin their lives. Graham, who remains one of my best friends, went on to be Deputy Secretary General of the British Arts Council. A section of *Poe* was performed in 1985 at the Sydney Opera House by the Australian Opera. And sometimes I watch *Sesame Street* with my daughter.

6.

Starting Again

As the Qantas flight made its descent into Sydney, 'Waltzing Matilda' played in the economy cabin. It was the Cloncurry tune, which I prefer to the standard tune, and I assumed Qantas always did this to welcome visitors and returning travellers, though I've never heard it since. It was August 1983, and I was coming to Australia for what I imagined – and had told my parents – would be five years.

I knew almost immediately I'd be staying longer. Before leaving England, I had taken the precaution of obtaining permanent residence, so my options would be open, and Australia quickly felt like home. I liked the apparent optimism of the place, as well as its informality. On my second day I walked into a branch of Westpac Bank to open an account. When the manager emerged to take me into his office, he was wearing shorts.

'Barry,' he said, extending his hand and telling me his first name but not his last.

During my final year in Bradford, I had begun to think it might be good to undertake some further study with a composition teacher. It had also occurred to me that I could combine this with living in another country. I wrote to Bernard Rands in San Diego, Sven-David Sandström in Stockholm and György Ligeti in Hamburg. Ligeti replied to say he couldn't take more students, Sandström didn't reply at all and I had a pleasant late-night phone conversation with Rands, at the end of which the whole thing felt a bit impractical. Then, on 1 October 1982, my final day of employment at Bradford University, the mail contained a postcard from Edward Cowie. On the front was a painting by Arthur Boyd of the surf crashing on a beach as a dog runs alongside (it hangs in Wollongong Art Gallery); on the back, a short message from Edward advised me to accept no job offers – 'I have a job for you.' Since I had no obvious prospects, I took Edward's advice and stopped searching. Meanwhile, I composed music and drew the dole like thousands of young artists before me and since.

Edward was almost as good as his word. It transpired that the job, in the School of Creative Arts at the University of Wollongong, was not his to offer. It would have to be advertised and I would have to apply. At some point there was a phone interview and the whole process took nearly a year. While I waited, I continued to send scores to potential performers and promoters, and had some success. *Portraits*, three pieces for piano, was shortlisted for the Yorkshire Arts Composer's Award at the 1982 Huddersfield Contemporary Music Festival, where Peter Donohoe gave the first performance. The judges were the composers David Bedford and Nicholas Maw, and they awarded me joint first prize along with Mark-Anthony Turnage, who would quickly go on to greater things. The concert was broadcast on BBC Radio 3. Another piece, *Bright Ringing Morning*, was taken up by the BBC for a studio recording. There were a couple of new commissions, including one from Adrian Jack at the Institute of Contemporary Arts (ICA) in London. This became Chamber Concerto No 2: *Cries in Summer*, the title adapted from a line in Wallace Stevens's poem 'Asides on the Oboe' (twenty years later, I would borrow Stevens's title, too, for a solo piece for the oboist David Nuttall).

The first performance of the ICA piece was scheduled to take place the weekend after I left for Australia, but I heard from friends who attended the concert that it hadn't been performed. When I asked Adrian Jack what had occurred, he reported that the program of six new pieces had turned out to be too long, and since I wasn't there my piece had been dropped. It seemed a clear indication that, for a young composer, out of sight was more or less out of mind. And so it proved, well beyond the point at which I ceased being young. Since I came to Australia, my music has only occasionally been played or broadcast in the UK. Chamber Concerto No 2 was one of my first pieces to have its premiere in Australia, when the Australia Ensemble devoted a Sunday afternoon workshop/concert to my music in late 1984. I took the cancelled London performance and subsequent Sydney premiere to be evidence I was starting my career all over again.

The School of Creative Arts was new and had grown from the recent merging of the University of Wollongong with the neighbouring teachers' college. As part of the amalgamation, the staff of the latter were guaranteed their jobs in the new set-up, notwithstanding the fact that they were no longer training teachers, but, ostensibly, artists. Not all these men and women were suited to their new task. The school included strands in theatre, the visual arts, creative writing and music, and the degree was interdisciplinary. Students took a major course in painting, say, and a minor in acting, or perhaps a major in music performance and a minor in ceramics. Applicants who wanted to do only music were encouraged to look elsewhere. New staff were appointed, all practising artists, and one of the first was the celebrated sculptor Bert Flugelman.

Looking back at the school (later it became a faculty) through a twenty-first-century lens of rationalisation, efficiency and vocational training, it all looks a bit pie-in-the-sky, but I believed in the school's aims and still do. The most interesting people I know are curious about all the arts (and other things besides), but in music they are quite rare. Traditional music education tends to focus closely on technique – as it must – but often in a way that encourages tunnel vision. I think the flute player who can throw a pot or write a sonnet or design the lighting for a play will tend to be more interesting than the player who has only mastered Boehm's studies.

In my first week at the school, the *Illawarra Mercury* – Wollongong locals often refer to it as 'the mockery' – sent a reporter to interview me, the newly imported member of staff. I could tell she wasn't really paying attention as I enthused about the courses, about the school's willingness to experiment, about how risk was vital to artistic success and how an element of *danger* inherent in the course was what made it so exciting.

'SCHOOL OF CREATIVE ARTS "DANGEROUS" SAYS LECTURER' was the following day's headline, above a picture of me smiling cheerfully in front of a sculpture. The department received a number of phone calls that morning, the first from the Deputy Vice-Chancellor's office.

I was surprised to discover that tertiary education in Australia is quite local. In the United Kingdom, going to university usually involves leaving home and moving to the other side of the country. It's part of the rite of passage. But nearly all the students at Wollongong University were from Wollongong, the majority still living with their parents. Our first students came based largely on word of mouth, and they were good – independent-minded, open to ideas, driven and creative. Each week there was a lecture in a course called History of the Arts, which the whole school attended, including most of the staff. It wasn't really a history in any strict sense, but individual lecturers speaking about great art or artists – occasionally it might be a single work – that fascinated them. I gave the first lecture, about *The Rite of Spring*, and others in the series on Beethoven's late string quartets (with quite a lot about Eliot's *Four Quartets*) and Samuel Beckett. These days it is so easy to find clips of things to show in lectures, but then if you wanted your students to see the opening of *Krapp's Last Tape*, you had to find an actor. I ended up doing it myself, my ambition in this area never fully vanquished, and presented the departmental secretary with a petty cash receipt for the bananas Krapp must consume at the start of the play. In the years that followed I gave lectures on the origins of rock'n'roll, the films of Alfred Hitchcock, and themes in English folk song: we didn't just cover 'high art'. The lectures given by others were just as wide-ranging in their topics, and the History of the Arts course was important in terms of bringing and binding together a hundred or so staff and students.

Those early years were full of excitement and energy. Many of the courses had no plans. We taught from week to week. If I had discovered something interesting in Stravinsky's music, suddenly finding myself preoccupied with the rhythmic structure of *Symphonies of Wind Instruments*, we would listen to the piece, look at the score and discuss it. I would be doing my best teaching, because I'd be talking about something that was right at the front of my mind. But I wouldn't always be right, and it was important for the students to realise that just because I pointed something out, it wasn't necessarily true. There are always different ways of thinking about music.

Composition lessons were still more spontaneous. Students brought their latest scores and we looked at them together and talked about how they might be improved. All young artists are pursuing individual paths; they tend to flourish abruptly, often in unexpected ways, and then they might hit a rough patch; a good teacher tries to keep up and help them discover what they need, but they all need different things at different times. Suddenly a composition student will find that her work is taking her in a very contrapuntal direction, at which point it's time to talk about counterpoint, look at Bach maybe, look at Schoenberg. But another student will be doing something completely different and doing it well; he doesn't want his teacher forcing him to look at Schoenberg, when what he needs is a good dose of Xenakis, or possibly just to be left alone for a while.

You wouldn't get away with this now, and *we* didn't get away with it for long. When the school became a faculty, the individual subject strands had more autonomy, and some began to argue we'd attract a better standard of flute player if she were not obliged also to be a ceramicist or a poet. It was a fair argument, but my response was that there were plenty of other institutions catering for musicians who only wanted to play their instruments. Just try telling the director of the Sydney Conservatorium of Music you'd like to add sculpture to your course. But gradually the offerings of the Faculty of Creative Arts were standardised and the academic staff spent more time being accountable: filling out forms, writing reports and attending meetings. It happened everywhere, I know. We were expected to inform our students at the start of a semester what they would be taught each week and, significantly, what the outcome of this teaching would be. As if we knew! The notion of student artists as individuals, and of that individuality leading their education was bit by bit eroded as spontaneity went out of the window. If it said on the course outline that in Week 9 the students would learn about metrical modulation, that's what we did, whether anyone needed it or not (some of them might have needed it sooner). I believe the education we offered in the first years of the course was better than this regimentation, and the number of former students from those years now in gainful employment right across the arts would suggest I'm not entirely wrong. So I grew unhappy with academe. After four years at Wollongong, I became a part-time employee in order to devote more hours to composing, and after twelve years I abandoned my tenured university job to join the ABC as presenter of *The Music Show*.

But good things happened at Wollongong. We started a new music group, somewhat clumsily called the SCAW Ensemble (an acronym for School of Creative Arts, Wollongong), and as with Moonflower at Lancaster we performed as many student works as possible. We also played new or newish Australian pieces by Ross Edwards, Anne Boyd and Vincent Plush alongside twentieth-century classics by Webern, Stravinsky and Grainger, Janáček (*Capriccio*) and Kurt Weill (*Little Threepenny Music* and the songs from *Happy End*), Berio's *Folk Songs*, Gavin Bryar's *Jesus' Blood Never Failed Me Yet*, Birtwistle's *La Plage* and Boulez's *Dérive I*. Perhaps inevitably, we also did *Ylem*. Most memorably, we gave the first Australian performance of Stockhausen's *Stimmung* and staged one of John Cage's music circuses.

Stockhausen's music was notable for its inconsistency of style (Cage's too, for that matter). Great store is set by composers who are instantly recognisable; we feel their music must be good because it has such a strong idiolect. But this can be true of bad music just as much as good. In terms of its sound world, *Stimmung* could hardly be more different from *Ylem*, or any other piece by

Stockhausen. Scored for six, closely miked voices, it explores, for more than an hour, the harmonics of a single B flat ninth chord. The singers, three female and three male, must learn to produce overtones with their voices, rhythmically animating them by chanting the names of divinities from many of the world's cultures. There are moments of precise syncronisation between the voices, as different singers take turns to lead each of the fifty-one sections, but all the singers must be constantly aware of what the others are doing. I sang bass.

We rehearsed *Stimmung* with great enjoyment for three months from December 1985, then performed it at Adelaide's Pilgrim Church during the 1986 Adelaide Festival. *During* the festival, but not as part of it: we had an audience of around sixteen. We sang it in Sydney, in Canberra, in Wollongong, and the experience was indelible. Apart from anything else, it is a piece that stops time. The composer stipulated that it should last between sixty and ninety minutes. Our performance generally took seventy but always felt as though it had gone by in about fifteen. To some extent, all performing is like this, but *Stimmung* is an extreme case in this as in nearly everything else. It is a piece, like Cage's *4'33"* – his so-called 'silent' piece – that is unique. It occupies a special niche of its own. You can't have another piece like it because it would be a straight-out copy.

Cage's ___, a ___ ___ *Circus on* ___ is almost the opposite of this, remaking itself with every performance. It is a set of instructions for turning any book into a piece of music, and there is a recording of a radiophonic version entitled *Roaratorio, an*

Irish Circus on 'Finnegans Wake'. The starting point is to take a book and randomise its text by means of a mesostic – like an acrostic, except that instead of running down the edge of a text, a mesostic runs down the middle. The word or phrase is applied to the book, one letter at a time, to isolate a word in the text so that a new text emerges. The original book is also read for its mentions of sound and place. The sounds are recorded and the places visited and recorded, the recordings played back while the new text is spoken or intoned. The book we chose was *Charivari*, the first novel by Martin Buzacott, who had recently joined the creative writing team at Wollongong. It was a good choice because the book's title describes the sound of rough music, while much of the plot is set in a circus, so Cage's idea of a music circus became nicely self-reflexive. Martin read what was left of his text while the ensemble played back recordings of the various sounds, some of which had been recorded on a field trip to a circus. *Jingle, a Bicentennial Circus on 'Charivari'* was the title we gave it. This was in 1988, the year in which nearly everything had to be a celebration of the bicentenary of White Australia.

o
o o
o

I suppose Edward Cowie had invited me to Wollongong because of my own interests and activities across the arts. While I knew my limits as an actor – I'd had no ambitions in this area since childhood – and had stopped writing poetry after trying to set it to music as a student, I still painted and drew. I'd had a solo exhibition at the Bradford Playhouse before I left England and now

I had another in Wollongong. I worked with a mixture of water-colour, ink, pastels and charcoal, and the results were not embarrassing like the poetry, but they also weren't consistent, depending too much on happy accidents. I had the sense that with a mighty effort I would have improved, but decided my time was better spent writing music. In 1994 I produced my final mixed-media work. It hangs in the spare bedroom of my friend and librettist Sue Smith, and whenever I stay over at her place I recognise both its merits and its shortcomings.

My composing was slow to get going in Australia, at least from a professional point of view. I knew no one and no one knew me. Moreover, I was aware that as a Pom I wouldn't be automatically welcomed by Australia's existing composers. A couple of years after I arrived, I was in the green room of the Sydney Opera House and got into conversation with some well-known Australian musicians, all of whom, by now, I'd worked with. One of them referred to me, in passing, as an 'Australian composer' – which technically I was, having acquired citizenship earlier that year. '*He's* not Australian!' said another, not nastily, but firmly.

Perhaps this is the place to say that I don't much care for nationalism or patriotism. I didn't when I lived in England, and I haven't since I've lived in Australia. Nationalism always seems an excuse to exclude people more than welcome them, and while I know that patriotism implies a love of one's country, I'm never sure what it is I'm meant to love. The people? I don't know most of them. I love some of those I do know, but some I dislike. The land? Much of the Australian landscape is awe-inspiring, but I seldom feel part of it. Perhaps it would be different if I'd been born here. Yet most days there's nowhere I'd rather live than my bit of Australia – it's felt like home almost from day one. Perhaps that is all that patriotism needs to mean, but I suspect there's more to it than this, and I'm suspicious of whatever that might be.

In my final year living in England I'd seen a bit of Oliver Knussen, both before and after he conducted my Concerto for Orchestra. The last time was in a pub near his home in London, just before my leaving for Australia.

'The thing about your music,' he said, 'is that I can't pick the influences.' I was surprised and must have looked it, because he went on to explain that with most young composers you could say, fairly quickly, if the music aligned itself stylistically with Harrison Birtwistle or Nicholas Maw or whomever. My music, apparently, came from nowhere. I took this to be the compliment he intended. But I often thought about the remark. For one thing, I *could* hear the influences – particularly Birtwistle, but also Tippett and Maxwell Davies. There was a trumpet figure in the Concerto for Orchestra that I had effectively stolen from Maxwell Davies's first symphony (to be clear, I had first written it, then recognised the provenance of the idea, then decided not to remove it). But, more troubling, if my music didn't display its influences (surely a good thing), did that mean it couldn't be readily pigeon-holed (also a good thing)? And would this, in turn, result in my music being ignored (obviously a bad thing) or thought worthless (a very bad thing indeed)? I was looking forward to living in a country where such categories didn't matter, but it turned out they did.

In 1983, my first impression of Australian composers was that they were always asking themselves what it meant to be Australian composers. I'd never come across a composer in Britain with similar concerns. It's true to say the issue was predominantly of interest to composers who were older than me, and it was probably inspired by Peter Sculthorpe, who in the 1960s had turned to Asia for cultural nourishment, finding inspiration in Indonesian gamelan and the court music of Japan. He wasn't alone in this or even the first. Percy Grainger had been attracted to the music of South-East Asia and so had Peter's friend Peggy Glanville-Hicks, in old age a vital spark in Australian music and after her death a significant benefactor who left her Sydney home to the nation for composers to live in rent-free. But Peter was the most prominent, and his students became caught up in his Asian explorations, Anne Boyd especially drawn to Bali, Japan and Korea, while Barry Conyngham had actually gone to Japan to study with the composer Toru Takemitsu.

The embrace of Asian influence was often considered to be anti-European in inspiration, notwithstanding Debussy's fascination with the gamelan, and some days Peter would encourage this interpretation – or not discourage it. Similarly, he came to believe, or at least repeat the notion, that Australian music was distinguished by long, flat melodic lines above slow-moving blocks of harmony, and that this was redolent of the Australian landscape. It was hardly true of all Australian music, but it was a good description of Peter's own, and such was the strength and individuality of his work that its sound implanted itself in the national consciousness. Peter, for many concertgoers, was the voice of Australia.

But if Peter and his colleagues and students felt they knew the nature of Australian music, and what it meant to be an Australian composer, there were some of my own generation – Gerard Brophy, Michael Smetanin and Mary Finsterer, for instance – who were rather antagonistic to what they regarded as a sort of parochialism. Most of them had studied with Richard Toop at the Sydney Conservatorium and been exposed to a wide range of music from postwar Europe and to a lesser extent the United States, and many had gone on to study in Europe. It is important to understand that the discussion about national identity in music was at least as much to do with modernism as with geography, and those who we might broadly think of as nationalistic (in the sense that composers such as Smetana or Vaughan Williams or Copland were nationalistic) were also at odds with the modernism of the European avant-garde. Some, including Ross Edwards and his teacher Richard Meale, were recovering modernists. It's also important to note that the duality I appear to be describing was really nothing of the kind. There was, for instance, a third strand of composers, including Graeme Koehne and Carl Vine, who, while antagonistic to modernism, were pursuing a sort of cosmopolitan neo-romanticism far removed from Sculthorpe's aesthetic. There was a fourth strand of experimental composers, most of them in

Melbourne, who had little to do with any of the music I've described (though they held Grainger in great esteem). And there were plenty of individual composers – Larry Sitsky, Nigel Butterley, Moya Henderson – who stuck to their individuality and were never drawn into the debate. I like to think this is where I sat.

Why did any of this matter? To the general public, it didn't. But in musical circles it escalated, until around the time of the Australian bicentenary a sporadically entertaining guerrilla war had broken out – 'style wars' someone labelled it. On the one hand there was an article by Toop referring to the official bicentennial commissions as a 'whore's carnival'; on the other, there was a succession of leaflets poking heavy-handed fun at complex modernism, mailed to composers around the country by the so-called Adelaide Pastoral Company, an anonymous source that as far as I know remains anonymous still. While the strife was primarily internecine, it also spilled over a bit to the ABC, which was criticised for favouring certain composers in its orchestral programming. The favoured composers were those of the Sculthorpe school and the neo-romantics; the critics were everyone else.

My feeling is that none of this would have happened had Peter Sculthorpe not been a great composer. Because of the strength of his musical voice he gave Australian musicians something to care about (one way or the other) and Australian audiences something they felt might be their own. His music has a richness and detail that aren't always immediately obvious, though they are very much part of its power and distinction. But the sound is unmistakable, and outwardly the music is simple and direct.

I suppose you might have said the same about Peter himself. I was never a close friend of his – I certainly wasn't part of the inner circle of (mostly) former students – but I had many conversations with him over thirty years, and when I was a near neighbour in Sydney for the two years I spent in the Glanville-Hicks house, sometimes the conversations stretched into the early hours of the morning, fuelled by bottles of Australian sparkling wine. What emerged were contradictions, and while we all have those, in Peter's case they were surprising because he and his music had such a strong reputation for being nationalistic, anti-European and devoted to all things Asian. It wasn't always true. He was, for example, quite the Anglophile, and one particular night, following the launch of his memoir *Sun Music* in 1999, we sat in his backyard discussing the forthcoming referendum on the Australian republic. I was for it, and he was against it, saying it was 'window-dressing', though he wouldn't be drawn on what he meant by that.

'I can't believe you're saying this, Peter,' I kept repeating. 'You're meant to be the voice of Australia. Do you want the Queen of England as your head of state?'

'But you're English!' he kept countering.

The conversation went round and round, his notion of Australia, this night at least, more old-fashioned and even colonial than I'd supposed.

Peter was good company and impossible to dislike. He was well known for being polite and always remembered the names of others' girlfriends and boyfriends, spouses and offspring. But he was a terrible gossip, and you learnt not to tell him secrets. A couple of things he shared with me about mutual friends turned out to be completely untrue, and occasionally he could be unkind about people, though always in the guise of a joke.

His favourite joke was to drop his trousers at parties. I witnessed this three times, the first in a crowded restaurant. I assumed, as I was meant to, that the trousers had fallen down of their own accord, but Belinda Webster, who was present, said she'd seen it all before. Peter's technique was to go into a corner of the room and surreptitiously loosen his belt, then return to the others in the room and look astonished when the trousers fell round his ankles ('Oh, no! My pants have fallen down!'). The last time I saw him perform the trick was in the street outside the Glanville-Hicks house following a party. It was five o'clock on a summer's morning and Peter, typically, was the last to leave. Since it was broad daylight, there was every chance that someone would look out of their bedroom window and see Australia's most famous composer, seventy years old, standing in the middle of the road in his white boxer shorts, and maybe that's what he was hoping for. I can't believe it was just for my benefit.

For all that, I think Peter was probably shy. He loved the acclaim of an audience better than anyone I've known, but in his dealings with me, at least, I detected a reserve, a protective layer that stopped you getting too close, and some of the things he said had a rehearsed quality about them. I'm pretty sure Peter didn't like my music, and I wasn't certain he liked me until one day he rang out of the blue to ask if he might dedicate his *Beethoven Variations* to me. This was one of his last orchestral works and I'm proud to have my name at the top of its first page.

o o o

With expatriation and immigration, perspectives change. You see your old country differently, while expectations of your new country have to be modified. Things that had seemed important in Britain – including Britain itself – no longer seemed so important from the other side of the world. Where I had once found Margaret Thatcher appalling, not so much for her policies as for the gleefully heartless manner in which she executed them, now all that Iron Lady stuff looked faintly ridiculous. She also sounded ridiculous. I think it was George Melly who described her voice as like a 'perfumed fart'. That's certainly how it sounded from Australia.

One expectation of Australia that had to be revised was to do with the way people lived. Everyone outside Australia knows about the Outback and the cities – especially Sydney – so it comes as a shock to discover that most Australians live in suburbs. I also expected Australians to be forthright and bold, possibly based on the way they played cricket, and was surprised to discover a degree of timidity and conservatism. Not wanting to let go of the monarchy seemed part of that.

Before coming to Australia, one of the strongest attractions I felt about the place was its multiculturalism, and this did not disappoint me. There was multiculturalism in England, too, but it was fundamentally different because it went back so far. The first waves of British immigrants were invaders: Celts, Romans, Angles and Saxons, Vikings and the Norman French. If we speak of Britishness today, we are really describing a thousand-year consolidation of those influences. Midway through that thousand years, Britain became an imperial superpower, and in the middle of the twentieth century, its empire in rapid decline, more waves of immigrants came, some assimilating, some not. But by now there was a strong, mostly unspoken sense of what it meant to be British, as well as a strong seam of racism to which it gave rise.

In Australia, anyone who isn't Aboriginal or Torres Strait Islander is either an immigrant or the descendant of a fairly recent immigrant – what, after all, is 200 years? – so multiculturalism, though not without its frightened detractors, is taken for granted and mostly easygoing. I like the way cultures hang on to their traditions, and I like the way they adapt and sometimes mix together. If there were ever to be a genuine Australian musical style, it seems to me it would surely be the result of this melting pot of international influences.

After a few months in Australia, I began to meet colleagues and make friends. I also met my first wife. Margaret Morgan was a law student when she lobbed suddenly into my life, and she later practised as a solicitor, before moving, for a while, into television writing. We didn't have a lot in common and our marriage lasted only seven years, but we were good friends and shared a love of books and films. By 1992, we'd both reached the conclusion we could do better than each other, and in time we both did, but we parted on good terms and for the next seven years wrote pieces together.

When couples separate cordially, it's always difficult for friends. Acrimonious divorces are far easier to understand. I think we all have a stake in the success of others' relationships, and when one simply fizzles, it's like an early death – it makes you aware of your own vulnerability. Some of our friends seemed sadder than we were at our parting.

Three people who were particularly good to me in my first years in Australia were the clarinettist Murray Khouri, who organised my Australia Ensemble concert, the composer Vincent Plush, who gave me one of my first Australian commissions for his group the Magpie Musicians, and the entrepreneur James Murdoch, who gave me a list of people I should meet. I discovered much later that each man disliked the other two, though I never found out why. Among the people on Murdoch's list was Belinda Webster, a sort of patron saint of musicians in Australia, working tirelessly on our behalf, always either underpaid or unpaid. At the Sydney community radio station 2MBS, she interviewed composers and performers and recorded their concerts. At one point, she drove a taxi to support herself. In 1991 she formed Tall Poppies records, acting as producer, engineer, designer, head of A&R and manager, and building up an indispensable catalogue of Australian music. She was always honest in her opinions – if you asked what she thought of your new piece you had to steel yourself for her reply – and in contrast to some of the petty squabbles I found elsewhere, Belinda was one figure in Australian music who seemed to be universally loved.

Gradually I began to feel part of a community of musicians, and in 1985 I was appointed composer-in-residence at the Bennelong Programme, the education scheme run by the Sydney Opera House Trust. The idea was to devise a multimedia work with a hundred 'young people', aged from fourteen to twenty-five. We would meet at the Opera House every Sunday for six months, putting on a show at the end of the year in the Recording Hall (now the Studio). It was an ambitious project, never more so than at the beginning when the applicants had to be winnowed. Approximately 250 people turned up on that first Sunday and I had just a day to choose the ones I wanted. We split into small groups all over the Opera House and played some pretty intense theatre games – trust exercises, movement exercises, improvisations – as well as vocal and rhythm exercises. Anyone who played an instrument had been asked to bring it, and there were improvisations that involved voices and instruments. Storytelling was the final element in the auditioning process, and in some ways most important, since urban myths were to be the subject of the piece.

I knew I couldn't assess 250 people on my own, so I enlisted the aid of fifteen of my best students from Wollongong University. The students and I had worked through all these various games and improvisations, and everyone was familiar with how they went. I put one student in each group, while I went around observing, joining in, attempting to work out who were the talented applicants. To complicate the matter, we were looking for a range of skills, including the ability to work constructively in a group. At the end of the day, I met with my students, who'd been keeping notes, and we pooled our impressions of this great sea of people. I'm sure we missed some fabulous talent, but from the 250 applicants we chose 150. My feeling was that there would be a significant drop-out rate over six months, and that by choosing fifty more participants than we required, we'd end up with the right number. I was correct about that at least.

So *Tall Stories* went into development, but very, very slowly. Each Sunday we'd begin with more games and improvisations, the rest of the day devoted to workshops designed to produce the hour-long piece we were tasked with presenting in November. I was insistent the participants come up with the piece themselves. It seemed to me they'd have a far more valuable experience than if I simply told them what to do. And I'd worked like this before, back in England, both with Graham Devlin's Major Road Theatre Company and Big Bird. We'd gone into schools and colleges, worked with youth groups and, as with *Tall Stories*, devised public pieces with volunteers. But there were significant differences. In the English projects there were always at least four of us leading the process and never more than fifty participants, usually fewer. The workshops would go for a fortnight, sometimes just a week, and we'd meet daily – they were intensive affairs. With *Tall Stories*, I was leading over a hundred people on my own, once a week for six months. With just a month to go, the Wollongong students had mostly dropped out, as was always intended, and the couple that remained had long ago taken a back seat to allow the other participants to run the show.

The trouble was we *had* no show. We had lots of ideas, but nothing remotely cohesive. It wasn't hard to see the problem: too much democracy was delaying progress. I continued to resist taking over. Instead, I talked to the whole group and suggested it was time to appoint some leaders. It was also time for these leaders to meet on weeknights. Nothing was going to happen if we restricted ourselves to the four remaining Sundays. And so a committee of six pulled all the ideas together, deciding what to leave out and what to develop, and delegating further responsibilities relating to design, lighting and sound. People had jobs; at last they all knew what they were doing.

In the end, the performances were all right. They weren't groundbreaking but they weren't meant to be. Built on a framework of individual urban myths, *Tall Stories* was an episodic blend of music, theatre and movement. It had quite an intense atmosphere, and people were pleased – the participants, the audiences, the Bennelong Programme. But with a project of this nature, it is always the process leading to the performance that is significant. I learnt a good deal from it, though I'd done this sort of thing before. For most of the participants, the experience was new, and for some of them it was literally life-changing, leading to careers in the arts as writers, actors, filmmakers. Friendships were formed and also deeper relationships. More than twenty years later, I bumped into a *Tall Stories* alumna at the ABC. She told me that she had married one of the other participants, that he had recently died, and that he had been buried in his *Tall Stories* T-shirt.

The same year as *Tall Stories*, music commissions began to come my way, performances too. By the year's end the Sydney Symphony Orchestra and the Australian Opera (later Opera Australia) had both performed my music. The Australian Opera included the final third of *Poe* in their first National Opera Workshop. The baritone Garrick Jones sang the title role in a cast that included a number of up-and-coming singers as well as some operatic veterans. Brian Fitzgerald and John Wregg co-directed with considerable imagination and care. At the start of the process, I had an emergency appendectomy and Brian and John travelled down to Wollongong from Sydney for a meeting, since I was recuperating. I pointed out various things that were in the score, but they'd already spotted them and had ideas about how to realise the moments on stage. I was in good hands. It felt collaborative.

It was the Australia Ensemble concert, though, that seemed to launch my music in Australia. Quite a few of Sydney's musical luminaries came along, including the conductor Stuart Challender, and I spoke about the pieces before the performances. The *Sydney Morning Herald* ran a complimentary review written by Fred Blanks, who said that 'Ford's music not only touches the heart but stimulates the mind'. I was so pleased with the line, I put it in my published catalogue of works, and it was quoted for years until *24 Hours* magazine misprinted it as 'Ford's music not only touches the heart but stimulates the wind'.

In addition to the first performance of the chamber concerto dropped by the ICA, the Australia Ensemble concert included a solo violin piece written for the occasion and played by Dene Olding. *Like Icarus Ascending* – its title filched from Joni Mitchell's song 'Amelia' – would become an important piece for me, one that has been played in several countries. In 1988 I took the piece as the basis for a third chamber concerto, building layers of music (for flute, clarinet, percussion, piano and cello) around the solo line. This piece was commissioned by Terra Australis Incognita, a group of Australian expats living in New York, formed with a view to playing Australian music around the United States during the bicentennial year. The group's pianist, Lisa Moore, had already played two of my pieces, one of which she'd commissioned. I travelled to the US to conduct the chamber concerto at the June in Buffalo festival in upstate New York and as Visiting Composer at the Aspen Festival, and there I met another musician who would become important for my music, the violinist Rohan Smith, who was my soloist in these performances. Later still, Rohan made a spectacularly good recording of *Like Icarus Ascending* and commissioned a new piece, which I called *Icarus Drowning*, for his Kowmung Music Festival in central New South Wales.

That chain of events is typical of how, in professional music making, one thing leads to another, and of how composers and performers work together. Collaboration is important for both sides. Most performers of classical music spend their time communing with the dead. Bach and Beethoven are two of the greatest composers who ever lived, but you can't ask them questions; by comparison, most living composers, while a long way from the accomplishments of their German forebears, are happy to discuss possible wrong notes and matters of interpretation.

This is to the composer's advantage as well as the player's. You might think you have made your intentions clear in the score, but it is surprising how often misunderstandings occur. If you are invited to rehearsals, you must attend, though it's a good idea to avoid the first one or you'll end up depressed; if you're not invited to rehearsals, you should try to attend anyway. Once a piece has been played a few times by different performers, it's another matter, but when a piece is new, the composer should hover. Often, of course, performances happen without your knowledge; sometimes recordings do, too. *Like Icarus Ascending* first appeared on CD in 1999. I was not involved at all and only discovered later that the recording had taken place. I didn't know the violinist and although I asked to hear the recording prior to its release, the tape never arrived. When I saw the CD, I assumed that the timing of my twelve-minute piece at seven minutes was a typo. It wasn't; the performance was nearly twice as fast as intended. It was also full of mistakes. Pizzicato notes were bowed, bowed notes plucked, and at the end of the piece, where Icarus floats off to his doom like Major Tom (he doesn't crash into the Aegean Sea in this piece), and the violin plays long, quiet and stratospherically high notes, my artificial harmonics were read as regular double stops and the music remained stubbornly earthbound in a chain of parallel fourths. I complained, but it was too late and the CD is still for sale. Fortunately, Rohan Smith's excellent recording of the piece came out the following year on Tall Poppies.

Performers often inspire composers, and sometimes they imprint themselves on a composer's sound. Peter Pears influenced the vocal lines of Benjamin Britten so strongly that it is hard for another tenor to sing Britten's music without sounding a bit like Pears. It was something to do with the colour of Pears's voice, the effect certain pitches created when applied to certain vowel sounds, and also the fact that Pears had his great vocal strength around the note E, where a lot of tenors have a weakness since it's where the full chest voice changes to a head voice. Britten was an intensely practical composer, and in writing well for Pears, he naturally exploited the singer's qualities. He may even have done it without thinking, having that familiar voice in his head.

Something similar happened to me. I had worked with Lisa Moore more than any other pianist when, in 1997, Ian Munro rang to ask me if I'd write him a big piece, 'like a sonata'. Over the next four and a half years I composed Ian a very big piece that was nothing like a sonata. *The Waltz Book* consists of sixty individual movements each lasting a minute (on paper at least) that may be played separately or in groups, but taken together add up to a continuous hour of music. It's a musical mosaic, each piece drawing on at least an aspect of the classical waltz, while many are full-blown waltzes.

Ian is a wonderful pianist, a fine composer, a dear friend and a Schubertian through and through. He brought to my music a kind of old-world sophistication, a wistfulness that often seemed to elevate the music and clarify the connections with waltzes of the past (because there are oblique references in my pieces to Schubert and Chopin, Schoenberg and Ravel). Ian began to perform individual waltzes as I wrote them. He played the first one ('Waltz for Jasper') at the 1998 Dartington Summer School in England, before the other fifty-nine were written and even before the commission was finalised. Other pianists played them too. Roger Smalley performed a group of the waltzes in 2000 when I was composer-in-residence at his New Music Week in Perth; my niece Kirsty played some in her first-year university exam.

The premiere of the complete hour, an unusually nerve-racking occasion for me, was in 2003, the final waltzes having been written late the previous year. I was concerned that sixty of these pieces played back to back would be too much for any audience, but Ian was magnificent and the longer he played, the more enthralled the Hobart listeners became. He gave three more complete performances that year, including one at the Sydney Opera House and another at the Melbourne Festival. I heard them all, and with each performance Ian made *The Waltz Book* more his own, discovering new details all the time while finding ever more ways of turning the pieces into a seamless entity.

Then something curious happened. At the Australian Youth Orchestra's National Music Camp in January 2004, Lisa Moore was the piano tutor. She had planned a sort of tag-team performance of *The Waltz Book* in which she and her three students would share the pieces between them. I was a tutor myself that year, and as I walked through the Canberra School of Music, where the camp was based, I heard one of my waltzes being played in a practice room. The sound of the music forced me to stop. I recognised something familiar in the playing. It was Lisa. It wasn't just her interpretation, her sound was part of the music. It's hard to put this into words – it's like describing wine – but there's a crisp clarity to Lisa's playing that I like very much. It suits her approach to Beethoven, it suits her Janáček, and it suits contemporary music, of which she has played a vast amount; perhaps her sound was forged by contemporary music. Since I first met her in 1984, I'd heard her play my music quite a lot, and while I hadn't realised it at the time, I had composed *The Waltz Book* for Ian with Lisa's sound in my head. What I recognised coming through the practice room door was my original inspiration.

But if Lisa was giving me exactly what I'd imagined, Ian had given me something I hadn't imagined, which in a way was more valuable. He had shown me new possibilities. You can learn a lot about your music from interpreters, and *The Waltz Book* has had a few. Besides those I've mentioned, they include Piers Lane, Gerard Willems (at the Adelaide Festival), Jenni Flemming, Sally Whitwell, Simon Docking (in Canada), George Lopez (in the USA), David Vance (in Vienna) and Vyacheslav Novikov (in Finland and Poland). I heard only a few of these performances, but the most memorable by far was Novikov at the Kuhmo Chamber Music Festival in Finland. The Ukrainian pianist played seventeen of the waltzes and – disregarding my tempo instructions, which would have brought his performance in at around seventeen minutes – took twenty-five minutes over them. A Schubert specialist, like Ian, Novikov played the pieces with great romantic freedom; indeed, there was as much Rakhmaninov as Schubert in his playing. It was a little shocking to hear, but fascinating, and gratifying that the music could stand up to such a wayward interpretation.

o   o
o

I've been fortunate to work with a number of fine and intelligent singers. I won't make another list, though I should mention the sopranos Jane Edwards and Jane Sheldon, who, between them, have commissioned, sung and recorded nearly all my music for that voice. But the most important collaborator I have ever had was the tenor Gerald English, for whom I composed a dozen pieces across a range of media, from song cycles to music-theatre pieces, from a role in a children's opera to a part in a radiophonic work.

I had been a fan of Gerald English's since I was a teenager and often heard him on the radio and at concerts in London. I heard him sing Tippett's *Songs for Dov* (of which he'd given the first performance) and, at a Prom concert at the Round House, Elisabeth Lutyens's *And Suddenly It's Evening* with the London Sinfonietta and a 21-year-old conductor called Simon Rattle. I was queuing before that concert and remember the frisson of excitement as the tenor bounded up the steps past me. English's career had always embraced very new music and very old – baroque and earlier. In 1950 he'd been a founder member of the

Deller Consort, one of the first vocal groups to specialise in early music, leaving only when he came to believe that Alfred Deller was keeping fifty per cent of the takings for himself and distributing the rest among the other five singers. He was part of Raymond Leppard's Glyndebourne Opera revivals of Monteverdi in the 1960s. Under Britten, he sang Peter Quint in *The Turn of the Screw* when Peter Pears had double-booked himself. In Lisbon he sang the title role in *Oedipus Rex* with Stravinsky conducting. He sang Berlioz with Thomas Beecham, Vaughan Williams with Adrian Boult, and Britten with John Barbirolli. He even sang the Evangelist in Bach's *St Matthew Passion* for Vaughan Williams. Berio and Henze both composed operatic roles for him, and he returned to La Scala several years in a row to sing in Berg's *Wozzeck* under Claudio Abbado. At the BBC, Boulez regularly engaged him to sing Stravinsky, Schoenberg and Ravel.

When I was organising concerts in Bradford, I tried to book Gerry more than once, only to be told by his agent that 'Mr English is in Australia'. I assumed he must be on tour almost continuously and it was only when I arrived in Australia that I discovered he'd been living in Melbourne since the late 1970s as founder and director of the Opera Studio at the Victorian College of the Arts. I met him for the first time when he visited Wollongong University and sat in on a rehearsal I was leading of Birtwistle's *Bow Down*. I was hardly less in awe of him than I'd been as a teenager at the Round House Prom. I wanted to ask if I could write him something but couldn't summon the courage, so I sent him a letter. Gerry wrote straight back saying he'd be delighted to sing something of mine, and so the Seymour Group, Sydney's new music ensemble, commissioned *Sacred Places*, to words by the poet Christopher Reid. I composed most of the piece in hotel rooms in Amsterdam and Los Angeles, while on a honeymoon of sorts with Margaret, and I conducted the first performance in the Sydney Opera House's Recording Hall in 1986, Gerry singing Berio's *Melodrama* on the same program. Later, Margaret would write me two sets of words for Gerry. The first was for the song cycle *Harbour* with the Australian Chamber Orchestra, a piece we wrote at the start of 1992, just as our marriage was ending. The other, in 1999, was *Night and Dreams: the Death of Sigmund Freud.*, which Gerry performed at the Adelaide Festival in 2000, and at the Sydney and Melbourne festivals the following year.

By this time Gerry was seventy-five and no longer had his very top (or bottom) notes, but was in good voice and in no mood to retire. I composed *Night and Dreams* for his singing voice as it then was and Margaret's libretto also required him to speak to the audience, quite naturally, in the character of Freud. It was an immense challenge for him at many levels. Naturalistic acting isn't the strong suit of most classical singers, and Gerry had never done anything like it, though he pulled it off supremely well, thanks in no small part to the direction of the ever-patient George Whaley. After the first performance, Robyn Archer, directing that year's Adelaide Festival, commented that she knew actors who couldn't act that well. The piece also required Gerry to be alone on stage for an hour, so it was quite a feat of memory for a man in his mid seventies, especially since there was no instrumental ensemble, so no conductor giving cues.

In place of live instruments, I had made a backing track in the studio, bringing in Ian Munro (Gerry's son-in-law) to play piano, and two harpists, Marshall McGuire and Alice Giles, the latter playing an electro-acoustic harp, and then supplementing their contribution with sound effects and historical recordings of Hitler and Chamberlain – *Night and Dreams* is set in the exiled Freud's London home in 1939, with Britain declaring war on Germany in the final weeks of Freud's life. A backing track can be a straitjacket for a performer because once it starts, it keeps going. I wanted Gerry to have as much flexibility as possible, so I divided the cues between two CDs, allowing tracks to overlap. This meant that Gerry not only took cues from the recording, but was also able to give cues, certain words or notes or gestures prompting the start of the next CD track. The operation of the CDs was quite a collaborative and rather virtuosic role, requiring a technically minded sound projectionist who was also a musician, her role, essentially, to accompany Gerry like a pianist in a *lieder* recital, except that instead of a piano she had two CD players. Fortunately this is where Wollongong's Faculty of Creative Arts came into its own, Ingrid Rahlén having studied both theatre technology and music.

Gerry English had a gloriously clear tone and the best diction I have ever heard from a classical singer. Many singers are uncomfortable with new music. It's partly that some of them don't read music terribly well, so a score without a recording

poses problems, and partly that a singer's training is pretty conservative in terms of repertoire, so the music of the singer's own time seems foreign to them. Often, when faced with a piece that isn't tonal, they disguise their inadequacy by widening their vibrato so you can't really hear a precise pitch. I suppose they would argue that the right note is in there somewhere. This doesn't happen as much as it used to, but it still happens. With Gerry, the note was always hit smack in the middle.

Working with him was a pleasure, partly because he was so straightforward. He was a thorough professional and regarded it as his job to get the piece right; if he made a mistake, he wanted to be told. I've worked with prima donnas (some of them men), where any critical remark was instantly deflected. For example:

ME: In bar 83 on the final quaver, you're singing an E flat instead of E natural.

PRIMA DONNA: [*Huffily.*] Yes, I know. I'm doing it on purpose. I thought E flat sounded better.

ME: Really?

PRIMA DONNA: Yes, it's more 'in character'.

ME: But it doesn't fit the tonality. The flute's got an E natural.

PRIMA DONNA: Yes, see, that's what I mean. It makes me sound more mysterious. Like a sort of outsider.

This is very time-consuming when you just want him to sing the note you wrote in the score, so you have to find a way to lead into the correction:

ME: Now, that is amazing! I can't begin to ... How do you *do* that? I mean, you've nearly memorised it. And I loved what you did in bar 72, the way you floated that high A. It was perfect. Oh, just before I forget, I think my notation in 83 might be a little unclear. The last note is an E natural, not a flat.

PRIMA DONNA: [*Triumphantly.*] Yes, I did wonder about that. You composers!

But with Gerry, the conversation would go like this:

ME: Gerry? Bar 83 – the last note's a natural.

GERALD ENGLISH: Ha! So it is! [*Takes pencil from behind ear, puts circle round offending note. Never wrong again.*]

Sometimes Gerry was a little too quick to learn a piece. When I'm composing for a specific performer, which is most of the time, I like to send through a photocopy of the pencil score for comments before the piece is typeset. Sometimes, if it's a long piece, I'll send the pages in little bundles as sections are completed. This was dangerous with Gerry. He rang on one occasion to see how a piece was going.

'Have you done any more?' he asked. 'I've learnt that bit you sent the other day.'

'Stop learning it, Gerry!' I said. 'I'm still changing notes.'

I gave up sending him excerpts from pieces after that. But still he would turn up to a first rehearsal with scruffy photocopies of my handwritten manuscript, even though I had sent him a nice, clean, *accurate* printed score. I put it down to his background in early music, where original manuscripts often provide a clearer picture of what the composer intended than a published edition. When a composer has been dead for 300 years, the manuscript is a way of being in touch with Purcell or Handel.

Gerry gave me some remarkable performances. One of the best was of the premiere of the second piece I wrote for him, *A Martian Sends a Postcard Home*, a setting for tenor, horn and piano of Craig Raine's poem. I'm not sure I'd have had the nerve to set this poem to music had I still lived in England, because its notoriety was so great. The poem was published in the *New Statesman* in 1977 and Raine's extreme use of metaphor and metonymy was instantly taken up by others, including Christopher Reid, who were quickly styled the Martian school.

The conceit is that a Martian comes to Earth then writes a typical holiday postcard describing the local customs, either getting the names of things wrong or mistaking their function or purpose: 'Caxtons [books] are mechanical birds with many wings / ... / they cause the eyes to melt [tears] / or the body to shriek without pain [laughter].'

Normally, when setting a poem to music, the last thing you should do is illustrate the words. If the poem mentions a dull thud, you do not need to hear it in the music. It would be banal, nothing more than a sound effect. But this poem was different. The Martian never calls a spade a spade, and the innocent listener will likely find it hard to understand his postcard. At one level, then, my music aims to explain the poem. When the Martian is telling of a 'haunted apparatus' that sleeps in every home, 'snores when you pick it up' and is soothed to sleep when it cries, the horn and piano are going through a gamut of telephone dial tones, ringtones and engaged signals; when he speaks of 'Model T', 'a room with the lock inside' and a key 'turned to free the world / for movement', the horn becomes a police siren, complete with Doppler effect.

I hadn't been able to attend any rehearsals for this piece – they were in Hobart – and had never even met the horn player and pianist, so when I arrived for the premiere I had still only heard the music in my head. At the concert that night, Gerry and the others brought it vividly to life, performing it as though it were a repertoire piece. It didn't sound like new music, but as though it had always existed.

Above all, I suppose, I saw Gerry's enthusiasm for my work and his regular requests for new pieces as a vote of confidence. This singer who had worked with Britten and Boulez, Stravinsky and Tippett had faith in me; this man who I'd watched in awe climb the stairs to the Round House in London now came to stay whenever he was in Sydney, and we talked about everything. Although he was two years older than my father, sometimes Gerry forgot we weren't contemporaries. One conversation began: 'Andy, you remember before refrigeration ...'

o
o   o

A form of musical collaboration I was keen to pursue was conducting. In my four years at Bradford, I'd conducted approximately a hundred concerts with the widest repertoire and learnt a lot about music and about performing, But only a handful of these concerts had been with professional musicians. Working with amateur choirs and orchestras, you have to do a bit of clowning around; you have to make the rehearsals enjoyable, because you want the singers and players to come back next week. None of that is necessary with professional musicians. What professionals want is a conductor who is as competent as they are but, ideally, knows more than them. In Australia I'd conducted the Australia Ensemble, the Seymour Group and the Magpie Musicians. Then came the Australian Chamber Orchestra.

In 1992 the artistic director Richard Tognetti invited me to be the ACO's composer-in-residence, but my association with the orchestra had begun three years earlier, at the Huntington Estate Music Festival in Mudgee, New South Wales, where Richard was also artistic director. Some of the pieces I conducted were my own suggestions – *The Unanswered Question* of Charles Ives, Berio's *O King* (with Emma Matthews), Maxwell Davies's *Eight Songs for a Mad King* (Lyndon Terracini) and Stockhausen's *Ylem* – but quite often I was roped in at the last minute to conduct pieces that Richard would normally have directed from the first violin desk. There was never enough rehearsal time at these festivals, and the theory was that if I beat time and Richard concentrated on playing, the allotted thirty minutes might be used more efficiently.

On one occasion, Richard handed me a score of Britten's *Lachrymae* for viola and string orchestra just before lunch, telling me the rehearsal would be at four p.m. with a performance that night. *Lachrymae*, based on John Dowland's Elizabethan pavan of the same name, is a wonderful piece in the broad tradition of Vaughan Williams's *Fantasia on a Theme by Thomas Tallis* and Tippett's *Fantasia Concertante on a Theme of Corelli*, but I didn't know it. I took the score back to my room and spent the next few hours marking it up. The viola soloist was Hartmut Lindemann, a magnificent player and an old friend of the ACO, and the rehearsal went well enough. The performance, however, was close to disastrous. Hartmut, it transpired, was a very spontaneous player and nothing we had decided at the rehearsal happened in the performance, though lots of things we'd never discussed did. In particular, his approach to tempo was suddenly exceptionally elastic, pushing ahead in semiquaver passages then slamming on the brakes just before a cadence. It was all very musical, but I couldn't follow him and so the orchestra couldn't follow me. In fact, I was in the way. The best chance for the performance to hold together would have been for everyone to watch Hartmut.

'Such a great player,' said the violinist Monica Curro as I walked off shell-shocked. 'It's always different on the night.'

This incident should probably have served as a warning as far as professional conducting went, but as the orchestra's composer-in-residence in 1993 and 1994 part of my duties involved programming and conducting concerts of contemporary repertoire. The first, for strings alone, was a particularly ambitious program containing Webern's Five Movements, Op 5, Gerard Brophy's sparkling *Orfeo*, Michael Whiticker's little flute concerto *Ad marginem* (played by Geoffrey Collins) and Birtwistle's *Still Movement*, a wonderful piece, since withdrawn by the composer. At the centre of it all was the world premiere of a large-scale song cycle by Larry Sitsky for the great soprano Marilyn Richardson, *In pace requiescat* to words by Edgar Allan Poe.

I prepared like mad for this concert and knew the scores inside out. The Birtwistle was full of changing time signatures and metrical modulation and I sat at my kitchen table, beating the air until I could conduct all the transitions smoothly. At the end of the first rehearsal, the players actually applauded. But there was something missing, something that wasn't happening, and if I knew that, the orchestra certainly knew it. My beat was clear and individual players were getting their cues, but that special rapport, that telepathic bond that puts performers inside each other's heads, *that* wasn't there. And to be fair, I also had technical problems. I've always felt that *Pierrot lunaire* was the hardest piece I've ever conducted because there never seem to be more than four bars in a row in the same tempo, the music always speeding up or slowing down. Webern's Five Movements are similar, and Sitsky's song cycle isn't far behind. But what do you do with your hands to indicate this fluctuation? That was my problem. That was where telepathy would have been useful.

'This is very hard,' I said at one point, rehearsing the Webern.

'For you, maybe,' said Tognetti, and he wasn't being mean.

If you're playing an instrument – if you're actually making a sound – it is far easier to control tiny shifts in tempo than if you're simply moving your hands through the air. Now, any professional conductor reading those words will immediately recognise my problem, because of course there *are* ways in which you can indicate these fluctuations. It was just that I didn't know them, and I still don't.

The concert, in Sydney's Eugene Goossens Hall, was by no means a disaster – the reviews were mostly positive – and a few weeks later the second concert, featuring, the first performance of my piece *The Widening Gyre*, together with music by Boulez, Berio and Sculthorpe, was rather successful. But I had to recognise that I wasn't a conductor.

'You know, Andy, you're not the worst we've had,' said another violinist, Leigh Middenway. It was sweet of her, but if I was going to conduct, then it wasn't enough to be 'not the worst'; I wanted to do it well. I'm sure I could have improved over time, but I didn't really have time and the ACO certainly didn't. So conducting went the way of painting, my creative life becoming ever more focused on writing music. I have since occasionally conducted my own works – when I stand on the podium to do one of my pieces I am, after all, the world authority, whatever my technical shortcomings as a conductor – but for the most part I've left other composers' music alone.

In December 1994, my two years with the ACO ended and I returned to Wollongong University, walking straight into a day-long faculty meeting. A condition of my leave from the university had been my return, but by the end of this day, I knew I had to escape.

On New Year's Eve, my friend Cathy Strickland asked for my New Year's resolution. I told her I intended to spend 1995 extricating myself from academe and wheedling my way into the ABC. In the middle of January, Penny Lomax rang from Radio National. She explained that the presenter of *The Music Show* was leaving and that they were looking for a replacement: would I be interested? It would be two days a week, the same as my university job.

'Yes,' I said.

'Well, obviously you'll want to think about it,' Penny said.

'I already have,' I said.

7

Words About Music

Writing well about music – or anything else – isn't the same as talking well about it. Some people can do one thing but not the other. Andrew Porter was a case in point.

Porter was perhaps my favourite classical music critic, his writing a mixture of deep knowledge, elegant literary style and shrewd judgement, always expressed as kindly as possible. He was on the *Financial Times* from 1953 to 1972, then the *New Yorker* until 1992, and finally, back in London, the *Observer* and the *Times Literary Supplement*. He generally wrote at greater length than his fellow critics – unimaginably greater length than most music critics are permitted today – and was an expert provider of context, which I have always believed to be the critic's main job. In 2003, Lyndon Terracini, then artistic director of the Queensland Music Festival, invited Porter to Brisbane and asked me if I'd hold a conversation with him. I jumped at the chance and the producers of *The Music Show* were equally keen, arranging to record the session for later broadcast.

Before our lunchtime session, I met the famous critic for a coffee. He was charming and interested in everything. He'd even read my latest book, *Undue Noise*. But as we walked on stage at the Spiegeltent, he said, 'You know, I'm not very good at this sort of thing. I'm really a writer.'

And it was true, except that it was an understatement. It was as though the moment he sat down in front of an audience, his mind froze. Over coffee, he had been open and free with his opinions, but now, when he felt his pronouncements ought to carry some weight, this most knowledgeable and eloquent of critics became diffident and tongue-tied. It wasn't long before people started to leave, and at the end of the session there were no questions.

'Sorry,' he said to me, as we walked off. The conversation was never broadcast.

When Andrew Porter died in 2015, I read, in his friend Nicholas Kenyon's obituary, how Porter had needed the discipline of the written word – and, who knows, perhaps a deadline – in order to formulate his thoughts. Kenyon told a story from Porter's days on the *Financial Times*, when he had arrived at the newspaper's office one night following the first performance of a song cycle by Britten. He didn't know what he thought; he doubted Britten's talent for setting words to music and wondered aloud whether Peter Pears was really much of a singer. Then he shut himself in his office, sat down at his typewriter and began banging away. An hour later, his review written, Porter opened the door to announce that the song cycle was Britten's finest to date, a masterpiece.

When I begin writing an article about music, I often don't know what I think; sometimes I'm not even sure what the topic is. I find out by writing. In that sense, at least, writing about music is similar to writing music or making any other kind of art. You discover what you're doing by doing it. As far as I'm aware of having a writing style at all, I know that it is similar to the way I speak – or would speak if I were better at marshalling my thoughts on the spot. I read aloud everything I write, because I want it to sound natural, I want it to flow; I want my reader to feel as though I'm addressing her. But it's a confection; it's not real speech. When I read my actual speech transcribed – in an interview, say – I frequently cringe at the lumpy dullness of it.

In my first book, a collection of conversations called *Composer to Composer*, I ran up against this distinction. I interviewed thirty composers, some of them very famous: Cage, Reich, Tippett, Boulez, Stockhausen, Gubaidulina, Carter. Transcribing these interviews, I noticed that while some of the conversations worked well on the page in a question-and-answer format, many did not. My aim wasn't solely to present a composer's ideas but to paint a sort of portrait of each composer as a person. I wanted their personalities to emerge and, much of the time, found I had to write the interview up as a profile in order to achieve this. It wasn't because the composers were inarticulate. On the contrary, some of the most articulate needed this extra help because the meaning wasn't just in their words, but in their delivery and tone of voice, and these didn't translate to the page.

Talking about music – notwithstanding the difficulty of the subject itself – is fundamentally different to writing about it because, like music, it depends on sound, and musical sound at that. This is true of talking about anything. We are seldom aware of it, but, when we speak, our rhetorical devices are precisely the same tools a composer employs. First there's pitch. Our voices rise and fall to varying degrees (more so in South Wales than in New South Wales); if they didn't, we would sound mechanical and no one would listen to a word we said. We use rhythm and tempo to give variety and structure to our speech. We employ dynamics (loud and soft) and different forms of articulation for emphasis, and we use repetition to drive a point home. Without these musical devices, our speech would lack meaning or interest. This is how we bring subtlety to our communications with each other, and also how we divine truth. A person's words might point in one direction, but the sound of the words gives us a different sense. Some politicians use the music of rhetoric to disguise the fact that they're not really saying anything at all.

Vocal ticks can be part of that music. Peter Sculthorpe was famous for his ums. Ask any Australian radio producer who has worked in the arts and they will tell you they have spent hours removing ums from interviews with Sculthorpe. I once heard him slip an um into 'Wagga Wagga'. But you have to be careful, with someone like this, not to tidy up the speech too much or it will lose its character.

Once on *The Music Show* I interviewed a man with a savage stammer. He was an academic and the expert in his field. The interview was from a New York studio and until the man gave his first answer we had no idea of his speech impediment, let alone the scale of it. It was Friday, and the interview and its topic had already been announced for the following morning. Had it been just a few remarks, we might have run it unedited, but we were supposed to be devoting an hour to this topic, and he, our one guest, was very difficult to listen to. From a moral standpoint I'm not sure we should have done it, but the interview was cut in three, and three producers each spent hours going through their third of the tape, removing the ticks, hesitations and repetitions from his speech. By the time the editing was done, there wasn't a trace of the stammer, but while the man's words now flowed, they were curiously monotonous. All the expression in his speech had been in those stammers. Without them, he sounded flat and robotic, like Stephen Hawking's voice generator. A number of listeners commented.

Because expressive speech is musical, we often get a sense of a musician's art through the sound of their speaking voices. This is plainly true of singers, particularly when they sing their own songs. To hear Paul Kelly interviewed about his songwriting is to hear the same laconic vocal delivery that sings those songs; moreover, since he writes his songs using that voice, his answers bring together the songwriting and the speech, the singing and the song. Something similar, though less obvious, happens when classical musicians speak. I'm not so much thinking of how they might sing examples, as the pianist Mitsuko Uchida once did for me with Beethoven sonatas via a bad phone line from

London. I'm thinking of how the orotund impetuosity of Steven Isserlis's speech somehow mirrors his cello playing, how Pekka Kuusisto's tendency to stop mid-sentence and reach for an unexpected reference or analogy is not dissimilar to the way he plays the violin.

o
o o
o

The Music Show began on ABC Radio National in 1991. It was a nationwide consolidation of half a dozen different state-based programs, all called *In Tempo*, that had focused on classical music in their respective capital cities and regions. Not only did the new program cover the whole country, it covered the waterfront in terms of musical style. It was the invention of Maureen Cooney and Penny Lomax, and for the next twenty-six years they produced it together. Christopher Lawrence was the first presenter (I was occasionally a guest), followed briefly by Julie Steiner. I took over in February 1995. Like most programs on Radio National, *The Music Show* is producer-led. The producers, who are music specialists, choose the guests I will be speaking with and the music I will play; they research the interviews and precis their research in the form of suggested questions on which I then base my interview. It's also the producers' job to hone the presenter's on-air skills, pointing out bad verbal habits and refining the timing of an interview — one of the most frequent instructions I hear in my headphones is 'Move on now'. Practically everything I have learnt about radio, I learnt from Maureen and Penny.

When I began at Radio National, I did what all new ABC presenters do and attended seminars run by more experienced broadcasters. These are intensive sessions held over a few days, aimed at making the newcomers into better readers of scripts and askers of questions. On the first morning, our seminar leader said, 'Of course we all aspire to present *The 7.30 Report*,' mentioning ABC TV's flagship current affairs program. I have never aspired to do this. I am not a career journalist and, in my third decade of presenting this long-running radio show, I still feel like a complete amateur. Naturally, over the years I have picked up some of the skills and tools of the broadcaster's trade: I have always operated my own panel – microphones, CD players and so on – and I am confident enough on air not to use a script. If, as I hope, *The Music Show* sounds spontaneous, it's because it mostly is. So when I say I'm an 'amateur', I'm not fishing for compliments – after all this time, I think I'm quite good at presenting the show and asking questions. What I mean is that my approach to the program is that of a musician, more than a journalist.

The most important skill for an interviewer happens to be identical to the composer's most important skill – the ability to listen hard and critically. For a composer, it's about hearing all the possibilities in your musical material, spotting those with the greatest potential and understanding how they might develop or fit together. When composing is going well, the music itself is telling you what to write next, and that also comes down to listening. It's the same with an interview. The producers' research is essential background on which to build an interview, and their questions – usually expanded and reordered by me, then reduced to a series of keywords – are the framework. You might say they are the equivalent of a composer's basic musical material. But just as that material does not make a piece of music on its own, so the list of questions doesn't make an interview. You have to listen to the answers.

In my early days on *The Music Show*, I was interviewing an Irish folk musician. He was in a phone box somewhere in rural Victoria. Computer screens had recently been installed in our broadcast studio, so that producers, rather than speak into their presenter's headphones all the time, could also type instructions or suggestions. As the Irishman spoke, Penny Lomax was typing and I was reading. Suddenly the Irishman stopped speaking.

'Are you *listening* to me?' he asked. I wasn't.

'Of course I am,' I lied. Then I posed a question, more or less off the top of my head, that happened to be relevant to what he'd just been saying. I was lucky and I never forgot the lesson.

The idea of *The Music Show* is to talk about music: how it's made, what it's made of, how it's heard, how it's used. I speak to musicians – to singers, instrumentalists and composers in all areas of music – and my job is to help them talk. We want to hear their insights, experiences and points of view. Listening is the key, as it is to any good conversation. You listen so you can prod for more information, the single interjection 'Why?' one of an interviewer's most valuable tools; you listen in order to pick up on information that wasn't in the research, information that might colour the other questions you were intending to ask; you listen to help the speaker move the story along, because sometimes they can become bogged mid-explanation; and you listen in order to identify when the speaker is struggling with a subject. Often that subject is music itself, and it's wise not to push if the guest seems reluctant. But you won't notice this if you're not listening.

Whenever I'm asked to talk to journalism students about interviewing, I play them my interview with the jazz singer Annie Ross. This was a good interview that turned into a train wreck, and it was my fault for not listening. The first part of the interview was so compelling that it begins *The Music Show*'s book, *Talking to Kinky and Karlheinz*.

Annie Ross is speaking about growing up in a family of vaudevillians, becoming a singer and finally going to the Apollo Theatre in Harlem one night to replace Billie Holiday, who's indisposed. She's evidently told the story many times, but she tells it well, controlling the dramatic pacing, delaying information and delivering punchlines with a singer's timing. For good measure, she throws in impersonations of her agent, the mob-connected Joe Glaser; Duke Ellington, who 'had the band' at the Apollo; and Billie Holiday herself. It's a bravura performance.

Then I ask her about music and, specifically, about what makes an enduring jazz standard. She hesitates, then says that it must have 'a beginning, a middle and an end'. She doesn't elucidate. I hear her answer, but I'm not listening. What I hear is that she hasn't understood my excellent question. Were I listening properly, I'd notice that she has deflected the question away from music, and I might guess that this is because she's not much good at speaking about music. Some musicians aren't; some of the more instinctive musicians, brilliant though they may be, can't talk technically.

I hear none of this. Instead, I rephrase my question and ask if perhaps a certain level of harmonic sophistication is necessary for a standard to be open to a variety of different interpretations.

'No,' she replies, with as much dignity as she can muster, given that she's being tortured on live radio. Deaf to her discomfort, I plough on – because, after all, I know I'm right – pointing out that while some of Bob Dylan's songs are classics, they lack the richness of harmony necessary to a jazz standard. I'm no longer interviewing her, just trying to get her to agree with me. The interview is off the rails, and all I had needed to do, following her engaging story and brilliant impersonations, was to ask if perhaps she'd care to tell us about some other famous musicians she'd worked with. The presenter's job is to help the guest sound good, but in trying to sound good myself, I embarrassed Annie Ross.

Some guests require a lot of help – the Tibetan singer Yungchen Lhamo, who at the time didn't have much English, once nodded her answers to my questions – and some require very little. Occasionally, the hardest thing is to stop someone talking. When Malcolm McLaren, the former manager of the Sex Pistols, came on the show, I only managed to ask three questions in half an hour. He spoke well and interestingly, but in a sort of stream of consciousness. In those days we recorded to tape, and eventually my producer informed me the tape was about to run out; we had a minute left and McLaren was in full flight. Because he was wearing sunglasses I couldn't see his eyes, but he seemed to be staring past me at the view of Sydney through the studio window. At any rate, I couldn't get his attention and his speech contained no pauses for me to interrupt. I had two choices, one of which was to speak over him, which would have sounded rude. Instead, I wrote him a note – 'The tape is running out' – and pushed it across the desk. Still talking, he glanced down at the slip of paper, then brought his disquisition to an elegant and reasonably logical conclusion with just seconds remaining on the tape.

Occasionally the guest goes too far in answering the first question and touches on questions that haven't yet been asked. Pete Seeger did this when I visited him at Beacon on the Hudson River in upstate New York. Meeting me off the train from Grand Central, he took me down to an old boathouse that doubled as a community hall. I'd been looking forward to this interview, and had prepared my questions carefully. He was coming up to his eightieth birthday, and it seemed to me the best approach to our conversation was to guide him through some of the main events of his life and career. I'd been told that Pete was sometimes a little confused these days, so before we began I explained what I wanted to do. I switched on the recorder and asked my first question, but his answer rambled off into so many other areas that after five minutes he had completely destroyed my interview plan. I had approximately ten questions on my list and he had part-answered eight of them. His was one of the most popular

interviews we ever broadcast, but it depended for its success on two days of surgical editing by Penny, who cut down a sprawling hour of reminiscences, anecdotes and oft-repeated stories, to a tight and surprisingly cogent twenty minutes.

The best interviews are always those in which the guest also listens. There are some regulars on *The Music Show* who we're always happy to have back because they engage with the questions. I always look forward, for instance, to talking to Robyn Archer and Paul Grabowsky, or the conductors Simone Young and Roland Peelman, all of whom are real conversationalists. They listen to the questions and think about their answers. Pierre Boulez was like that, as were k.d. lang and John McLaughlin. I like to hear people think. In my early days on the show, the guitarist John Williams proved himself to be one of the best interviewees, always listening and never dodging a question. We often talked politics and I once asked him if he believed that, like politicians, music was capable of lying. He thought for a moment and then, without actually naming Andrew Lloyd Webber, left no one in any doubt that he believed the composer of *Jesus Christ Superstar* fitted the bill.

While you hope that your guests listen as hard as you do yourself, sometimes they don't, and especially if they are in the middle of a promotional tour, they can be on automatic pilot. When I interviewed Elvis Costello about his doorstop of a memoir, he didn't wait for me to finish questions, but jumped in as soon as a phrase or word set him off on a train of thought. It was entertaining and informative, but not a conversation. (I might say that his wife, Diana Krall, is one of the best listeners I've ever interviewed.) Some guests have given so many interviews in their lifetime it is hard to know what to ask them, but it's worth trying to come up with something new, because you might prick their interest and provoke a genuine conversation. I asked Eric Idle and John Cleese about the uses of music in comedy and about comedy in music. It turned out they had never really talked about this subject – Cleese gave the impression he'd never even *thought* about it – and the resulting interview was fascinating, especially when the two men forgot about me and had a conversation with each other that they'd never had before.

Another sort of guest is the legend. I count myself fortunate to have spoken to some ridiculously famous musicians, from Odetta to Ornette Coleman, Tom Jones to Patti Smith, Joan Baez to Boy George. For the most part they wear their fame lightly, but sometimes you feel the legend has claimed them. Marianne Faithfull was one, though she was undoubtedly entertaining.

'If I thought I was no better than little Alanis [Morissette],' she announced, when that singer's name came up, 'I'd cut my fucking throat.' We edited the comment out and I wish we hadn't. Another guest who had become his own legend was Yehudi Menuhin.

'I'm just a child, you see,' he told me in 1998, and I'm afraid I didn't believe him. All I could think of was Harold Skimpole in Dickens's *Bleak House*. Surely anyone who was really 'just a child' would not even know. During our half-hour together, Menuhin made some profound comments about the nature of music and especially about Bach, but I didn't warm to him.

My earliest interviews were all with composers and mostly for newspapers and magazines, particularly, in the early 1990s, the ABC's magazine *24 Hours*, under the inspired editorship of Suzy Baldwin, and it was some of these interviews that ended up in *Composer to Composer*. At the time I felt I was on reasonably safe ground, even though a few of the interviews were daunting. Because I didn't want to risk being late, I arrived an hour early at the Greenwich Village building in which John Cage had his loft. I waited in a cafe round the corner, where I became increasingly nervous as it dawned on me I would never be able to think of a question he hadn't answered a hundred times before. But Cage was very kind, and if I failed to ask him anything new, he treated all my questions as though they were interesting propositions he was keen to explore for the first time.

Brian Ferneyhough was daunting in a different way. Unable to meet in person, we opted to do the interview by fax. Ferneyhough, an Englishman in San Diego, said that he preferred written interviews anyway, and he agreed to answer my questions as spontaneously as he could bear to in an attempt to bring a conversational feel to the exchange. When I read through his answers, I found there were parts that made no sense. Ferneyhough had a well-deserved reputation for composing extremely complex music, and another reputation, only slightly less deserved, for giving extremely complex answers in interviews. So I tried harder to comprehend his sentence structures and use of obscure words, but the more closely I read his fax, the more it seemed to me that those bits I couldn't grasp were a result of his having used the wrong words. There were half a dozen such places. In each case, the words were all long and fancy, and I felt I could see the words that he had meant to use, words that would make his answers, though still arcane, at least intelligible. But how do you suggest to a fellow of Ferneyhough's stature that he's misusing the English language?

I faxed back a politely tentative letter, apologising if, through my own stupidity, I had misunderstood his answers, but wondering if it was possible that in the following instances he had used the wrong word. I sent him my suggested replacements. The next morning, his reply lay in the fax machine tray, cheerfully accepting all my corrections. I couldn't help wondering whether some of the more obscure utterances I'd read elsewhere, attributed to Ferneyhough, were a result of his interviewer or editor failing to challenge his word choices.

One or two people to whom I've told this story took it to be evidence that Ferneyhough was a charlatan. I don't think that at all. Assuming it wasn't an isolated case, I think a tendency to succumb to grand malapropisms is charming. It humanises him. It's like Boulez's comb-over.

There are really only two reasons to write or broadcast about music. The first is to encourage people to listen harder; the second is to encourage them to think musically – with a view to listening harder. Interviews are a good vehicle for the latter because they bring different points of view. In some of my books, I've included interviews alongside my own writing to present opinions other than mine. In *Earth Dances*, for instance, straight after my chapter on the significance of *The Rite of Spring*, there's an interview with the composer Martin Bresnick that begins with his judgement that *The Rite* is far from Stravinsky's most interesting piece, and he explains why. My broader point in doing this is that while it might be possible to be precise about musical mechanics, it is almost impossible to be precise about meaning, and therefore about significance. Perhaps, for this reason, I'm open to other people's suggestions for writing articles or books. It's a way of engaging with an idea I hadn't previously considered and discovering what I think about it.

Two of my books came from other people's ideas. *Earth Dances*, which also became a radio series, was the suggestion of my publisher, Chris Feik. *Illegal Harmonies*, which began as a radio series, was proposed by Maureen Cooney. She rang me one day in the early 1990s, even before I began working with her on *The Music Show*, to point out that the twentieth century was going to end, that someone ought to make a radio series about the century's music, and that perhaps it should be me and her. It would be a big job and we should start as soon as possible. In 1994 we took the idea to the new head of ABC Classic FM, Peter James. We wanted to make ten ninety-minute episodes, one for each decade, and asked for $35,000 for me as a freelancer to write and co-produce the series. As it turned out, the project took far longer than anticipated, and the money wasn't nearly enough, but it seemed like a hell of a lot at the time and Peter blanched, asking that we leave the proposal with him. The following morning he rang, telling me to go ahead. Such was the freedom accorded to heads of the ABC's networks in those days, and such was their control of budgets.

Illegal Harmonies was always primarily about the music of the concert hall and opera house – it was, after all, commissioned by a classical music station. Yet because the twentieth century was also the century of the sound recording, of mass production and commercialisation, and of popular music going global, Maureen and I felt it was important to talk about this too, at least in so far as pop music had affected classical music. On a small scale and at a local level composers had been drawn to vernacular music since the Middle Ages, but the twentieth century was different. From its earliest days, American jazz reached out across the Atlantic, its syncopations and, to a lesser extent, its harmonies enchanting European composers from Debussy to Stravinsky to Ravel. By the 1960s, pop music had more or less eclipsed all other music so far as the mass media were concerned. Some modern classical composers, including Berio and Stockhausen, were changed by it; those who were not, those who had chosen to ignore the Beatles and the Beach Boys and Jimi Hendrix, were arguably composing in opposition to popular taste. So besides Stravinsky and Schoenberg, Bartók and Berg, *Illegal Harmonies* also considered Irving Berlin and Ethel Merman, Duke Ellington and Charlie Parker, Buddy Holly, the Beatles and Run DMC. The radio series was first broadcast in monthly episodes in 1997 and the book published in the middle of that year. In 2011 it went into its third edition.

Making a series such as *Illegal Harmonies* is hugely enjoyable, the highly produced programs more collaborative than the weekly *The Music Show* can possibly be. I write scripts, the producer edits them, we choose music and maybe other sounds, and then the collaboration really starts; for once the script is recorded, we start to lay it out. It is rather like composing, but with a producer and engineer to bounce ideas off and, occasionally, overrule me. Sometimes the music or other sounds are woven through the words; more often the words are woven through the music. Either way, it's counterpoint. And how you use the music helps tell the story.

In the eighth episode of *Illegal Harmonies*, about the music of the 1970s, we wanted to look at minimalism, but minimalist music tends to last a long time and using little excerpts would have been misleading. So we had the idea of running music continuously under my voice, cross-fading different works as my script took us from one piece to another. Because of the repetition inherent in minimalism, it works quite well as a sonic bed: you can talk over it in a way you can't with, say, Stockhausen's *Gruppen*, which is a series of big events. By leaving the music under my voice we were able to show the continuity that most minimalism offers, bringing the music to the fore between my paragraphs to show different colours or textures. The music didn't stop for the first forty minutes of the program, as Bryars's *Jesus' Blood Never Failed Me Yet* gave way to the first-movement development of Beethoven's *Pastoral* symphony (to show that minimalist devices weren't new), then Reich's *Music for Eighteen Musicians*, La Monte Young's *Composition 1960 #7* (lasting as long as its single chord continued to resonate), Riley's *In C*,

Reich's *It's Gonna Rain*, Reich's *Drumming*, Glass's *Music in Twelve Parts*, Glass's *Einstein on the Beach*, Pärt's *Cantus in memoriam Benjamin Britten*, Anne Boyd's *Angklung* and Mike Oldfield's *Tubular Bells*. By the end of our work on *Illegal Harmonies*, I felt Maureen and I had created a kind of house style for our radio features, and our next project allowed us to develop it.

Dots on the Landscape was a six-part series about Australian composition that Maureen and I made for ABC Classic FM in 2001. In contrast to *Illegal Harmonies*, which was ten extended radio 'essays', *Dots* was an oral history, the story of music since colonial times told by more than thirty composers and a few critics. My voice introduced each episode and popped up occasionally to move the program along or to identify a speaker, but essentially each episode was a collage of voices, music and ambient sounds, most of the interviews having been conducted on location. The series looked at what is unique in Australian music – or if not unique, then heightened: colonialism and Aboriginality; the role of opera in the national psyche; attitudes to Europe, Asia and the landscape; and finally expatriation, Australia having more immigrant and emigrant composers than any other country I can think of. I avoided certain topics – such as modernism and postmodernism – because there wasn't a specifically Australian angle: that debate had happened everywhere. Inevitably, there were some well-known composers whose voices we didn't hear, because they didn't fit my themes.

In the third episode, the only one devoted to a single composer – because it struck me that Percy Grainger was a theme unto himself – I recorded nearly everything at the Grainger Museum in Melbourne. The museum, established by the composer in the 1930s, is a fascinating place for many reasons, and some of the displays are laid out like Victorian or Edwardian drawing rooms, stuffed with furniture and other objects. I tried to make the Grainger episode in *Dots* reflect this, with a multiplicity of voices edited into small sound bites, jostling to be heard among the fragments of music. In contrast, the fifth episode, about the influence of landscape, uses very few voices and allows them time to be expansive. To begin, we hear David Lumsdaine and Barry Conyngham speaking in turn about the bush and the city, and there is no music at all, just birdsong and insects behind Lumsdaine's voice and the sounds of Sydney Harbour behind Conyngham's. Barry and I had recorded our conversation one warm Saturday evening, sitting on a bench outside the Opera House, the ferries and passing concertgoers giving us all the ambiance we needed.

Dots on the Landscape, though it was designed as a history and functions as one, was close to being a musical composition. The production techniques were similar to those I had used on *Night and Dreams* and would go on to use in *Elegy in a Country Graveyard*. It's an indication of the size of the role that the ABC's producers and sound engineers have played in my professional life, not only by training me up as an on-air presenter, but also in broadening my outlook as a composer.

Writing books, inevitably a more solitary business than making radio, is a different kind of pleasure and always demanding.

I have also sometimes found it to be a form of exorcism, and wonder how many other writers have had this experience. Before Martin Buzacott and I wrote *Speaking in Tongues* in 2005, we were two of the biggest Van Morrison fans in Australia. We would devour his new albums and discuss individual songs whenever we met, until one day one of us said to the other that we should write a book about them. So we did.

We divided the task between us. Martin wrote the introduction to the book and most of Part Two, about Morrison's albums up to 1990; I wrote Part One, about the themes in his songs, the final section of Part Two (the albums since 1990) and the Epilogue. Then we swapped chapters and edited each other. But by the time we came to do publicity for the book, sitting in a small studio chatting remotely with ABC Kalgoorlie or wherever, we realised our hearts weren't quite in it anymore. It was as though, having spent so long listening to the songs, thinking about them, and dissecting and discussing them, we had lost the sense of fandom that had driven us to write the book in the first place. It wasn't that we'd gone off Van the Man – when the presenter in Kalgoorlie introduced our conversation with the opening of 'Madam George', Martin and I exchanged happy smiles – but there was no longer the urge to seek out his music. Of course the more recent material hasn't been up to much, but even the classics – *Astral Weeks, Common One, Into the Music*, whatever – have tended to gather dust on my CD shelves since the book came out.

Is it that I know the music too well and in consequence it lacks the interest it used to have? I don't *think* so. When remastered editions of *Astral Weeks* and *His Band and the Street Choir* were released in 2015, my wife gave me them for Christmas. I listened again in wonder. I still love that voice and marvel at its flexibility and emotional depth; my admiration for his singing is undimmed. Perhaps it's simply that the mystery is gone, that I've worked out what I think about Van Morrison and would now rather listen to something I haven't worked out.

There are those, of course, who feel that you shouldn't write seriously – let alone analytically – about popular culture. These people come in two varieties: the academics and the anti-intellectuals. The first group think pop is worthless, and that musical analysis should be about Buxtehude; the others think that pop music becomes less cool if you study it, and it's enough to give it a thumbs up or thumbs down. I think they're all wrong. With anything you like – people, food, books, cars – it's worth wondering why. You don't have to be Socrates to feel you will get more from life if you subject it to a little scrutiny.

I'm fond of quoting a remark I once heard Wilfrid Mellers make in a lecture. He said that if you're not talking technically about music, you're not talking about music at all. He was right, and most pop journalism dodges the music to discuss the lyrics of a song or the attitude of the singer. But from time to time you meet people who are suspicious of scrutinising any music too closely, let alone trying to put that scrutiny into words. Not many people now feel comfortable speaking about the structure of a bass line, the insistence of a rhythmic figure, the unfolding of a melody. It wasn't always so.

In my book *In Defence of Classical Music*, I wrote about Donald Tovey and his seven volumes of *Essays in Musical Analysis*. If we pick up one of these books today, we will see specialist writing about classical music, filled with extracts from scores, apparently aimed at music students. But Tovey, who published his books in the 1930s, was writing for ordinary music lovers, in a plain, direct style reminiscent of George Orwell's. Tovey's readership, perhaps more than averagely well-educated, lived at a time when an interest in classical music was not regarded as anything out of the ordinary. His *Essays in Musical Analysis* had begun as program notes for public concerts, and the books were aimed at readers who weren't only interested in classical music, but were also able to prop open his books on the piano in their front parlour and make some sense of the examples. In the mid twentieth century, amateur musicians and music lovers were the bedrock of musical life, their love of music a matter of engagement. I'm talking about the middle class, the bourgeoisie that had invented the notion of classical music for a paying public in the nineteenth century. They still exist, and though their numbers are dwindling, they are not to be scorned. In Australia, Musica Viva was founded by people like this.

In 1979, when I was at Bradford, I received an invitation to a conference at the University of East Anglia in its recently opened Sainsbury Centre, all steel and glass and light. The conference was about the arts and education, and brought together educators and practising artists from all areas of the arts. It was organised by the Arts Council of Great Britain together with

Penguin Books, and I never discovered why I'd been invited, because most of the other conferees were famous. I was a 22-year-old nobody swanning around with the likes of Sir Peter Hall, director of the National Theatre, and the novelist Malcolm Bradbury (I bought him a drink). One day I shared a lunch table with three others, including the actor Patrick Stewart ('call me Paddy'), who at the time was still only moderately famous as a star of the Royal Shakespeare Company, his roles including the best Enobarbas I've ever seen. But the encounter that left the most lasting impression on me was with Basil Deane and Lord Boyle.

It's important to understand that while I was nominally the third person in this conversation, I said practically nothing. Deane, who early in his career had been a lecturer at Melbourne University, was now Professor of Music at Manchester; Lord Boyle, as Edward Boyle, had been a parliamentary secretary in Churchill's postwar government and, in the early 1960s, Minister of Education. The conversation was about the chamber music of Fauré, in particular the two piano quartets (which I didn't know), and specifically the composer's handling of harmony. This was very much Deane's area – he was an international authority on French music of the early twentieth century – and yet here was his lordship explaining a few things to the professor, referring to chord progressions and details of texture. My impression of Boyle was that had the conversation suddenly veered off in the direction of Bach or Mozart or the piano music of Brahms – or the novels of George Eliot or the paintings of El Greco – he would have been equally well-informed. He was simply a cultured person, an enthusiastic amateur who wore his erudition charmingly.

Fauré's chamber music is sometimes mentioned as a sort of touchstone of musical sophistication. It isn't showy and is unlikely, perhaps, to imprint itself on one's memory with a single hearing. You might call it a connoisseur's music. It's possible that Lord Boyle was an extreme case and just happened to know more about chamber music than anyone else in mid-century British political life. I certainly detected a degree of surprise on Deane's part. But my feeling is that people of Boyle's generation, education and professional distinction – and also, let's say it, class – were once able to speak about culture in a way that is no longer common in public life. I don't simply mean that there aren't so many parliamentarians with a detailed knowledge of Fauré's piano quartets, but that there are few who would have the least interest in exploring them, and fewer still, perhaps, who would ever admit to it, lest identification as a connoisseur dent their public image as a man or woman of the people. In this regard, if in no other, public life reflects pretty closely the lives of the rest of us.

Part of the problem, I imagine, is that we listen less. This may seem an odd claim, when most people you see in the street or on public transport are wearing earphones of one sort or another, but that's private listening. Public listening – including to the everyday sounds blocked out by those earphones – has been in decline for decades. Once children in schools sang and learnt poetry and chanted their multiplication tables – learning by ear, learning by heart. I still try to learn poems, because I think it's a way of understanding them. I wouldn't make the same claim for times tables – I'm perfectly sure that today's children comprehend mathematics better than children of my generation – but I do, at least, remember my tables and have no need of a calculator for arithmetic. Back in Tovey's day – and Lord Boyle's – radio listening would have been at its zenith; even when I was a child in the 1960s we listened to radio as much as we watched television. And the listening was active and communal. I'm told that, before TV, people would sit around the radio and look at it as they listened, the bakelite set a sort of meditation object. In Western countries, for at least the first two-thirds of the twentieth century, people attended church in far higher numbers than today. It wasn't necessarily anything to do with religious belief: it was a social practice. You sang hymns with others, some of them strangers, and listened to the repetition of familiar words and phrases – often beautiful words and phrases. Whether you believed in God or not, you remembered the tunes and the words, because the communality of listening intensified the experience.

Where do we find communal listening today? Really only at concerts. Radio and television are shared experiences less and less, because there's so much choice, not only of what to listen to or watch, but also when. In this context, all words *about* music can be understood in the same light, as a plea to listen, to think and to discuss – to restore something that's missing from our daily lives.

It is curious that the most popular segments on *The Music Show* are always the most technical, the segments in which we heed Wilfrid Mellers's advice and so *really* talk about music: a sitar player or a boogie-woogie pianist discusses his musical tradition, demonstrates techniques on his instrument and applies them in a performance; a musicologist, at a piano, takes us through the chord changes in an operatic scene, showing how the harmony gradually brightens; or a songwriter explains the way she constructed the layers of sound in her song, peeling them back, one at a time. We may feel shy talking about music ourselves, believing we lack the verbal tools, but when someone else goes into these details we are fascinated, and when they illustrate their explanation, we feel we understand. So that's what a diminished chord sounds like! So that's a hemiola!

In 2009, when I was resident composer at the Australian National Academy of Music (ANAM), there was an event for the Academy's supporters. The orchestra had given the first performance of my Symphony the previous year and was about to play it again the following week, but this evening was an open rehearsal for an invited audience of forty or fifty people who had been generous to the Academy in one way or another – a sort of thank you.

Nick Bailey, ANAM's manager, had the idea of placing the audience members in different sections of the orchestra, alongside the players. Brett Dean, the Academy's artistic director, conducted the orchestra, and after some general rehearsal, which the audience experienced from the players' point of view, he asked me if there was anything I wanted to say. We changed the balance in a few places, slowing the tempo in one section and exaggerating the woodwind's accented attacks in another. At the end of the piece, where the strings play a rather plangent coda, there are some tiny, decorative figures from the piano and glockenspiel, soft but sharply dissonant, like little flecks of light. One of these wasn't terribly effective, so I suggested to Brett (or perhaps he suggested to me) that the piano play its figure an octave higher. We tried it that way and it was an improvement. You could hear more clearly the gentle clashes I'd intended between the piano and the glockenspiel. It was a tiny detail – maybe two seconds of music, maybe less – but we'd brought it better into focus.

Following a complete performance of the Symphony, there were drinks. The event had been a success – for most of the audience, it was the first time they had sat in an orchestra and they had found the rehearsal a revelation. The room was buzzing. Nick Bailey sidled up to me, clearly pleased his idea had worked so well.

'Do you know what they're all talking about?' he said. 'They keep saying wasn't it amazing when the piano went up the octave!'

8.

Inventing Music

I dislike the expression 'music industry'. I don't think such a thing exists. There is – or was – a recording industry, but for what I do the term 'industry' is inaccurate. Being a composer is more like cottage gardening.

I'm often asked what composing entails from day to day. Do I keep office hours or wait for inspiration to strike? What do I physically do and what goes through my mind?

I do work office hours. If you wait for inspiration, you might wait a very long time. Also inspiration can be distracting when you're trying to get something right, because it usually means having a brand new idea. I work with my pencil and paper, sketching ideas to begin with, then writing a full score, still in pencil so I can rub out the mistakes. Gustav Holst said a composer's most valuable piece of equipment was an eraser. As for what I think about, it depends.

I listen. I listen to the sounds in my head – they are always there (often to the detriment of conversation) – and I listen to the sounds I make at the piano, repeating chords over and over, leaning in the better to hear them. When a piece is going well, I'm not thinking much at all about the music, just listening: the sounds are telling me how they relate to one another and how they want to be ordered. Sometimes the piece seems to be writing itself while I hang on for dear life, and that's one of the best feelings there is. You look at your day's work, come dinnertime, and wonder how all that music got to be on the page.

But I do think about the performers, especially if I know them (which is generally the case), and also about the commissioner.

Often commissions come from the performers themselves, but increasingly they are from private individuals. And they take three forms: a performer might approach a patron asking him or her to fund a new piece (Halcyon asked Barbara Blackman if she'd fund my song cycle *Willow Songs*); a commissioner might propose an open commission (Kim Williams asked me what I'd like to write, and the result was *Raga*, my electric guitar concerto); sometimes a commissioner will approach you with an idea for a piece. When private individuals put their hands in their pockets to pay you to compose, you naturally wonder what they will think of the piece and hope they'll feel their investment was worthwhile. But when they have the idea or some aspect of the idea, they are a collaborator. For example, the commission for *Oma kodu* came with the request that the piece feature a solo clarinet (Catherine McCorkill) and make reference to an Estonian folk song; *Hear the Bird of Day*, a setting for the Song Company of the poet David Campbell, was commissioned to commemorate 'lost loved ones';

Contradance, for the Omega Ensemble, was a birthday present, the commissioner telling me his partner had recently enjoyed the Symphonic Dances from *West Side Story*, so I should include some dance rhythms. These sorts of commissions are increasingly common, and I like them. Of course if you don't fancy Estonian folk music you can always say no, but I enjoy the challenge of coming up with something that gives the commissioner more than they asked for, taking their idea in an unexpected direction.

But how does a piece start in one's head? When I'm asked this question, which is surprisingly often, I tend to say every piece is different. Music can be inspired by a poem, a painting, a film, a short story, even a word. A couple of times I've had the title of the piece in my head before anything else. I knew, for instance, I wanted to write a piece called *Harbour* before I knew it would be a song cycle for Gerald English and the Australian Chamber Orchestra, let alone where the words would come from. Sometimes another piece of music can set me off on an idea of my own. The spark is always different, but the truth is that the moment the piece begins is always the same. It is a feeling of recognition. The piece suddenly exists – even though not a note of it has been written down or yet imagined – and at that moment I usually know how long it is. It's always the first piece of precise information I have, or I would be like a painter with no sense of where the edge of my canvas is. Certain ideas come in certain sizes – or lengths, in the case of a piece of music. The other thing I know from the start is the instrumental palette, the quality of the sound. Often this is given and immutable. If a string quartet has asked me for a piece, I can't write a part for tuba or xylophone. I did once try to convince a piano duet that a mooted piece for two pianos should also feature a French horn, but if you look down my list of works you'll notice there is no such piece (I still think it was a cracker of an idea). I also continue to regret that the orchestra in my viola concerto, *The Unquiet Grave*, lacks the banjo I so badly wanted to include.

Commissions take many forms. It is particularly gratifying when they come from strangers, because it suggests that the music has gone out there on its own and communicated with someone. I once composed a piece, *Ringing the Changes*, for the Dutch ensemble Het Trio. They took it to the United States and played it at a festival in Pittsburgh. I found out about this when I received a letter from the composer and conductor David Stock, telling me how much he had liked the trio and asking if I would write a larger piece for the Pittsburgh New Music Ensemble. This ended up being *Dance Maze* for seventeen players, which, some years later, came to the attention of Joel Sachs at the Juilliard School in New York. Joel conducted it in a concert by the New Juilliard Ensemble, leading to a continuing relationship with both Joel and the school and performances of several other works. One of these was *The Unquiet Grave*, with violist Jocelin Pan the impassioned soloist. One thing, if you're lucky, leads to another.

The composing of *The Unquiet Grave* is worth unpacking, because it sheds light on several aspects of a composer's life, and especially on how pieces develop beyond the first spark and that moment of recognition. In the case of this piece, the initial idea was to write a concerto for my friend Patricia Pollett, who had given numerous performances of my solo viola piece *Swansong*. It was always going to be a rather lyrical piece, and since Patricia hailed from Adelaide and the concerto seemed to require only a small orchestra, we took the idea to the Adelaide Chamber Orchestra and its conductor Richard Mills, who agreed to commission it. ('How many performances of the piece do you actually want, Andy?' asked Richard, when I mentioned the banjo.)

In January 1997 I was in Pittsburgh to conduct the first performance of *Dance Maze*. The following morning I flew to New York and checked into a hotel. In midwinter, New York hotels always have the heating turned up too high, so before I lay down for a restorative nap, after the previous night's post-concert celebration and an early start for the airport, I opened the window to let in some cold air.

I was awakened from a deep sleep by a noise from the street. Two noises, in fact: a truck horn and a metallic clang. The horn was loud and long-held, as though the truck driver was leaning on it; the clang, which was a whole tone higher, I took to be a piece of falling scaffolding. I don't know whether the sounds were related, but the noise of the scaffolding (or whatever it was) cut across the blaring horn, so they were related in my head. It was such an arresting sound that I got off the bed, took out some manuscript paper and wrote it down, putting 'horn' beside a long, fortissimo E flat, and 'tubular bells + harp' beside the F above. I also added a very short G for tubular bells alone immediately before the F, like a grace note. For good measure, I doodled a viola line emerging from the horn's E flat, accelerating into a dramatic flourish. Over these few bars of music I wrote 'Viola Concerto'. Then I went back to sleep.

Most of the rest of 1997 was taken up with finishing my radio series *Illegal Harmonies* and its accompanying book, so nothing further happened on the concerto until November. No, that's not right – one thing happened: I reread Cyril Connolly's curious little book *The Unquiet Grave*, his musings on life at forty, written under the pseudonym Palinurus. I was turning forty myself, which I suppose is why I picked it up again. There was something about the title that appealed to me and I wondered if I could steal it for the concerto. Connolly himself had taken it from an English folk song about a grieving lover at a graveside. The young man rends his garments and gnashes his teeth until, at length, his dead lover tells him to pipe down or she will never rest in peace. I looked up the tune. There are dozens of tunes for 'The Unquiet Grave' and dozens of versions of the words, but the one I had on my bookshelf was in the *Penguin Book of English Folk Songs* edited by Ralph Vaughan Williams and A.L. Lloyd. It was a good tune. If I was going to take the title, I reasoned, I should take the tune too.

In November, I went to stay with Belinda Webster in Kangaroo Valley, two hours south of Sydney, where she was house-sitting for the composer Martin Wesley-Smith. If I am kept from composing for long, the music pours out when I finally have some manuscript paper in front of me. With *Illegal Harmonies* done, the radio series on air and the book published, I returned eagerly to the viola concerto. To my surprise, the fragment of music I'd jotted down in the New York hotel room still made complete sense to me. I tweaked it a bit, adding an oboe, saxophone, bassoon and trumpet to the front of the French horn's E flat to kick-start it, prolonging the resonance of the bell and harp with some delicate string harmonics. Other than that, what you hear at the beginning of *The Unquiet Grave* is what I wrote down in that hotel. As for the rest of the piece, it is an exploration of the English folk song that had given Connolly his title. For four days, I sat at Martin's dining table and wrote music until Belinda decided it was time for gin and tonics. On the fifth morning I took the train back to Sydney with the first ten minutes of *The Unquiet Grave*, fully scored, in my bag. Peter Sculthorpe threw a party that weekend, where I told anyone who would listen about my astonishing progress on the piece. I had never had such a productive week of composing and, figuring it must be partly the country air, decided I must move out of Sydney. Two years later, I bought a house in the Southern Highlands, but first I was fortunate to have a couple of years in the Peggy Glanville-Hicks composers' house.

The Unquiet Grave was the first piece I completed in the house in 1998, the beginning of a very productive period. I was happy with the piece and eager to hear it performed. Unfortunately, I now learnt that the Adelaide Chamber Orchestra had ceased to exist. These things happen from time to time. Circumstances change while you are completing a commission – the person who requested and paid for it has moved on or, as in this case, the whole organisation has closed down – and your new piece has no scheduled performance. Martin Buzacott, who was devising musical events for the Queensland Biennial Festival of Music, came to the rescue, and in 1999 Patricia Pollett gave the premiere with an ensemble conducted by the composer James MacMillan.

Writing earlier about *From Hand to Mouth*, I mentioned the vibrancy that folk music can generate in one's own work, but there's something else that comes with the introduction of found musical objects of any stripe, folkloric or not. A preordained melody frees you: you write things that otherwise you might not. In *The Unquiet Grave*, the folk song is unrecognisable until the end of the piece, when the solo viola at last has the tune. For the first fifteen or sixteen minutes of this seventeen-minute concerto, fragments of the song provide the building blocks for my own melodic material. The tune contains a lot of minor seconds, and there is a moment in my piece where the viola ruminates on this interval. My music at that point sounds oddly Sculthorpean, and I would never have come up with it had I been inventing my own material, because I'd have spotted the similarity to lines in pieces such as *Irkanda IV* (there are minor seconds everywhere in Sculthorpe), and I'd have edited myself. As it was, I didn't notice the resemblance to Sculthorpe's music until my piece was in rehearsal, because while I was composing, my imagination had been in the folk song. The source material had prevented me being too selfconscious and allowed me to expand my harmonic palette in a new direction. It was a step towards finding my voice.

As a young composer, this was something I'd worried about. What kind of music should I be writing? In what style? I loved Vaughan Williams, but I also loved Stockhausen; I loved Britten, but also Boulez. In which directions should I take my own music? Michael Tippett often used to talk about the importance of finding your own voice, possibly because it had been a struggle for him, but this only made matters worse. For it's all very well saying you have to find your voice, but where do you look for it? And how do you know when you've found it? These were daunting questions for a young composer, and there were no answers.

In the end, finding your voice as a composer is like finding your voice in life. It finds you, and you don't notice it happening. When you speak, other people hear and recognise your voice, but you don't hear it yourself, because you're focused on what you're saying. Composing is the same. The more you concentrate on getting the content of your piece right, the less you worry about style. Writing *The Unquiet Grave* consolidated this for me. The melodic material was given and it was calling the shots; I was writing very fast, barely stopping to think. When I did stop, I was surprised at what I had written. In the Glanville-Hicks house, I took the score to the piano. I was forty-one years old and this was the first time I had lived with a piano since I'd left home to go to university at the age of eighteen. Gingerly, falteringly, I played through the final pages of the concerto, where the viola states the folk tune, against a series of slowly descending scales. The music made me cry. I don't know why.

The folk song – this musical found object – had in a sense

distracted me from myself. It had focused me on the music, and I wrote a piece I would otherwise have been too selfconscious to write. But it's not just musical source material that can bring you out of yourself and send you further into the work. I have composed a number of pieces that had visual art as their starting point. There are, for instance, three pieces for flute and percussion entitled *Mondriaan* (the original Dutch spelling of the painter's name), and there's a work for string orchestra in five movements called *Manhattan Epiphanies*, consisting of musical responses to the work of four twentieth-century New York artists: Robert Motherwell, Mark Rothko (twice), Joseph Cornell and Jackson Pollock.

In the *Mondriaan* pieces, each based on a specific painting, I took the proportions of the artist's work and employed the same proportions in my music, allowing them to govern how long harmonies, textures and even individual notes should last. The most extreme of these pieces is 'Composition with Yellow Square', for piccolo and metal percussion, in which the piccolo plays long, mostly loud notes representing the yellow and white paint, interrupted by metallic clanging for the black lines.

In *Manhattan Epiphanies* I attempted to find musical equivalents for the works of art. I'd seen a Motherwell retrospective at the Guggenheim Museum in New York in late 1984, and I remembered how the painter's dark abstractions seemed to jump off the wall as I walked down the spiral ramp with that watery light pouring in through the ceiling. I called the piece 'Motherwell at the Guggenheim', and contrasted airy chords in violin harmonics with thick stabs of dissonance in the lower strings. With Cornell, whose art consisted of little boxes displaying tiny installations filled with fragments of theatre posters, dolls, small stuffed birds and so forth, I made thirteen of my own miniatures from little shards of Bach and Beethoven, Brahms and Webern. I also added toy instruments to the mix, since so many toys turn up in Cornell's childlike art. I had never worked like this before, but the source material was obliging me to. And it was the same with Rothko and Pollock. The two Rothko movements were great smudges of tone, seventeen solo strings wending their individual ways from their highest notes to their lowest in 'Rothko I', and back again in 'Rothko II', with lots of small details for the listener to attend to. If you walk up close to one of Rothko's canvases, what had seemed a monolithic slab of colour turns out to be quite varied, the surface patina of brush marks surprisingly subtle. The Pollock movement was the only one based on a particular painting, the so-called *Blue Poles*, which hangs in the National Gallery of Australia in Canberra (where this movement had its first performance). This time I tried to imagine my string orchestra playing the painting, the drips of colour running across the canvas like notes across a page, the slanting poles that gave the work its nickname functioning like bar lines. Apart from the first two bars of this piece, nothing is fully synchronised in the music, the players free to play their rather intricate material each in their own time. The 'poles' themselves are vaguely synchronised, but the effect is of a jagged line – like the poles in Pollock's painting.

Where the folk song in *The Unquiet Grave* had led me into a particular harmonic area, and the measurements in *Mondriaan* forced me to deal with formal restrictions, so in *Manhattan Epiphanies* the artists' techniques obliged me to come up with new approaches to composing – well, new for me. What I found particularly interesting was the way in which the abstract expressionism of Rothko and Pollock, so redolent of the 1950s and 1960s, led me, through adapting their techniques, to compose music that evoked the same era. My Rothko pieces had a good deal in common with the slow-moving wodges of sound in early 1960s Ligeti – pieces such as *Apparitions* and *Atmosphères*, and particularly the string orchestra piece *Ramifications* – while my 'Blue Poles' recalled pieces from that same era by Lutosławski, a mass of tangled lines, occasionally cut off by a big twelve-tone chord. Once again, it was only when I heard the pieces that I noticed the similarities, and it was only then that it struck me how close 1960s art and music had been.

Scenes from Bruegel, for small orchestra and recorded sounds, was mostly composed in 2005, and this time I didn't set out to ape the artist's techniques, but to compose equivalent pictures in sound, little tone poems for three of his paintings. I remember exactly how the idea for the piece came to me. It was in the new concert hall at Lahti in Finland. I can barely recall the concert itself – Osmo Vänskä was conducting – because there was something about the gleaming wooden stage that instantly conjured up the yellow ochre of Bruegel's *Children's Games*, and after that all I could think of was how I might make a musical version of the picture.

The answer lay at home. Most days I walk to the post office to pick up my mail. My route takes me past the local primary school, where there is sometimes a playground full of children engaged in a variety of games. One sunny morning, the penny dropped. This would be a piece about Robertson, New South Wales, as much as about the Low Countries in the sixteenth century. I arranged with the school to be in the playground with recording gear at recess time and my piece begins with the clunk of the school bell followed by approximately a hundred noisy children emptying out of their classrooms, their voices gradually replaced by scurrying strings and woodwind in the orchestra. At the end of the movement, as the orchestral pianist becomes fixated on Philip Glass-like arpeggios, children's voices chant the skipping rhyme, 'My Aunty Anna / Plays the pian-na / Twenty-four hours a / Day'.

Now that I had a Robertson recording alongside the orchestra in my first movement, it seemed appropriate to record some local sounds for the other movements. *The Hunters in the Snow* didn't immediately suggest anything, though it's true that Robertson is 700 metres above sea level and some years it does snow. But in Bruegel's leafless trees big black birds sit that presumably squawk at the hunters as they trudge homewards; in the central movement of my *Scenes from Bruegel*, then, as the brass swells and a blizzard issues from the accordion's bellows and a wind machine, I introduced recordings of Australian ravens and magpies, currawongs and gang-gang cockatoos.

Finding some local connection for the final movement, based

on *The Peasant Wedding Dance*, was more of a poser. Drunken peasants with giant codpieces, bagpipes, lascivious dancing: it was not obvious where to turn; probably not the monthly 'old-time dance' at the Robertson school of arts. But I had a tune in my head – a repetitive and rather annoying little march – that I thought might serve, and I suddenly remembered the Robertson Public School Band. They might not have been drunken peasants, but as you would expect from players between six and eleven years old, some of whom had been playing their instruments only a matter of months, they were never quite together or in tune, so perfect for my needs. I rehearsed them for a few weeks, and for the actual recording session a few friends came and played along, including my piano tuner, David Ricketts, whose trumpet playing added a certain lustre to the sound.

The children themselves were surprisingly savvy. I had told them their recording would be played at a concert in New York – the piece was co-commissioned by the New Julliard Ensemble and the West Australian Symphony Orchestra – and at the end of one rehearsal, I was approached by a boy who had clearly been elected the players' shop steward.

'Is there going to be a printed program with our names in it?' he asked. I wrote everyone's name down and sent them to Joel Sachs. A few months later, at the premiere of *Scenes from Bruegel* in Alice Tully Hall, the Lincoln Center Playbill listed all the Robertson Public School players alongside their counterparts from the Juilliard School.

There was something touching about being at a concert in

mid-town Manhattan and hearing those Australian birds. There's nothing like the calls of a currawong or an Australian magpie to make you homesick. A few of the Juilliard players wondered if the sounds were electronically produced, so remote and foreign did they seem. But equally touching was the way in which the Juilliard Ensemble morphed into the recording of the Robertson band playing my annoying march, and then finally took up the tune themselves, bringing it into Alice Tully Hall (suddenly in tune and in time) at the very end of the piece. Joel was happy with the commission and amused by the Robertson Band: 'Still, that kid on trumpet can certainly play.'

Having moved to Robertson in 2000, when my time in the Peggy Glanville-Hicks house was up, I had quickly come to feel part of this rural community – in fact, within minutes of my arrival. I reached my new house ahead of the removal van only to discover I had left my kettle in Sydney. With removalists due to turn up in the next hour and no way to make them a cup of tea, I walked into Robertson's General Store, figuring that 'General' might include electric kettles. It didn't, but Hope behind the counter told me she was about to drive to Moss Vale and could buy one for me. I handed her $50 and an hour later, as the removalists were unloading the first boxes, she arrived at my front door, with the kettle.

At the end of that year I married Anni Heino, so my life changed doubly and very much for the better. I first met Anni at an international conference of music information centres at the Sydney Opera House. She was there in her capacity as Head of

Classical Music at the Finnish Music Information Centre; I was there as a local composer. She was obviously smart, with a very dry sense of humour, not to mention beautiful, and without going into unnecessary details one thing led to another and eighteen months later we were married on the verandah of our Robertson home, though she wasn't able to leave her job in Helsinki for another six months.

I had never been to Finland before, so in addition to a new rural existence and a new wife, I was gaining a new country. We had often had Finnish musicians on *The Music Show* – classical, jazz and folk – because it's a country that treasures its culture and especially its music. There are approximately five million Finns, a million of whom sing in choirs, and while the population might be less than a quarter of Australia's, Finland has more orchestras. Most Australians interested in classical music would find it easier to list conductors from Finland than from Australia. Indeed, some of Australia's best conductors, such as Benjamin Northey, are from Finland in a sense, because that's where they went to study.

Even now when I visit Finland I feel an ineffable and beguiling foreignness. This is a pagan culture hiding beneath a thin veneer of Lutheranism: a culture where Father Christmas is a goat and effigies of witches are on display at Easter. It is a culture where the sauna is so much a way of life that for centuries babies were born in them and the dead taken there to be washed, where there is still one sauna for every three Finns, and where they think so little of nakedness you sometimes see it on children's television. So there are palpable differences between Finland and Australia, but also similarities. Perhaps it comes from being at the periphery of Europe (in Finland's case) or the world (in Australia's), but many Finns and Australians share a diffident manner, an uncertainty, perhaps, about how their countries fit with all the others. I'm told, by friends who attend international conferences, that the Finns and the Australians invariably end up together, drinking in the corner.

Finland has turned up in my music quite a bit in recent years. I've used its folk poetry in three of my song cycles – *Tales of the Supernatural*, *Learning to Howl* and *Domestic Advice* – especially words from the *Kanteletar*, a collection of short, often aphoristic writings with a domestic bent, the work of women, one imagines, in contrast to the heroic, epic *Kalevala*. But a moment of Finnish history inspired *Rauha*.

In 1929 the Imatrankoski rapids on the Vuoksi river in Southern Karelia was dammed for hydroelectricity. It was big news, a symbol of twentieth-century progress; foreign dignitaries visited for the occasion and Sibelius was asked to compose an Imatra symphony, which he failed to deliver. But only hours after the damming, the local people began to doubt the wisdom of it. Having grown up next to this raging torrent of water, they found the silence creepy. You can get an idea of the effect because in summer they open the dam each evening for about twenty minutes and let the water through. Anni's family comes from Imatra, and one June evening we went to see and hear the rapids. Anni told me the story of the damming and the people's reaction, and

I saw the potential for a piece of music that begins with its climax, a great roar from woodwinds, brass, bell plates and cowbells, the energy quickly dissipating, before fifteen minutes of mostly very quiet music with lots of silences (*rauha* is the Finnish word for peace). Sometimes the first idea for a musical work is structural.

But if Finland has found its way into my music, Robertson may be fairly said to have embedded itself. Shortly after I arrived in the Southern Highlands, Richard Buckham, then a manager at Radio National, emailed to say the ABC had a new fund for regional artists and producers, and that I should come up with a proposal. By the time he emailed the next day to explain that he'd discovered ABC employees (even part-time ones like me) were ineligible to apply, I'd had the idea for *Elegy in a Country Graveyard*, and it wouldn't go away.

You have to be a little careful hanging on to an idea for too long. The playwright Alan Bennett once spoke in an interview about how a perfectly good idea can go stale if you don't act on it swiftly, and his words chimed with my own experience. But I've discovered a strategy: if you are careful not to think too much about the idea and you do no planning, no sketching, it can remain fresh when you come back to it. I carried around the notion of an electric guitar concerto called *Raga* for nearly two decades before I finally composed it, but I committed nothing to paper during that time. Early sketches would have killed it off long before Kim Williams's generous commission allowed me to devote half of 2015 to writing the piece. With *Elegy in a Country Graveyard*, I had to wait only a couple of years until a grant from the New South Wales Arts Ministry and the promise of studio time at the ABC enabled me to work on the piece.

The Robertson cemetery is a little way out of town. You reach it by trekking down (and up and down and up) a dirt track. You pass rolling hills and paddocks crisscrossed by the crumbled remains of drystone walls. These used to puzzle me, because it was impossible to imagine what their function might have been. Finally someone explained they were part of the film set of *Babe*, which was shot in those paddocks, the walls never intended to stand for more than a few weeks. When you reach the cemetery, there is a spectacular view and graves dating back to the 1880s, though they look much older. Lichen-encrusted and in some cases quite dilapidated, they have been regularly lashed with rain, baked by the sun and bulldozed by wombats. I wondered what it must have been like in the late nineteenth century getting a coffin up the steep, stony lane in intense summer heat.

Thinking in general of Robertson's past, I decided to record the memories of some of the senior residents. To their voices, I added that of the young daughter of some friends reading the funeral sentences from the Book of Common Prayer, and then set about composing a slow procession of chords – fifty-five of them.

In the studio, we invited the harpist Marshall McGuire to play the sequence of chords very slowly and in his own time. He took more than fifteen minutes over them. Then, since Marshall is also a fine pianist, we asked him to do the same on piano. Percussionist Daryl Pratt played the same chords on a vibraphone and a second time on a harmonium. The Sydney

Conservatorium's harmonium was in a delicate state and we had to record it in situ, the producer Andrew McLennan lying under the instrument by Daryl's feet, working the bellows with his hands. Next we layered the four recordings on top of each other, lining up their first notes. Of course the ensuing chords were almost immediately out of synch, creating a marvellously blurred effect. I added to this, having brass players and members of the Sydney Chamber Choir listen to the passing chords, pick out a note, play or hum it very softly until out of breath, then choose a new note. By the time we had finished, my fifty-five chords had turned into twenty-minute smear of slowly shifting harmony, ready for the speaking voices to be added, along with recordings of bird song, thunder and rain.

Working with Andrew McLennan and the engineer Russell Stapleton – possessor of the most imaginative ears at the ABC – was a great luxury. So was the experience, rare for me, of starting the week with an idea, a page of chords and some recorded interviews, and ending it with a 24-minute piece in the can. When I write a score, it will usually be months before I hear it played, but building a radiophonic piece provided instant aural gratification. The ABC submitted *Elegy in a Country Graveyard* for the Prix Italia in 2007, and it nearly won, runner-up to a sassy French Radio entry (its high energy levels the very opposite of *Elegy*), created at IRCAM, the Paris Institute for Acoustic and Musical Research founded in the 1970s by Boulez.

I made a second version of *Elegy*, for live performance by a choir and instrumental ensemble, with a backing track of harp, piano, vibes and harmonium, the spoken voices and the environmental sounds, and I conducted it the same year at Belinda Webster's new Arts in the Valley festival in Kangaroo Valley. The performers were a choir from Berry on the New South Wales coast and the Southern Highlands Concert Band. Most of the band had never played anything like *Elegy* and they found it hard, at first, to stifle their amusement. They reminded me of the audience at a concert in Gouda, where the Bradford University Chamber Choir once gave a concert. It was in a big Calvinist church in the town square, and until the final item, the locals, mostly members of the congregation, were respectful and attentive, just what you'd expect of Dutch Calvinists. Then came Stockhausen's *Atmen gibt das Leben*. It's one of its composer's more fanciful pieces – music about breathing – in which the choir, half of them lying on the ground, not only sing on the out-breath but also while inhaling. It sounds quite strange (try it), and is made even stranger by the sporadic and unpredictable hiccuping of some of the singers. The devout burghers of Gouda tried terribly hard to hold it all together – you could actually hear the effort – but in the end gales of laughter filled the church.

I wasn't asking the Southern Highlands Concert Band to lie on their backs and hiccup, but in place of the lines of music they were used to, there were only a few indications of the notes they should play. Moreover, they were not expected to play in synch with each other, but to choose and sustain their notes individually and hold them as long as they were able. I'm not sure the band's conductor, Mike Butcher, had had much experience of this sort of music, either, but he was a complete pro and a gentleman to boot, calm and practical, with an air of the Beatles' George Martin. Though I conducted the piece, Mike's presence in the room and the seriousness with which he took the music helped the band settle. At the concert, they played the piece very beautifully.

Largely on the strength of this performance, another Southern Highlands project came about at the suggestion of Jenny Kena, the Cultural Development Officer at Wingecarribee Shire Council. This was *A Singing Quilt* (Jenny's title, which I initially resisted, then came to like), and as with *Elegy* it started with interviews. I spoke to people who had been born in the Southern Highlands and people who had come from other countries. I asked them to describe the landscape and their early memories of it. The big difference was that this time the large amateur choir had words to sing, and the words came from the interviews. This meant that in performance you might hear the recorded voice of an elderly man or a small girl speaking words that would later be sung. The large chorus consisted of seven local choirs, and some singers joined up just for *A Singing Quilt*. A few of the participants had never sung in a choir in their lives, but no one was turned away. Faced with having to make the music simple enough for such a motley bunch of singers, yet interesting enough to sustain an audience's attention for twenty minutes or more, I decided to compose canons. These would sound quite rich and complex, but for each canon the singers would only have to learn a single melodic line. The piece was in discrete sections, linked interludes played by five percussionists, the only instruments in the piece. This meant that the individual choirs could learn their canons on their own, coming together for final rehearsals with each other and the percussionists. It worked better than I'd hoped, and at the end of the first performance, something surprising occurred.

In the final minutes of the piece the recorded voices of the immigrants describe the view from their Southern Highlands window in their native languages, Italian, Irish, Dutch and Finnish (Anni, of course). Then we hear some words in the now largely forgotten Gundungurra language, spoken by an Aboriginal elder, Velma Mulcahy, known to all as 'Aunty Val'. Specifically, we hear the word for 'home'.

'I'm home,' Aunty Val then says in English. 'This is my grandmother's land. You can't get more home than that.' The choir has been softly humming under Aunty Val's recorded voice, an intense, almost hypnotic sound. Suddenly, on her final word, the humming cuts out, jolting us into the present. It's a Saturday afternoon in the Soldiers' Memorial Hall at Bundanoon. After a moment's silence, enthusiastic applause breaks out. I take my bow and begin walking off, but spot Aunty Val in the front row with tears in her eyes. So I walk over to give her a hug, but as soon as I do, I am wracked with sobs. I turn to look at the choir, and see that many of them are crying too. Later, people will keep mentioning 'your reconciliation piece', though it has never occurred to me that this is what I've written. I had put Aunty Val's words last because 'I'm home' seemed like a good place to stop, but others have heard it differently. 'All the spirits were here,' one Aboriginal woman tells me as she leaves the hall.

Of course if people listen to *A Singing Quilt* and hear a 'reconciliation piece', then that is what it is. Music is made in the mind of the listener as much as in the mind of the composer. I was happy to find I had composed such a work, even if it hadn't been my intention. This was an extreme case, but I often find that I don't know what I am doing until I have done it, and from conversations with colleagues in all areas of the arts, this seems to be a common experience, particularly if the work has come out well. It's that unselfconscious state, once more, and just as it can be brought about by the use of found material, like a folk song, or images such as paintings, so words can do it – it might be simply a title (as with *Harbour*) or a story (*Rauha*), but it might be the sound of voices, as with *A Singing Quilt*. It's especially true when one is setting words to music. I know a lot of composers who go searching for words to use in vocal pieces. I find that words nearly always come to me.

Sometimes one text guides me to another and I end up composing music to a small anthology of writings, as Britten often did. *In somnia*, *Last Words* and *Learning to Howl* are all examples of pieces that employ texts from different centuries and cultures, St John of the Cross rubbing shoulders with A.D. Hope, Dorothy Porter with Emily Brontë, Sappho with Elizabeth Smart.

I already knew Elizabeth Smart's writing from her novella-cum-memoir, *By Grand Central Station I Sat Down and Wept*, when in 1982 I found a slim volume of her poetry in a Yorkshire bookshop. It was called *A Bonus*. Several of the poems were about the business of writing, and I thought they'd make a sequence for music. One was called 'A Terrible Whiteness' – which struck me as a good title for the cycle as a whole – and described 'the horror / Of the blank page', something felt by composers as much as writers.

I sent her a letter via her publisher but heard nothing back. Not every poet wants her hard-won words put to someone else's music, and Smart's words seemed especially hard-won. Since I didn't have her permission, I gave up the idea. But in early 1984, on my first visit back to England from Australia, there was a reply from the writer. It turned out she'd been in Canada (she was in fact Canadian), standing in for Margaret Atwood on sabbatical, and by the time she returned to England I'd left for Australia. She said she was happy for me to set the poems to music.

A year later, I was back again in England with my five-song sequence *A Terrible Whiteness*, for mezzo-soprano and piano, just finished. I rang Elizabeth and we arranged to meet for a lunchtime drink at the Coach and Horses in Soho.

'You'll recognise me,' she said, 'I'm about a hundred and wild looking.' And it was true. I spotted her as soon as I walked in. She was seated at a table, wearing a workman's donkey-jacket. We got on well and plied each other with Bloody Marys, then went for pizza with two of her poet friends, Anthony Cronin and David Wright. I had a volume of poems by Christopher Reid in my bag – I was in the midst of setting some of them to music in *Sacred Places* – and Elizabeth asked David, who was deaf but had the sonorous voice of a prophet, to read one of the poems aloud. There was some sceptical talk about 'these Martian poets', but Reid's 'Numen' met with the older poets' approval. After pizza, Elizabeth and I repaired to her son Christopher's flat, taking a small detour so she could show me the blue plaque to William Blake just around the corner. When we got to the flat, she dug out some carbon copies of new poems to give me, along with a dog-eared copy of *The Mid Century: English Poetry 1940–60*, which included the work of George Barker, the father of her four children. By now, we had hatched a plan to write some cabaret songs together. I mentioned that I'd been commissioned to compose something for the Dutch singer Marianne Kweksilber, and Elizabeth said she'd always wanted to write song lyrics, especially 'The Grand Central Station Blues'.

It seemed too good to be true, and, alas, it was. Occasionally I would write from Australia to ask her how the lyrics were coming along, and sometimes there'd be a postcard from Elizabeth: 'SORRY SORRY SORRY!' Finally, after a silence of several months, a letter arrived from her son, Sebastian Barker, informing me of his mother's death, 'at my brother's flat, close to where the poet Blake lived'.

One of the advantages of meeting Elizabeth had been the chance to discuss my musical setting with her. She liked the fact that the title song, which comes first, began with voice alone, the piano eventually joining in with tentative single notes, like a one-finger typist. She was also amused that in the central, third song, 'Trying to Write', the mezzo-soprano would be obliged to sing

'Fuck off!'. (At the first performance in the foyer of the National Library in Canberra, Elizabeth Campbell sang the expletive with feeling, but at the Sydney Festival she sang 'Get lost!'. When I asked why she'd chickened out, she told me she'd spotted her elderly singing teacher in the front row.)

Some poets whose words I've set to music have been less sanguine about the possible results than Elizabeth Smart. The venerable Anne Ridler graciously gave me permission to use part of her poem 'Choosing a Name' in *Dancing with Smoke*, a cycle of songs about childhood for tenor and harp, written for Gerald English's seventieth-birthday concert (at which he performed thirteen world premieres). But when I sent her a recording of the performance, with Gerry and Marshall McGuire, she replied somewhat less graciously, saying how very much she disliked my music. Writers are often shocked by how their words sound when set to music, even when they are sympathetic to the composer's work.

My meeting Elizabeth Smart had one other advantage. I was able to check a typo in one of the published poems, and so, on this occasion at least, avoid setting the wrong word. I wish I could say I'd never set wrong words, but there are several instances of my doing this. When the music is coming out just right, you are in the world of the piece, and a good set of words quickly brings on that longed-for unselfconscious state. Paradoxically, this means you might lose sight of the precise details of the text you're setting. As the words turn into songs, the music takes over and you can begin to set words that aren't really there. Some writers notice and correct you. Lorrie Moore pointed out that at the start of *Learning to Howl,* the soprano was singing 'the sunflowers knocked bent by a deer', whereas in her novella, *Who Will Run the Frog Hospital?,* she had written 'knocked bent by deer' (no 'a'). But some writers are forgiving. Craig Raine, who, as a critic, has a reputation for eviscerating sloppy colleagues, has very sweetly never mentioned the fact that I accidentally omitted half a line of his poem in *A Martian Sends a Postcard Home.*

In writing music-theatre or opera, you have to change words. Sometimes there are simply more than you need for a particular scene; sometimes a word won't sing. It might be that it has its stress in the wrong place for the music, or has too many syllables, or has the wrong vowel sound for the high note you want to write. I have had only cordial collaborations with my librettists, all of whom have been happy for me to change their words – wittingly or not. Not all writers are so obliging to composers. When Elisabeth Lutyens was working with Elias Canetti on an operatic adaptation of his play, *The Numbered,* she rang him one day to ask how he would feel about a line change. There was a loud crash at the other end of the phone, followed by silence. After a few moments, Canetti's wife came on the line.

'Elias has fainted,' she told Lutyens.

Television writers make particularly good librettists, and part of it, no doubt, is that they're not precious. Indeed, they're used to network managers, producers, directors and actors riding roughshod over their scripts. At Victorian Opera's headquarters for the first week of rehearsals on *Rembrandt's Wife,* Sue Smith, one of Australia's most celebrated screenwriters, kept marvelling at the fact she was being asked for her opinion. But there's more to it than this. A lot of inexperienced librettists think they have to explain everything and that their words should be poetic and rather grand. In fact none of this is true, and TV writers know it. Television drama is about showing, not telling, and often the most compelling scenes have very few words, sometimes none at all. As a TV writer, you must leave room for the camera to do its work, moving in slowly on a face or pulling back to reveal a room. In opera, the music does the camera's work, and sometimes the composer requires only a few words for a scene.

A good libretto can take you over utterly. It will oblige you to work in certain ways, and some of those ways will be new to you. With *Rembrandt's Wife*, I made certain decisions in advance, particularly that my ensemble of nine players would have some of the dark hues of Rembrandt's paintings, bass clarinet, bassoon and French horn to the fore, as well as echoes of seventeenth-century music, lute and viols replaced by harp and low strings (there are no violins). Beyond that, though, I forgot all about the historical period and wrote the music that made best dramatic sense of the words. I was determined it would be a 'singing' opera, that's to say there would be no speech, no extended vocal techniques à la *Eight Songs for a Mad King*, and as little formal 'recitative' as I could get away with. So although there are not many songs in *Rembrandt's Wife*, nevertheless even the conversational music is quite melodic. My guide in this was Puccini.

I've never cared for the sound of Puccini's music – all those sugary vocal lines doubled in the orchestra give me musical indigestion – and there are no traces of his style in my opera. But in the opera house I am always impressed by Puccini's stagecraft, the way he doesn't muck about but jumps straight into the action, and then the way drama pours out in a stream of melody. It would be hard not to find *La Bohème* more obviously tuneful than *Rembrandt's Wife*, but from the point of view of musical drama Puccini was my model. Even so, the music for *Rembrandt's Wife* is often quite tonal and occasionally, you'd have to say, romantic; at the first read-through I was astonished at its lyricism, and my librettist was gratifyingly teary. As with the shades of Ligeti and Lutosławski in *Manhattan Epiphanies*, none of this was intentional, because I wasn't thinking about style. In Sue's libretto I had found another source of unselfconsciousness, and the style took care of itself.

Opera composers are like directors. As the composer, you lift the librettist's words off the page and breathe life and meaning into them – possibly a meaning the librettist never intended. Your music positions the text in time; you say how slowly or quickly a speech is delivered; you say which are the important words – by placing them on a high note or underlining them in the score or having a singer repeat them; you put in the pauses; you say how long there is for a singer to move from point A to point B, because you have composed six seconds or sixty seconds of music to cover it. And in attending to these things, in making the drama as vivid as you can, you forget about musical style. That's what happened with *Rembrandt's Wife*. 'Lyrical', 'romantic', 'accessible' and '*unashamedly* accessible' were some of the critics' adjectives. It was enough to make me wonder if I was still a modern composer. Fortunately, someone brought to my attention a blog post that called the piece 'cacophonous modernism' or some such. I was relieved.

Because opera composers do so much of the director's job for them, it is small wonder that directors go looking for ways to stamp their personality on a piece. One of the most common tricks is to uncover what they believe to be the psychological subtext of a work, and make that the principal motif (so of course it's no longer subtext). In Kasper Holten's staging of Szymanowski's *King Roger* for Opera Australia, the action took place in and around a giant head, because the director had decided the drama was in King Roger's head. That sort of thing.

In *Whispers*, the music-theatre piece that Rodney Hall and I wrote in 1990 for Gerald English, a conductor attempts to rehearse the finale of Mahler's fourth symphony and in the process reveals himself to be unhinged. The stage is a rehearsal room, the orchestra with their backs to the audience, the tenor/conductor facing us from his podium. All the music proceeds from Mahler, and at first the conductor seems simply to be rehearsing the piece, singing along as conductors will, especially when there is a vocal part and the soloist is late, which is the conceit in *Whispers*. Our conductor's an unpredictable fellow, bumptious to a fault, who likes stopping the rehearsal to tell stories. From time to time he says or sings something that seems only to matter to him, but then conductors do that too. Gradually, as Mahler gives way to Ford, and recorded voices intrude, we realise all is not well, and by the end of the half-hour piece our conductor is a broken man.

Whispers is tricky to pull off, especially for the tenor, who, in addition to playing a man going crazy while singing difficult music, must actually conduct the whole piece. The first production, at Sydney's Seymour Centre, was to be entrusted to Barrie Kosky, a 23-year-old wunderkind. He and I had had breakfast a few months earlier and got along well; the rehearsals also went well, right up until the one before the dress rehearsal. That's when the eleven members of the Seymour Group who made up the 'orchestra' were fitted for their costumes. It seemed they were to wear pyjamas, as would Gerry, except that he would also be wearing a shredded tail coat. Rodney's idea was that the piece should begin as naturalistically as possible, with players coming on in everyday clothes, as if for a rehearsal. Then, as the piece unfolded, we would gradually realise the conductor was deranged. Barrie's *Whispers*, however, was to be set in a mental hospital. There would be no gradual revelation of the conductor's state, no dramatic arc; the curtain would go up and the audience would think: 'Oh, right, they're all mad.'

Gerry, Rodney and I repaired to the kitchen of my terraced house, just round the corner in Chippendale. Rodney wanted to print pamphlets denouncing the production. He and I would stand outside the Seymour Centre and hand them to the first-night audience as they arrived.

'You won't have to do that,' Gerry said. 'If they don't scrap the pyjamas, I'm not going back.'

He wasn't being a prima donna; he was defending the work. For Gerry, it always came down to fidelity to the score, and there was nothing in this score about pyjamas. Moreover, after a full week of rehearsals with Barrie, and with the dress rehearsal twenty-four hours away, this was the first that Gerry, the star of the show, had heard about the costumes. He felt betrayed; this was not the production he thought he'd been working on.

I was given the task of conveying all this to the director and designer. Barrie argued his corner, but I explained that Gerry was simply not returning until the costumes were dropped. Barrie gave way with good grace, though really he had little choice.

Then came the opening night, and a new surprise. At the climax of the piece, with Gerry singing a wild vocal line, conducting the thorniest passage of ensemble music in the work and apparently going off his trolley, a loud hissing started up on stage, so loud it was hard to hear the music. All around the conductor's podium, plastic sex dolls began to inflate. It was one thing to keep elements of the production secret until the final stages of the rehearsal, quite another to distract the performer during the premiere of a demanding new piece that required all his concentration. Gerry was furious. If the dolls inflated the following night, he announced, he would stab them all with his conductor's baton. The next night, the dolls had gone.

Perhaps I should say that I have the highest regard for Barrie Kosky, and did at the time. I also like him personally, and our conversations on *The Music Show* over the years have been full of ideas and wise insights. If Barrie wants to stage *Nabucco* in a sea of shoes or interpolate Cole Porter songs in *The Coronation of Poppea*, I say good luck to him. Apart from the fact that these productions were theatrically compelling, *Nabucco*, Porter and *Poppea* can look after themselves. They existed before Barrie came along and will exist when he's gone. But it's different with the first performance of a brand new work. This is hardly the moment for reinterpretation. I was concerned that Barrie's production would spell the end for *Whispers*. The critics, however, were kind, Rosemary Neill in the *Australian* concluding that a good piece had been sabotaged by wilful staging, and *Whispers* had a number of subsequent productions.

It had been Gerry's idea that I write him a mad scene, and mine that we make him into a conductor, but usually the subjects of my operas and music-theatre pieces have come from my librettists. Graham Devlin proposed we use the life of Edgar Allan Poe and, later, creation myths bound by the Schopenhauerian notion of the 'World Knot' (in *The World Knot*, for Sydney Grammar School). It was Barbara Blackman's idea to do a piece about Icarus (*Parabola*), though she had been inspired by hearing my violin piece, *Like Icarus Ascending*. Margaret Morgan suggested both Casanova (*Casanova Confined*, for Lyndon Terracini) and Freud (*Night and Dreams*), and Sue Smith came up with Rembrandt. But it was Anni's idea that I ask our friend Cathy Strickland – another TV writer – to collaborate on a piece about William Crotch.

Anni has a remarkable knack of coming up with ideas for pieces. She told me the story that led to *Rauha* and has been a constant sounding board. *Blitz*, for instance, was a piece we dreamt up together. But usually she just announces her ideas, and they are always good.

'What should I write next?' I once asked her in a restaurant – this conversation always seems to happen when we're eating. 'What's my next big project?'

'I think you should make a vocal work for Jane Sheldon and the Seraphim Trio out of some famous last words,' she replied, as though she'd been expecting the question. 'You could use Captain Scott's diary.'

So I did, although it took me a while to work out that it would require final poems to give *Last Words* substance.

The Musical Child was all Anni's idea. Researching the radio series *Music and Fashion*, she had unearthed the story of William Crotch, the much put-upon child prodigy, exploited by his overbearing mother (she had him giving organ recitals at the age of three), who went on to be the first director of the Royal Academy of Music. My stint as resident composer at ANAM in 2009 allowed me to write a piece about him. There was something fitting about having the piece played by young musicians, many of whom had themselves been prodigies, if better treated than little William. *The Musical Child* would also be my last piece for Gerry English, who was no longer singing but, aged eighty-three, had recently taken the part of the reciter in Schoenberg's *Ode to Napoleon* at ANAM, and William would be a speaking role. Anni's idea to ask Cathy for a libretto was inspired. In her screenwriting, Cathy has always been good at characters whose outward confidence conceals a damaged soul, and that was William as an old man. Her libretto was funny and touching.

I finished composing *The Musical Child* only a year after Gerry's *Ode to Napoleon*, but when I sent him the finished score, Gerry wrote back saying his health hadn't been good and he no longer felt he could perform it. The concert, which would also contain the first performance of *Rauha*, was scheduled for May 2010 and would be conducted by Brett Dean in his final orchestral concert as ANAM's artistic director. Brett had the idea of asking Geoffrey Rush to perform *The Musical Child*. Hardly daring to hope, we sent his agent the score, and heard back that Rush was interested. He couldn't yet commit, pending receipt of the filming schedule for *Pirates of the Caribbean 4*, but we thought it was worth waiting.

So we waited eight months, before hearing that *Pirates of the Caribbean* had claimed him after all. By now it was March and I was in Finland. The premiere of *The Musical Child* was just over two months away, but we had no William, and there was no obvious replacement for Geoffrey Rush. The piece required not just an actor, but a musical actor. Someone who could read music and learn a score. We asked Lyndon Terracini, who was keen, but in his new role at Artistic Director of Opera Australia lacked the time to learn the piece. We were reaching the point where only one person did have the time, because he knew it already, and that was me.

The performance was not a success. ANAM's musicians were committed, Brett was impeccable and, in the first half, *Rauha* came off wonderfully well. But *The Musical Child* needed a real actor with real stage presence; I had cleared room for him in the score – a huge personality, someone you can't take your eyes off, a Gerald English, a Geoffrey Rush ... I was not that man, and without a central performance of the proper magnitude, the piece seemed thin. People were kind; everyone told me I'd done a good job – and I'd certainly given it my best shot – but from childhood I'd known there was something special about actors, and here was more evidence that I didn't have whatever that was. I felt I'd let Cathy down: for eight months she'd had reason to hope that her words would be spoken by one of the great actors of our time, but she'd ended up with someone who wasn't an actor at all. Sometimes, perhaps, the show mustn't go on.

What it came down to was professionalism. I wouldn't have accepted a player who hadn't had much experience of their instrument, so why had I thought that a non-actor could perform the role of William Crotch? A professional attitude is really at the heart of being a musician. It means being dependable, and not turning up to a rehearsal poorly prepared because you'll undermine the whole enterprise. Musicians guard their reputations – it's what stands between them and unemployment – and there is an unspoken rule that you are all there to make each other sound good. If you don't know or can't play your part, you put others' livelihoods on the line. You may be forgiven, but your unpreparedness will not be forgotten. Next time, someone else will get the gig. In this particular case, it was the reputation of *The Musical Child* that had been on the line. While *Whispers* had survived

Barrie Kosky, *The Musical Child* shows every sign of not having survived me.

For a composer, professionalism is just as important. You will be allowed only so many mistakes in your scores before performers give up on you. For that reason, I am more pleased by a compliment from a player than by anything else. No composer plays every instrument; we all write music we cannot play ourselves then put it in front of people who are experts. So when a violinist tells you that your writing fits her instrument well, or a cellist says that his part is a pleasure to play, it's a feather in your cap.

I once told John Williams I found the guitar the scariest instrument to write for, to which he replied that I should just write what I wanted to hear and 'we'll fix it up'. That seemed to me the sort of advice that is bound to get a composer into trouble, because it's the opposite of professionalism. I avoided the guitar for years.

Sometimes, professionalism is a matter of being practical and flexible, of a willingness to solve problems, which come in all manner of sizes. In 2011 I composed *Blitz* for the Tasmanian Symphony Orchestra. I had interviewed my parents and two of their friends about their recollections of the bombing of Liverpool in World War II. They'd all been children at the time. I'd also recorded the memories of elderly Germans concerning the fire-bombing of Hamburg and Berlin. There was a mismatch between the accounts, the English voices often cheery in telling stories of children's escapades, the Germans sombre, befitting the scale of destruction in their cities. As with *Elegy in a Country Graveyard* and *A Singing Quilt*, the edited interviews would form part of *Blitz*, but this time the context would be orchestral in a piece lasting nearly half an hour. The English voices would be heard first, then the Germans.

When Simon Rogers, artistic manager of the Tasmanian Symphony Orchestra, had first talked to me about the commission, he'd asked if I would like to use the TSO Chorus as well, but I couldn't imagine what words a choir might sing; the speaking voices were already so powerful and touching on their own. So I was surprised to receive, late in 2011, the orchestra's concert brochure for 2012, announcing *Blitz* as a work for chorus and orchestra. I rang Simon to point out the error.

'Shit,' he said; then, barely pausing for breath: 'Are you sure you don't want a choir?'

Blitz was more than half written, but I was approaching a point where a change of mood was needed. The final speaker in the piece, Ursula Ezimora, is describing her present-day walks though the Hamburg neighbourhood of Barmbek. This is where she had lived as a child, when the whole area had been flattened by RAF bombing in July 1943. Approximately 45,000 people had died in three nights. She says it feels pleasant enough to walk around the neighbourhood today, but she can't go near the place where her childhood home stood. I wanted to introduce some element of hope at this point, a new harmony, maybe, that would lift Frau Ezimora's words and help her story and the music to turn a corner. So I brought in Simon's choir, softly and wordlessly, the orchestra dropping away save for a few tiny flickers of percussion. The magical effect, which was due to an administrative error, was many people's favourite moment in the piece.

Perhaps the most important aspect of a composer's professionalism is their willingness and ability to recognise when something is wrong with a piece. Of course you hope to solve all musical problems at your work desk but it doesn't always happen.

'A poem is never finished; it is only abandoned,' W.H. Auden wrote in 1966, paraphrasing an observation by the French poet Paul Valéry. The Frenchman had been more precise. 'A work is never completed,' Valéry had said, 'except by some accident such as weariness, satisfaction, the need to deliver, or death'. Satisfaction, of course, can wear off.

Sometimes, the moment of abandonment comes too soon. Hearing your music played or sung when previously you had only imagined it in your head will always be a shock. It's not that you are surprised by what you hear – though sometimes you are – but the physical sound of an orchestra or a string quartet or a soprano voice is bound to take you aback in some way, often a good way. If you know someone only from a photograph, then meet them in the flesh, you may recognise them, but they will be shorter or thinner or darker than you'd imagined.

The rehearsal room is full of these little shocks. A chord you had marked fortissimo isn't as loud as you expected. Perhaps it's to do with the spacing of the notes in the chord; repositioned, they might be more vibrant. You discover that an important line of counterpoint is getting lost in the texture. Perhaps it is an octave too low; perhaps the other instruments are too loud.

From time to time, you write a piece that needs no further work, but most require some last-minute tweaking, and some need more than that. The hardest thing, as always, is to get the timing right.

In 2007 the Sydney Symphony Orchestra gave the first performances of my short piece *Headlong*, a work commissioned for its seventy-fifth birthday season. Jeffrey Tate was the excellent conductor and he drew a particularly fine, clear, even passionate performance from the orchestra. The work was meant to be a celebration, but something seemed wrong.

Headlong was a piece with a plan. Its structure involved a seventy-five note melodic line – a tone row – that shot around the orchestra, its rhythm always fluctuating, leaving its harmony in its wake. The row repeats a semitone higher, then a semitone higher, then a semitone higher, until finally it runs smack into a suitably jubilant chord of A major. It was a display piece for the orchestra – everyone gets a little solo – and, bar for bar, the music sounded fine. But the ending appeared to come from nowhere.

Apart from devising my long tone row, the only thing I'd decided in advance was that it would be unstoppable; this line would rush through the piece – *headlong* – from start to finish, now in one octave, now in another, now in the violins, now on the tuba, slowing in the middle of the piece to enter a dense, dark thicket, but never stopping. Yet that final chord never felt earned; the arrival at A major lacked inevitability, even if my long and winding row insisted that it *was* inevitable.

At the end of the first performance, I thanked the conductor and asked if the following night he might bring himself to play the central section a little more slowly; after the second performance, I asked him to play it more slowly still; finally, following the third performance, I asked him to slow the whole piece down. Sir Jeffrey is a lovely man and did as I asked. I have a CD of all four performances, each longer than the last. *Headlong* wasn't a disaster – the ABC sent the final performance to the European Broadcasting Union and, for the next few years, radio royalties trickled in from all over Europe – but I still wasn't satisfied. When the Sydney Symphony Orchestra informed me they would be playing the piece again in their 2017 season, this time with Ben Northey, I decided it was time to pull it apart and fix it.

There is nothing wrong with using a system. It functions like a clamp on some aspect of the music, usually rhythm or, as in this case, pitch. Composers have been doing it since the Middle Ages, and there can be something powerful in a work of art that contains fixed elements (my tone row) alongside free elements (everything else in the piece). But sometimes a system can lead you into trouble, because having established the rules of the game, you tend to follow them. The tone row in *Headlong* ran through the piece without stopping. That was the point of it. But it *ought* to have stopped. The listeners – I include myself – needed more time to take in all that information, and slowing the music down wasn't enough. So I cut a hole in the music just after it reaches the central section. There's a silence, a moment to breathe and reflect on the story so far. After the music picks up and carries on, there are numerous places in which a note is held longer, a couple of bars are inserted to draw out a harmony, a rhythmic figure extended. I felt the piece was a tight-fitting garment that I was letting out. In the process, of course, I was breaking my own rules. There were now places where the line of notes didn't move forward, but lingered or doubled back on itself. Well, they were only my rules.

So is *Headlong* now finished or merely abandoned again? One of the changes I made to the score when I revised it was to add a new last bar. It didn't replace the old last bar, but was in addition to it. A second thought, an *esprit d'escalier*. The final peroration happens as before, though at slightly greater length and leading more purposefully to the A major chord. But where once a big fat pause sat on that chord, now it is played in strict tempo, followed by a sharp attack on the same chord, then a (sort of) F sharp minor eleventh chord (in case you're interested) that splinters apart as individual woodwind and percussion instruments execute little figures that slow down, independently, to nothing.

So the music disintegrates. Far from the triumphant blast that ended the original version, this time the piece actually *sounds* as though it's been abandoned.

9.

The Point of It

When I was a child, my father and I would go to watch cricket. We were at Lord's late one afternoon, when the newspaper seller came round with the *Evening Standard*. The headline announced that someone was 'helping police with their enquiries' over a string of murders.

'They've got him,' said the man in front of us, clearly very pleased.

'Let's hope he's the right one,' Dad said.

'He'll do!' the man replied, slightly belligerently.

With some people, the desire for vengeance is greater than the desire for truth. The man at Lord's was unconcerned that a murderer might still be on the streets, happy merely that someone was in custody. I was twelve or thirteen years old and thought he must be mad, but I've since come to realise this man was not so unusual. There are people who feel somehow vindicated by the punishment of others, whether or not it's deserved. You see them on the nightly news. They're the ones in the street outside the criminal court, banging on the side of the police van.

For them there is no nuance in life, there are no shades of grey. They are keener to restrict than to encourage; they like the death penalty and feel the occasional execution of a wholly innocent person is a small price to pay (of course, they're not the ones paying it), and when military action is mooted, for whatever reason, they're always in favour. In the weeks leading up to the invasion of Iraq, world leaders and their supporters were so keen on the war that, like the man at Lord's, they weren't interested in veracity. If Saddam Hussein's arsenal of nuclear and biological weapons couldn't be verified, evidence would be invented. It was to be war and there was no going back.

I'm not a pacifist. At the time of the Falklands War I considered joining the Peace Pledge Union, having read somewhere that Benjamin Britten had been a member. I sent for the forms, but having read them and understood that a pledge was indeed a pledge – never to fight in a war in any circumstance – I couldn't bring myself to sign; I could imagine situations in which I might feel obliged to fight. Still, pacifism is at least a logical and defensible position; always being in favour of war is insane.

What I'm trying to describe is a certain mindset. On the surface, it is aggressive, drawn to conflict, punishment and revenge, though generally at arm's length. But at heart it's defensive, because beneath the bluster is a kind of general fear, perhaps of change, perhaps of the modern world, perhaps of the unknown. It's understandable, I suppose, though no way to live.

Composing music – creating art of any sort – is more or less the opposite of this. I don't mean to suggest that all artists have sunny dispositions because, quite obviously, all don't. But the act of writing a piece of music or painting a picture, of making 'a hat / Where there never was a hat' (to quote Stephen Sondheim) is essentially optimistic, even if the optimism is short-lived. Philip Larkin projected a gloomy persona, especially in his poetry, and was apparently haunted by the notion of death. In his magnificent, late 'Aubade', he writes about waking early to contemplate 'Unresting death, a whole day nearer now'. And yet the business of crafting this poem, of slowly getting it right, of perfecting the seeming nonchalance of its opening iambic pentameter – 'I work all day and get half drunk at night' – can only be construed as a positive act.

In my book *In Defence of Classical Music*, I wrote about my response to the 9/11 attacks on the World Trade Center towers and the Pentagon, and how, in their immediate aftermath, I felt not only that I couldn't compose, but that music itself was something I didn't want to hear. It wasn't so much a reaction to the horror of what had happened – or not only that – but of what might happen next, and the prospect of the United States and its allies using the attack as a reason for further violence. Knowing that innocent people have died is bad enough, but knowing that innocent people are about to die is somehow paralysing.

After a short time, I took solace in Brahms's string quartets, not because I knew and loved them, but because I didn't. Brahms was a favourite composer – a composer I could depend on – but

I had never found time before for his string quartets and this seemed like the moment. I wanted to engage with a generous mind, and a great one at that. Brahms's three quartets restored me to some extent. They didn't just offer solace, but context. Yes, there might be crazed, violent terrorists in the world and governments who would grasp the opportunity to consolidate their own ambitions, but once there had been Brahms. What's more, we'd had terrorism and despotism before, yet Brahms's music was still here; it had been strong enough to survive.

The piece I was meant to be composing at the time of 9/11 was *Learning to Howl*, a song cycle for Jane Edwards, its structure proceeding from Lorrie Moore's words, 'When I was a child, I tried hard for a time to split my voice.' The piece describes the arc of a woman's life from childhood to old age, in texts by Sappho and Emily Dickinson, Christina Rossetti, Emily Brontë and Elizabeth Smart ('This old woman / Waddles towards love'). My creative paralysis came down to one question: what's the point? It seemed to me, and doubtless to many others at the time, that artists should be making some sort of response to the human destruction that had happened and would continue to happen.

I had felt this once before, in 1982, in the weeks preceding the Falklands War. Prior to Argentina's invasion, few people in Britain had heard of the Falkland Islands and fewer still could have found them on a map. Now, it seemed, we were going to war over them, and the only beneficiary would be either President Leopoldo Galtieri of Argentina or the British prime minister, Margaret Thatcher, both highly unpopular leaders seeking to bolster support in their respective countries. The fact that it would be weeks before war could commence, the British fleet first having to sail to the South Atlantic, somehow made the prospect more ridiculous and appalling. We were going to war in slow motion; there was time to stop it, but not the will. As the popular press did what they always do and egged Thatcher on, wars selling newspapers, I felt angry and began to imagine angry music. Pacing around my small Bradford apartment, I was overtaken by the brutality of the orchestra pounding away in my head. I had the feeling that if only it could be heard by everyone else, this music would stop the war.

Absurd, I know, but sometimes that is how the music comes, suddenly, urgently and in response to a non-musical event. Once, after the break-up of a relationship, I was feeling pretty devastated and began to imagine beautiful, lyrical music – consoling music, you might say. In my wretched lethargy I lacked both the concentration and the will to get any of it down on paper, so you'll have to accept my word that the music was beautiful, but my Falklands piece was finally written in 1986, by which time I was in Australia. Four years on, my anger had shifted focus. The war was now a small piece of history, but Thatcher, buoyed by her military triumph, had won re-election in a landslide. At the postwar victory parade though the City of London, she had received the salute with the Lord Mayor on the steps of Mansion House. Initially only able-bodied soldiers and sailors were invited to participate in the parade, but after a public outcry hundreds of maimed and wounded service men were also permitted to march. A newspaper reported that Thatcher had asked a blinded sailor: 'How are you enjoying the day?'

My piece, *The Big Parade*, was written without a commission for the largest orchestra I have ever employed, and it took the form of a twenty-minute funeral march that erupts midway into a distorted parody of 'Rule, Britannia!'. Not a very subtle gesture, but looking at it now I find the piece as a whole has a certain relentless power. I sent the score to the head of ABC Concert Music, which at the time ran Australia's orchestras, but it was never performed, possibly due to its seven instrumental soloists and extra string players on raised platforms behind the orchestra. I offered it to the BBC, suggesting it (tongue-in-cheek) for the Last Night of the Proms, and received an amused letter of rejection. Thatcher had recently appointed her stooge Marmaduke Hussey to chair the BBC, and my correspondent was moved to imagine Hussey's apoplexy occasioned by a performance of *The Big Parade*.

In the end, my response to 9/11 was completely different. I imagined some sort of musical protest, involving especially dark brass sonorities, but nothing eventuated. I simply went back to work on my song cycle. I reasoned that creating something new, seeing it through and getting the details right was more or less the opposite of terrorism. It wasn't just that life goes on, though that was part of it; neither was it written in the spirit of 'Take that, Osama bin Laden!' But it seemed to me that if there were enough positive acts in the world, they might counterbalance acts of aggression. If my own contribution was relatively modest, it was sincere. So this time my response was not, I hope, absurd, but it was arguably quixotic.

Sometimes I wish a composer could do more. When I was married to my first wife and she was still a lawyer, she would come home each evening having won compensation for an injured worker or spent the day prosecuting some child molester.

'What have you done?' Margaret would ask, and the answer would be that I'd written some really nice chords, or just as likely failed to.

I don't avoid political issues in my work. A piece such as my choral setting of Constantine Cavafy's poem 'Waiting for the Barbarians' can certainly be read as a double-barrelled protest at pusillanimous, do-nothing politicians who appease violent oppressors. When, at the end of the poem, and after all that waiting, the barbarians fail to appear, everyone is disappointed. They'd have been 'a kind of solution', certainly better than our own lacklustre leaders. Cavafy wrote his poem in 1898, and it only seems to have become more topical with the passing of time, though you might argue that, these days, the waiting is over: to borrow again from Sondheim, 'Don't bother, they're here.'

My *Waiting for the Barbarians* is an angry piece – the anger born of the pent-up frustration in Cavafy's poem – and the ending is desolate but, even if the words have driven and coloured the music, I didn't choose the poem in order to make a protest. I chose it because I was looking for words that would be suitable for a joint commission from the Melbourne Symphony Orchestra Chorus and the Sydney Philharmonia Choirs, two big groups of singers, and 'Waiting for the Barbarians' is that rare thing, a poetic crowd scene.

In his commonplace book, *A Certain World*, Auden wrote, on the subject of 'Commitment', that it was well and good for a poet to produce '*engagé*' poetry, but that he (*sic*) will be the only one to gain, his reputation enhanced 'among those who feel as he does'.

'The evil or injustice,' Auden goes on, 'will remain exactly what it would have been if he had kept his mouth shut.'

It's harsh, perhaps, but Auden is not sparing himself (he never did). This, after all, is the author of 'September 1, 1939', as *engagé* a poem as you could wish to read, and one that he had recently culled from his *Collected Shorter Poems*, labelling it dishonest.

Still, political art is not useless.

It's true that Picasso's *Guernica* didn't alter the course of the Spanish Civil War, let alone stop people massacring each other or being fascists, but it stands as a memorial to a horrific act, and as long as we have horrific acts we will need memorials. Though Picasso painted it in anger, and though it is evidently a work of great emotional power, it offers us an artistic context for the bombing of the Basque town of Guernica in April 1937, and a way to think about the event. You might counter that it also sanitises it, but I don't agree. It brings distance, certainly, but a photograph of the destruction would do that. I think when we look at *Guernica* – a mural on a grand scale – we see the time and care that went into the painting, the work and the energy Picasso spent on it. Looking at *Guernica* sets in motion a process of contemplation and understanding that bypasses words. We can't come to terms with something as grotesque as that massacre, the Luftwaffe and Italian air force invited to bomb the Basques by Spanish nationalists, but the mural offers a degree of perspective.

Some of Brett Dean's music has started with his concern for the plight of displaced people and refugees; it's the same with the paintings and installations of my Robertson neighbour Ben Quilty. And if it's not refugees, it's the death penalty or soldiers with post-traumatic stress disorder. By putting subjects such as these in his work, Ben opens himself to the charge of being a 'bleeding heart', though that doesn't strike me as much of a condemnation. What's the alternative? To be hard-hearted? Heartless? Who wants to look at heartless art?

I don't think that these causes drive Ben to paint – he is an artist and so already driven – but they guide and shape the nature of his work. Still, when you look at his large canvases in a show such as *After Afghanistan*, you are aware of the mental pain these soldiers have experienced and in some cases are still experiencing. Painting has it over music in that it can show us things. In the case of Brett Dean's first string quartet, entitled *Eclipse*, you wouldn't know, unless you were told, that the music was a response to the Tampa crisis of 2001 and the hardening of Australia's policy concerning asylum seekers who arrived by sea. Music without words is abstract sound, and in this case even the title isn't much help. *Eclipse* is a fine piece, gripping in its emotional intensity, but even if its composer had intended the music as a blow-by-blow account of the unfolding drama, a listener could have no idea. As it happens, the *Tampa* was simply the starting point for the music – Brett's inspiration, if that's not too positive a word for a boatload of desperate people.

My own musical ideas seldom begin this way, and when they do – say, with 9/11 – they generally amount to nothing. Increasingly, I find, a piece of music begins with musical concerns. If it ends up 'political', like *Waiting for the Barbarians*, this will be a result of the compositional process. Indeed it may even be an accident, as with *A Singing Quilt*, a statement about reconciliation between Indigenous and non-Indigenous Australians that others heard and had to point out to me.

Music is primarily about structure, about itself. It may claim to be about other things, and the composer may sincerely believe it to be about other things, but without words (or perhaps a musical quotation, such as my distorted 'Rule, Britannia!'), no one will ever guess. So why do we give our pieces titles at all? Why call a purely musical work *Like Icarus Ascending* or *Swansong*?

T.S. Eliot once argued that meaning in poetry was a deliberate distraction on the part of the poet. The poet, he said, is like a burglar who throws a piece of meat to the guard dog. The meat is a poem's meaning and the dog is our conscious mind. While our conscious mind gnaws on the juicy meaning, the poet goes though the drawers of our subconscious. Perhaps this is the function of an evocative title given to a piece of music; if not exactly a distraction, perhaps the title is the focal point in a musical meditation, holding our attention as those patterns of sound do their work on our subconscious minds. Or perhaps titles serve to prime us for the music, and make us receptive.

I once said to Peter Sculthorpe that, next to a doctor or a firefighter, a composer's work could seem pretty insignificant, but he demurred.

'I think what we do is very important,' he said. 'Music brings people together.'

He was right, no doubt. Shared experiences may be in decline in the modern world, but, as I have suggested, concerts still provide them. And shared experiences operate on many levels. There is, for instance, the sense of community that comes from attending a concert, and it's not simply among the musicians on stage or the audience in the hall, it's between them. A great performance is an act of communication, of reaching out – the listener reaching out as much as the performer. Part of what is being communicated by music is the onstage collegiality necessary for such a performance. A musical performance offers us an idealised model of society. This is not to say that all the musicians on stage love or even like each other, but in order to produce great music they must cooperate. There are myriad stories of rock bands and jazz musicians who play well together though they can't abide one another. Once, as a student, I spied on the Amadeus Quartet in rehearsal from the gallery in the Great Hall of Lancaster University. It was not like any other string quartet rehearsal I've witnessed. The players seemed profoundly irritated by each other, all talking all the time, occasionally shouting; individual players would suddenly stand up and walk off or wander upstage to practise a completely different piece; they were never all seated at the same moment. At the concert in the evening, they played like angels.

But of course there are also deep friendships between musicians, even between composers. There are, perhaps, a handful of my composer colleagues I would be loath to trust with my secrets, but by and large we wish each other well, and a success for one composer is regarded as a success for us all. I have been quite close to certain colleagues at different points in my life. Perhaps the most important was Roger Smalley, a wonderful composer, who was an inveterate supporter of my music, conducting it, playing it on the piano and programming it with his WASO New Music Ensemble and sometimes farther afield, yet never calling in the favour. I have had friendships with composers where we have shown each other new scores and given each other feedback; sometimes we've given each other moral support; sometimes just shared gossip.

Perhaps even more valuable than friendships with composers, though, are friendships with other musicians. As a composer who is not a performer, you often feel a little like an outsider. You work on your own and send your music off to players, waiting anxiously for their response.

The cellist Sue-Ellen Paulsen kept me waiting more than a month after I'd sent her *The Great Memory*, the cello concerto I'd written for her. I was nearly ready to tear the piece up when she finally rang, her first words – 'I'm not a flute player, you know' – doing little to assuage my mounting anxiety. Sue-Ellen could be quite scary when she was younger, rumour having it that she'd once made a conductor cry in rehearsal. Fortunately, I already knew Sue-Ellen and loved her dearly. In the end she gave me a magnificent performance of *The Great Memory*, her reputation for fierceness working in my favour, because the conductor, whose energies, hitherto, had all gone into his first *Petrushka*, found himself obliged to believe in my concerto as much as Sue-Ellen did. This is the sort of soloist you want playing your music.

One performer who never played a note of my music was the pianist Geoffrey Tozer. We weren't constantly in touch, but I treasure our conversations about everything from the music of Medtner to the films of Powell and Pressburger. He had an astonishing musical memory. At one Huntington Festival, he accompanied Jeannie Marsh in Elgar's song cycle *Sea Pictures*. He had no music in front of him, which is very unusual for an accompanist, and after the concert I asked him why he had done it. Why would anyone bother to memorise Elgar's piano part?

'I didn't,' he replied. 'I don't like Elgar's piano part. I was playing the orchestral version.' What he meant was that he had the sound of the orchestra running in his head, while he made his own piano reduction on the fly.

At that same festival, Geoffrey, Gerald English, Belinda Webster and I went for a drive one morning. We found ourselves in Gulgong, the neighbouring town to Mudgee, where there's a tiny theatre that calls itself the Prince of Wales Opera House. I'm not sure how much opera it's seen, but everyone from a young Nellie Melba to the boxer Les Darcy has appeared there. The door was open, so we walked in. There was a grand piano and it was unlocked. Geoffrey struck up the opening chords of 'Let the Florid Music Praise', the first song of *On This Island*, Britten's early song cycle to words by Auden. Gerry began singing and, quite remarkably, Geoffrey kept playing. How he came to have this piano part in his head in anyone's guess. At the end of the first song, they moved on to the second. By the end of the second, a small audience had gathered, mostly elderly women with shopping bags who had heard the singing as they passed by and now occupied the front row. They began calling out requests, which Gerry and Geoffrey did their best to fulfil. It was a wonderful morning.

I have a good memory for music, but Geoffrey's was different because he had the memory in his fingers as much as his head. And it is poignant to remember because, ten or fifteen years later, as his drinking took hold, it was the memory that went. In concerts, he would talk more and more and play less and less; it was as though he talked to put off the playing. Belinda told me that the last time she heard Geoffrey play, at a lunchtime concert in Melbourne, he couldn't remember some of the simple children's pieces he had recorded for her on the very first Tall Poppies CD. He would get lost in the middle of quite a short piece and be unable to find his way back to the music, sometimes for minutes, sometimes at all, improvising his way out. When they went for lunch after the concert, Belinda gently brought this up, but Geoffrey didn't know what she was talking about.

The memory of music is a curious thing. As a child of seven or eight, I had a book of American folk songs – cowboy songs, mostly – one of which was 'The Streets of Laredo'. It's a song about a cowboy who's been shot and knows he is dying. My sister, Kate, three years my junior, found 'The Streets of Laredo' unbearably sad, and so I would sing the song around the house, regularly reducing her to tears. I was not a good brother. But if it was the words that upset her, I quickly worked out that the tune alone would have the desired effect, and that even the first line of the tune, softly whistled so my parents couldn't hear, might tip her over the edge. It is an example of a musical signature that encapsulates a whole piece, and no different in this regard to the opening chord of 'A Hard Day's Night' or the first phrase of Beethoven's fifth. It is hard to remember the whole of a Beethoven symphony unless you've studied it, so the opening bars function as a mental sound-bite that embodies the whole structure. This is how we carry music around.

In 2003 I was fortunate to visit Bob Copper at his home in Peacehaven, near Rottingdean in Sussex on the south coast of England. Bob's family had lived here since before the Spanish Armada sailed by, up the English Channel. They had also sung together for generations. As a small boy, Bob had learnt traditional songs from his parents and grandparents, uncles and cousins. In the early 1950s, the Copper Family – Bob and his cousin Ron, together with their fathers – were recorded by the BBC and went on to make some records. When I interviewed Bob for *The Music Show*, he was an 88-year-old paterfamilias singing with his children and grandchildren. Since his death the following year, the Copper Family continues to sing, a centuries-old repository of musical tradition. Bob's grandfather, known as Brasser, had written down the words of their songs in his bold copperplate (what else?), but Bob talked to me about the way the songs had been preserved in people's memories.

'I find myself singing instinctively,' he told me. 'I go out here onto the lawn on a lovely May morning, you know, and you start singing: "How pleasant and delightful on a bright summer's morn …" A set of circumstances can trigger a song off in your head straight away, and it echoes, and you know that back down that long line of ancestors from which we all come [there] was a person who felt the same as you did about a certain thing: the weather or rough luck or good luck. Through these songs you can get a pretty good feeling and imagination of what it was like to live in those days. Some of them are sheer poetry, by the way, and all preserved in those old people's minds – most of them illiterate, remember, and yet: "Come write me down, ye powers above, / The man who first created love, / For I've a diamond in my eye / Wherein all my joys and comforts lie."

'What lovely poetry that was! And it was in those ignorant old men: dirty old men, chewbaccers, spit down on the floor as soon as look at you. And yet they'd got in their head these little bits of poetry and these tender feelings about the sadness of people lost at sea and battles and what have you.'

That's how music works in our memories and in our lives. Sometimes, when the memory is jogged – by a 'lovely May morning', say – the music comes pouring out, and when it is jogged by music, all sorts of things pour out.

When Anni and I became parents, somewhat late in the day, I discovered that being a dad unlocked a surprising number of memories from my own childhood, many of them musical. As I sang to my baby daughter, songs from my own early childhood half a century earlier kept popping into my head, often with complete sets of words.

A baby changes everything, as I was the last among my friends to discover, and if your work involves dredging up music from your imagination, a baby will certainly affect that. The day after Elsie was born, I sat down to write a musical setting of Jane Taylor's poem, 'Twinkle, Twinkle, Little Star', all five verses of it. I called my version 'Little Star' and wrote a gently meandering harp accompaniment to my vocal line. Looking at my daughter, still only hours old, it seemed apt to ask the existential question 'How I wonder what you are.'

The next piece I wrote, *You Must Sleep, but I Must Dance*, for viola and percussion, was inspired by pram-pushing. Not only did the exercise in pursuit of a sleeping infant remind me of Cormac McCarthy's line (misquoted, by the way, from Theodor Storm, who had it the other way round), but the tune that dominates the final movement occurred to me while out pushing, our walk, on this occasion, curtailed so I could get home to write it all down.

The idea of *Blitz* had already occurred to me before Elsie was even conceived, but when I came to write it the year after her birth, it was impossible not to think of children under dropping bombs without thinking of Syria, and, as every parent knows, it is hard to see children in harm's way on the nightly news without personalising it. Children get everywhere in your life.

Becoming a father is daunting, especially if you've reached the age of fifty-three without it happening before. I spoke to several colleagues with experience in the area and received advice about time management. Brett Dean told me I'd learn to do seven hours work in forty-five minutes; Damien Ricketson said I'd learn new respect for first thoughts, though I can't say this has always been the case. When Elsie was born, nearly everyone told me to treasure the first weeks, months, years, because 'they grow up so fast' – a cliché, obviously, but no less true for that. Only one person, the soprano Jane Edwards, said that it gets better, but this is what I've found.

What I was not prepared for was how fascinating it would be, watching and hearing a child grow up, and part of that is the forming of her musical tastes. It started with Bach. As a newborn baby, Elsie responded visibly to *The Well-tempered Clavier* (played on the piano by Roger Woodward), the preludes and fugues seeming to attract her attention and hold it for a while. No other music did this. I guess it must have been the constant affect of the pieces, the unchanging pulse, and that it would be the same for most babies and most baroque music. But the first taste she formed for herself was a love of the Beatles. I'd been sent CDs of *The Beatles at the BBC*, radio recordings from *Saturday Club* and *Easybeat*, which in some cases I had heard as a child. I thought I might write about them for *Inside Story*, the online journal to which I contribute a monthly music column. So I put the CDs in the car and listened as I drove around. Often enough Elsie, now three years old, was in the back, and it wasn't long before she was calling out requests: 'Play "Yeah Yeah", Daddy!' Then came demands for more songs and for information about the singers. Before I knew it she had Beatlemania, and I was obliged to attempt 'Dizzy Miss Lizzy' (she called it 'Busy Miss Lizzy') as a bedtime lullaby.

I was listening to the Beatles more than at any time since my own childhood, the house suddenly and repeatedly ringing to *Rubber Soul* and *Revolver*. And the sound of our house changed in another significant way. We became a bilingual home, Anni speaking to Elsie only in Finnish, as Elsie's command of the language quickly surpassed my own feeble attempts to learn it.

The main musical project Elsie inspired was an album of children's songs, *There Was a Man Lived in the Moon*. Some of them were composed by me – for instance, 'Little Star' – but most were arrangements of traditional nursery rhymes. I had come to feel as though I was a conduit for these rhymes, put in my head by my mother in the late 1950s and early 1960s and now being passed on to my daughter, and this CD was a tangible result. 'Have You Seen the Muffin Man?', 'Incy Wincy Spider' and 'Lavender's Blue' are songs that everyone knows in one version or another, and it was both a pleasure and also quite hard work finding new chords and instrumental colours for the songs, freshening them up without spoiling their simplicity.

I made each arrangement for a different combination of instruments (I wanted the album to function as a 'Young Person's Guide' to instruments of the orchestra), but the singing was shared between Teddy Tahu Rhodes and Jane Sheldon, two artists for whom I have enormous respect. In addition to the well-known songs, I also included some that were childhood favourites of mine and my mum's. 'The Tailor and the Mouse', for example, is a song I associate only with Mum. I can't remember anyone else singing it or ever hearing it on the radio: we're in the realms, here, of oral tradition. The song had quickly become a favourite of Elsie's, but in the recording studio it turned out no one else knew it – not Teddy, not the players, not Virginia Read the producer. Since the album came out, I've received a number of letters from members of the public saying it's become their favourite track. So the oral tradition is apparently alive; the conduit is functioning.

Because composers tend to work at home, it is inevitable that their home lives will impinge on their work, and not always in a helpful way. It is also inevitable that the events of their lives will affect their music. When my father died unexpectedly at the end of 2012, I was in a busy period of composing, with two pieces nearly finished – a fourth string quartet and *On Reflection* for the two-piano team of Liam Viney and Anna Grinberg; there was also a fifth quartet waiting in the wings. I managed to complete the fourth quartet before flying to England for the funeral, and *On Reflection* on my return. Both turned out to be angrier pieces than I was expecting. But the fifth quartet, which I dedicated to my father's memory, was the piece I was always intending to write, except in one particular.

When I was commissioned by the Australian String Quartet to write a piece for their 2013 season, I immediately had the structure in my head. My fifth quartet would be in a single continuous movement of approximately fifteen minutes, and at its heart would be an expansive tune to which everything else would relate. The only hymn sung at Dad's funeral was 'He Who Would Valiant Be', better known as 'To Be a Pilgrim', which had been Dad's school song. It's a great hymn: John Bunyan's words, tidied up to suit modern Christian sensibilities (sadly, the 'hobgoblin' had to go) and put to a folk tune adapted by Vaughan Williams for *The English Hymnal*. Vaughan Williams, in fact, had collected the tune himself from Mrs Harriet Verrall of Monk's Gate in Sussex, about twenty-five miles north of the Coppers' home down on the coast. In the hymn book, the tune is called 'Monk's Gate'. It wasn't the expansive tune I'd first imagined (it's actually rather jaunty), but after the funeral I couldn't get it out of my head – I found myself whistling it at Dubai airport on the journey home – so I decided to use it in the quartet. Fragments of the tune are heard from the very start as they build towards a complete statement of 'Monk's Gate' around the ten-minute mark, and there's hardly a bar of the piece that doesn't make some reference to it.

As I was completing my quartet, Margaret Thatcher died, and 'To Be a Pilgrim' was sung at her funeral by 2000 people in St Paul's Cathedral. My father had loathed 'that woman', and not only because her policies had cost him his job. Shortly after she arrived at Downing Street in 1979, with a prayer from St Francis of Assisi and a package of neo-liberal austerity, Dad had been one of her earliest casualties, BAT suddenly able to manage without his clerking. But if he felt sorry for himself – and he did – he felt sorrier for those who didn't have a solid pension to fall back on, or a wife who was by now a school principal. The point is that had Thatcher died before Dad, we would surely not have sung 'To Be a Pilgrim' at his funeral, knowing it had been sung at hers, and so my fifth string quartet would sound very different.

'Monk's Gate' is a generous tune. By that, I mean its melody is wide-ranging, its rhythm unpredictable and its metrical gait delightfully lopsided. There is also something generous about the way Vaughan Williams used it. A lifelong believer in musical communities, he conducted amateur choirs and encouraged ordinary people to sing. I'm sure this is why, although an atheist, he accepted the editorship of the *The English Hymnal*. He believed, as Peter Sculthorpe did, that music brings people together. In putting 'Monk's Gate' in the hymn book, he was liberating the tune from Mrs Verrall's memory and making it available to millions of others.

One reason I wanted to use it in my quartet was that Dad was a generous man. Generous to his family, but also to numerous charities and to strangers who came calling at the house. I learnt, after his death, that he'd been on first-name terms with a couple of Jehovah's Witnesses who had become semi-regulars on his doorstep, and with whom he was always happy to chat. In the unlikely event that Margaret Thatcher had dropped by, I dare say even she'd have been offered a cup of tea.

I'm talking, I suppose, about generosity of spirit, about openness. This is the only useful attitude to adopt in the face of art. If you are suspicious of a new piece of music, demanding that it prove itself to you, you are unlikely to get much from it. If you're open-minded, open-eared, open-hearted, if you have a little faith, the music may speak to you. That isn't to say you will necessarily like it or that it will be any good. You might be grievously disappointed. That's the price frequently paid by the open-hearted. You believe the best of someone and they let you down. But the alternative is to put up the shutters, to harden your heart, to close your ears and your mind. Then you're like the man at Lord's.

o
o o
o

Music is participatory. Not necessarily in the way Vaughan Williams hoped for – you don't have to sing along. If you bring your ears to it, your imagination and your memory, you will be participating.

Some music can appear forbidding, but it's not usually the music's fault. If you worry you're not cool enough for hip-hop or serious enough for jazz, or not sufficiently like the late Lord Boyle to appreciate the piano quartets of Fauré, you are worrying about the wrong thing. Music isn't like advanced physics, which would be hard to grasp without a knowledge of elementary physics. With music you can jump in anywhere: Snoop Dogg, Sonny Rollins, Joni Mitchell, Wagner, Sami yoiking, klezmer, Pauline Oliveros. If the music doesn't appeal to you, get out and jump in somewhere else. You will find something that does appeal and, before you know it, like Elsie with the Beatles, you'll want to know more.

But you may also discover that some music which didn't, at first, speak to you has lodged in your memory and is calling you back to listen again, for often enough the memory of music has little to do with reason or good sense. On the contrary, it is mostly *non*-sense, and it lies too deep for words.

Acknowledgements

A few of these words have appeared in print before in slightly different forms. The paragraphs about my school choir, *Headlong* and a couple of paragraphs from the introduction appeared first in *Inside Story*; the first part of Chapter 3 was written for *Meanjin* (Summer 2016) under the title 'God and I'. My thanks to the editors, respectively, Peter Browne and Jonathan Green. At Black Inc. I must thank Chris Feik, Patrizia di Biase-Dyson, Julian Welch, Kirstie Innes-Will and Georgina Garner.

Thanks to my mother and sister for helping with my memory; likewise Mark Lawrence, Roger Ashton-Griffiths, Graham Devlin, John Davis, Maureen Cooney, Penny Lomax and Belinda Webster. Thanks to Cathy Strickland and Tim Pye for lending me their beach house to finish the book, and to Cathy for enthusiastically reading chapters. My main thanks, as always, go to Anni Heino, who read everything first and made unfailingly useful and constructive criticisms, and also to our daughter, Elsie, who, in a way, inspired this book.

Chronological selection of pieces by Andrew Ford

1976   A Salt Girl (lost)

       Rounds and Hollows (lost)

1977   Flowers of Orcus (lost)

1978   Sonata for Four Instruments

1979   Chamber Concerto No 1

1980   Concerto for Orchestra

1981   Portraits

       Wedding Songs

       Est il paradis?

1982   Boatsong

       Epilogue to an Opera

1983   Chamber Concerto No 2: Cries in Summer

       Poe

1984   Like Icarus Ascending

       A Terrible Whiteness

1985 Sacred Places
      From Hand to Mouth
      String Quartet No 1
1986 The Big Parade
      Five Cabaret Songs
      A Martian Sends a Postcard Home
      On Canaan's Happier Shore
1987 Swansong
      A Kumquat for John Keats
1988 The Piper's Promise
      The World Knot
      Chamber Concerto No 3: In Constant Flight
1989 Wassails & Lullabies
      The Art of Puffing: 17 Elegies for Thomas Chatterton
      Parabola
1990 Ringing the Changes
      Whispers
1991 Pastoral
      The Laughter of Mermaids
      Piano Concerto: Imaginings
1992 Harbour
      … les débris d'un rêve
      In somnia
1993 Jouissance
      The Widening Gyre
      Mondriaan
      Composition in Blue, Grey and Pink

1994   The Great Memory
       A Salt Girl (recomposed)

1995   Casanova Confined
       Dancing with Smoke

1996   Rough Magic
       Dance Maze

1997   The Past

1998   The Unquiet Grave
       Tattoo
       Icarus Drowning

1999   Hymn to the Sun
       Manhattan Epiphanies
       Night and Dreams: the Death of Sigmund Freud
       The Furry Dance

2000   The Very End of Harvest

2001   Learning to Howl

2002   Tales of the Supernatural
       The Waltz Book
       Asides on the Oboe
       Chamber Concerto No 4

2003   Fear No More …

2004   The Crantock Gulls
       The Armed Man
       War and Peace

2005   Sad Jigs
       An die Musik

2006   Scenes from Bruegel

Barleycorn
Oma kodu
A Reel, a Fling and a Ghostly Galliard
    (String Quartet No 2)
Headlong
2007 Elegy in a Country Graveyard
Thin Air
Bagpipe Music
Domestic Advice
2008 The Tears of Geertje Dircx
Symphony
A Singing Quilt
2009 Rembrandt's Wife
Bright Shiners
Willow Songs
The Musical Child
Rauha
2010 Nine Fantasies About Brahms
The Rising
Little Star
The Scattering of Light
You Must Sleep, but I Must Dance
2011 Blitz
Waiting for the Barbarians
2012 Hear the Bird of Day
String Quartet No 3
String Quartet No 4

2013 On Reflection
     Uproar
     String Quartet No 5
     Untuning the Sky
     Australian Aphorisms
     Last Words
     Once Upon a Time There Were Two Brothers ...
2014 Slow Air
     A Pitch Dark Night
     After the Visitors
     Common Ground
2015 There Was a Man Lived in the Moon
     The Drowners
     Missa Brevis
     Contradance
2016 Raga
     In transit
     Comeclose and Sleepnow
     Never
2017 No One Could Relax around Jezebel
     Peter Pan

For more details about these pieces,
visit www.andrewford.net.au.

Discography

Numerous individual pieces by Andrew Ford can be found on releases from ABC Classics, Attacca-Babel, Halcyon, Move, Tall Poppies, Vexations 840 and Vox Australis, and there are plenty of pieces on YouTube and Ford's own Soundcloud (www.sound-cloud.com/drandrewford).

The following are discs devoted to Ford's music.

There Was a Man Lived in the Moon (ABC Classics)
Little Star, Nonsense, Golden Slumbers and arrangements of nursery rhymes and folk songs
Jane Sheldon, Teddy Tahu Rhodes

Learning to Howl (ABC Classics)
Learning to Howl, Snatches of Old Lauds, Sounds and Sweet Airs, Elegy in a Country Graveyard, The Birthday of My Life
Jane Sheldon, Marshall McGuire, Richard Haynes, Sydney Chamber Choir et al

The Waltz Book (Tall Poppies)
Ian Munro

Night and Dreams: the Death of Sigmund Freud
    (Decca Eloquence)
also Schoenberg's *Ode to Napoleon*
Gerald English

Icarus (Tall Poppies)
Hymn to the Sun, *Like Icarus Ascending*, Chamber Concerto
    No 3: *In Constant Flight*, *Parabola*, *Icarus Drowning*
Rohan Smith, Terra Australis Incognita, Kowmung Festival
    Ensemble

Harbour (Tall Poppies)
A Martian Sends a Postcard Home, Clarion, Epithalamium,
    Harbour, Composition in Blue, Grey and Pink, Dancing with
    Smoke, A Salt Girl, Female Nude, And Now, Five Cabaret Songs
Gerald English, Australian Chamber Orchestra et al

Whispers (Tall Poppies)
The Art of Puffing: 17 Elegies for Thomas Chatterton, Sacred Places,
    Pastoral, Whispers
Gerald English, Duo Contemporain, Tasmanian Symphony
    Chamber Players et al